HUMAN ABILITIES

AN
INFORMATION-PROCESSING
APPROACH

D0145353

HUMAN ABILITIES

AN
INFORMATION-PROCESSING
APPROACH

Edited by

ROBERT J. STERNBERG

Yale University

W. H. FREEMAN AND COMPANY

New York

Library of Congress Cataloging in Publication Data

Sternberg, Robert J.
  Human abilities.

  (A Series of books in psychology)
  Includes bibliographies and indexes.
  1. Human information processing.   2. Intellect.
3. Ability.   I. Title.   II. Series.
BF455.S674   1984   153   84-19124
ISBN 0-7167-1618-6
ISBN 0-7167-1619-4 (pbk.)

Printed in the United States of America

3 4 5 6 7 8 9   VB   5 4 3 2 1 0 8 9 8 7

This book is dedicated to Lee J. Cronbach, whose plea for the unification of the two disciplines of scientific psychology provided the impetus for much of the theory and research presented in this book.

CONTENTS

PREFACE

The decision to prepare a book can come about through any of a number of distinct motivations. The decision to prepare this one came about through frustration—namely, my own frustration with the absence of an undergraduate or beginning graduate level text on human abilities that adequately represented the great strides that have been made during the past decade in our understanding of the information-processing bases of human abilities.

There is no lack of books on the subject of human abilities, broadly defined. But none of them have come even close to suiting me and my students as a text. After examining all the available books, I found that they fell into one (or more) of the following four classes:

1. Books on human abilities that adequately represent the psychometric, or differential, point of view, but that give either little or no coverage to the information-processing approach that dominates current attempts to understand the nature of abilities.

2. Books on human abilities that represent the information-processing approach, but that are at a level that assumes at least advanced graduate-level competence for a reasonable level of understanding. Such books are simply inadequate as texts, for whatever their value may be to advanced graduate students and professionals.

3. Books on human abilities representing the information-processing approach whose coverage is motivated by the range of authors' interests rather than by an attempt to provide reasonably complete coverage of the human abilities field as it exists today. Used as texts, such books give an incomplete and even distorted view of current information-processing research on human abilities.

4. Books on human abilities that provide some elementary coverage of information-processing approaches to human abilities, but that seem based on the assumption that information-processing approaches to human abilities can be conveyed to the reader in the same way as psychometric approaches can be—namely, with a few paragraphs or even pages covering the "main theories" as they exist today. Such an assumption may have worked for psychometric theorizing, but it does not work for information-processing theorizing: Information-processing psychologists seek to understand in detail the cognitive bases of abilities that were named but not explained by psychometric theories. Thus, whereas it might be adequate to mention that a given psychometric theory postulates an ability called "verbal ability," one could do justice to information-processing theorizing about verbal ability only in the context of one or several chapters, because information-processing theorizing attempts to understand in detail the cognitive bases of verbal ability.

What, exactly, is an "information-processing" approach to human abilities? Different investigators will define such an approach in different ways, but all seem to have in common the goal to understand the component processes, strategies, and mental representations of information, as well as interactions among processes, strategies, and representations that give rise to measured individual differences in abilities. All the chapters of this book seek to convey to the student just what the cognitive bases are of the various human abilities that have been identified but not thoroughly understood through psychometric and other kinds of analysis.

Obviously, this book is biased in its approach to, although I hope not in its coverage of, the range of human abilities. Although some of the chapters, and particularly the first chapter, review psychometric theories and research, no attempt is made to provide extensive coverage of this or many other approaches. There exist any number of texts that cover the psychometric approach in detail. Moreover, because there have been relatively few recent developments in this approach (at least as it is traditionally defined), I believe that any of a number of texts, not all of them recent, will provide adequate coverage of this approach. But I believe that this text is unique in providing extensive and intensive coverage of the human abilities field as seen from an information-processing point of view. Here, a new book is a must, because by far the largest share of the relevant research has been done in the last decade.

It is something of an oddity to present an "edited" text, but my decision to solicit contributions from top experts in the field rather than to write the book myself was a carefully deliberated one. Whereas the human-abilities field as seen from a psychometric point of view required detailed knowledge of a relatively small number of global theories, and of the machinery of factor analysis and other psychometric techniques, the human-abilities field as seen from an information-processing point of view requires detailed knowledge of a vast array of theories—some of them global and some of them quite specific—as well as of the experimental techniques of a wide range of subfields of cognitive psychology. I doubt there is anyone today who could claim the kind of wide-ranging expertise in the information-processing approach that could more easily be claimed by a number of individuals for the psychometric approach. In any case, I cannot claim such broad-ranging expertise. Hence, I decided to have each chapter cover a distinct information-processing ability and have it written by a distinguished expert on that ability. Although each chapter author could undoubtedly have written about other abilities as well, I doubt that such writing could be done with the authority and expertise that characterizes the individual's contribution to his or her primary area of endeavor. Thus, I have sought a quality in the chapters that I believe only a multiplicity of authors can provide. I, at least, believe that the quality I hoped for, as well as the elementary level of presentation I requested, have been attained.

This book is intended as an introductory text and is suitable for courses such as "Human Abilities," "Individual Differences," "Thinking," "Intelligence," and "Complex Information Processing." It might also be used as a supplementary text in courses on cognitive psychology, tests and measure-ments, and educational psychology.

In sum, the authors and I offer this book as what we believe to be the first text on human abilities that provides a broad and balanced exposure to the field of abilities as seen from an information-processing point of view. We believe we have met a need that only a book such as this one could fulfill.

Robert J. Sternberg

INTRODUCTION: WHAT IS AN INFORMATION-PROCESSING APPROACH TO HUMAN ABILITIES?

Robert J. Sternberg

This book's ten chapters present much of what we know about human abilities as viewed in terms of information processing. What, exactly, is an information-processing approach to human abilities? In this introduction, I will seek to describe just what such an approach is, and how it is similar to and different from other approaches, particularly, the so-called "psychometric" approach to abilities.

Information-processing psychology seeks to study the mind, in general, and intelligence, in particular, in terms of the mental representations and processes that underlie observable behavior. Information-processing researchers usually address five main points, as follows.

1. What are the mental processes that constitute intelligent performance on various tasks?
2. How rapidly and accurately are these processes performed?

3. Into what strategies for task performance do these mental processes combine?

4. Upon what forms of mental representation do these processes and strategies act?

5. What is the knowledge base that is organized into these forms of representation, and how does it affect, and how is it affected by, the processes, strategies, and representations that individuals use?

The information-processing approach to human abilities has arisen during the last 20 years as a response to the psychometric or differential approach to abilities. In this latter approach, psychologists sought to understand abilities largely in terms of factors, or mental structures, believed to be responsible for individual differences in observed performance on intelligence tests and in academic and other kinds of work (see Chapter 1). Information-processing psychologists were dissatisfied with the emphasis on structure in the psychometric approach. In particular, they wanted to find out more about the processes that underlie intelligent behavior, and they found psychometric theorists to be rather silent about what these processes might be. Information-processing psychologists have therefore seen their mission as different from that of psychometricians, with the latter emphasizing static structures, the former, dynamic processes. Indeed, the kinds of findings that have emerged from information-processing research and that are reported in this book are quite different from many of the findings that have emerged from the psychometric study of abilities. For example, psychometricians have started their investigations of human abilities with the study of individual differences among people, but information-processing psychologists have started their investigations with the study of how people perform on tasks; only then have they sought to look at individual differences in task performance. Whereas a psychometrician might be content to identify a factor (structure) of "human reasoning," information-processing psychologists would seek to identify the processes that underlie human reasoning.

Although many psychologists have tended to emphasize the difference between the two approaches, it is important to look as well at the similarities, both conceptually and historically.

Conceptually, both psychometricians and information-processing psychologists have investigated what it is that gives rise to observable individual differences in task performance. Much of the time, they have examined identical tasks, differing only in what aspects of task performance they feel ought to receive the lion's share of their attention. Moreover, both types of psychologists have attempted to construct theories of just what the basic human abilities are, and of how they are manifested in task performance.

Historically, many of the major psychologists identified primarily as "psychometricians" have also maintained a strong interest in the processes that underlie human abilities. For instance, Sir Francis Galton, an avid experimentalist, invented the correlational method, which underlies psychometric analyses of abilities. Alfred Binet invented the prototype for the most widely used psychometric intelligence test, and yet a close reading of his writing will show that his often neglected theorizing was just as concerned with processing as any of the theories being proposed today. Charles Spearman invented factor analysis, which is the cornerstone of psychometric analyses of abilities; yet his 1923 treatise on the "principles of cognition" was a cognitive monograph, and provided the basis for much contemporary information-processing theorizing about abilities, particularly in the domain of inductive reasoning. Edward Thorndike is best known for his experimental work on animal learning, and yet was the author of a major book on the subject of psychometrically measured intelligence. Clark Hull, another famous learning theorist, wrote his first book on the subject of aptitude testing. Louis Thurstone, a psychometrician if ever there was one, advocated factorial methods as preliminaries to experimental ones, not as replacements for them. J. P. Guilford, clearly identified as a psychometrician, has proposed a theory of intelligence in which one of the three facets he believes crucial to intelligence describes the processes of intelligence. The list could go on and on, but I think the point should by now be clear: Psychometric and information-processing approaches to human abilities are largely complementary, and can be pursued in conjunction rather than as totally separate entities.

How do information-processing psychologists go about studying human abilities? In general, they analyze how people go about solving difficult mental tasks. They often construct explicit models of just how these tasks are solved. These models may take the form of computer programs, flow charts, or other schematizations of the flow of processing during task performance, but their goal is always to understand the processes, strategies, and mental representations that people use in task performance.

Although information-processing psychologists agree in their emphasis on mental processing, they disagree in just how this emphasis should be reflected in research on human abilities. Consider a brief sampling of the kinds of emphases and approaches that have characterized the research of information-processing psychologists.

1. *The cognitive-correlates method.* In this approach to understanding human abilities, subjects are tested on their performance of tasks that contemporary information-processing psychologists believe measure basic human information-processing abilities. Such tasks include, for example, the letter-matching task, in which subjects are asked to state as quickly as possible whether the letters in a pair such as "A a" constitute a physical match (which they don't) or a name match (which they do). Such researchers often use extreme-group designs, comparing high-ability and low-ability subjects (as identified by standard psychometric ability tests) in their performance of the basic information-processing tasks studied in the laboratories of information-processing psychologists.

2. *The cognitive-components method.* In this approach, subjects are tested on their performance of tasks of the kinds actually found on standard psychometric tests of mental abilities—for example, analogies, series comple-

tions, and syllogisms. The tasks studied tend to be more complex than those studied by cognitive-correlates researchers. Rather than starting from very simple tasks and building up to complicated tasks, cognitive-components researchers tend to start with more complicated tasks and work their way down to the simple processing components that generate performance on these more complicated tasks.

3. *Cognitive-training methodology.* This approach to understanding human abilities can be used in conjunction with either of the two preceding approaches or with some other approach. The idea is to study the trainability of cognitive processes, which is taken to indicate both the existence and the importance of these processes for performance on tests of mental abilities. Researchers using this methodology are interested not only in getting improvement on a single task in a single situation, but also in showing durability of training over time, and transfer of training from the task on which performance is trained to other similar tasks.

4. *Cognitive-content methodology.* This approach to understanding abilities seeks to understand differences in the contents and structures of the knowledge that higher- and lower-ability subjects bring to bear on cognitive tasks. Often experts in a given field of endeavor, such as chess or physics, are compared to novices in the field in order to discover the nature of the differences between the two groups in their knowledge bases, and in how they bring these knowledge bases to bear on problem solving.

Of course, these are not the only approaches that have been used by information-processing psychologists: the categorization is neither exhaustive nor mutually exclusive. But it does convey some sense of the variety of ways in which information-processing psychologists have sought to understand the nature of human abilities.

To conclude, then, information-processing psychologists seek to understand human abilities in terms of the basic mental mechanisms that underlie intelligent behavior. Their work is complementary to the work of psychometricians and others who have sought to study abilities in different ways. In this book, you will be introduced to what information-processing psychologists have discovered about the nature of human abilities. You should end up with a clear, basic grasp of the processes that underlie the main human abilities that have, during the last hundred years, been measured as part of research on the nature of human intelligence.

1

GENERAL
INTELLECTUAL
ABILITY

Robert J. Sternberg
Yale University

General intellectual ability, or general intelligence, is among the most elusive of concepts. Certainly, few other concepts of any kind have been conceptualized in as many different ways. Although the emphasis in this book is on information-processing concepts of human abilities, I will here also discuss the psychometric view of abilities (which gave rise to IQ and other ability tests). It was because of dissatisfaction with this view that information-processing views have come to dominate contemporary theory and research on human abilities. In order to understand information-processing views, we must first understand psychometric views, and the ways in which they have been considered unsatisfactory.*

*Although these two views have probably been the most influential in forming North American and British concepts of the nature of intelligence, they are not the only views that have been advanced (see, e.g., Hebb, 1949; Hendrickson, 1982, for physiological views; and Piaget, 1972, for a genetic-epistemological view). These other views are not discussed here, but descriptions can be found elsewhere (see, e.g., Dockrell, 1970; Eysenck, 1982; Resnick, 1976; Sternberg, 1982b).

Before considering the information-processing view, and the psychometric view that gave rise to it, I would like to introduce you to one of the simpler ways to get some idea of what intelligence is: This way is to have experts or laypersons define the concept. Although such definitions are not likely to give us a detailed understanding of the nature of general intelligence, they may well give us some general, if vague, notions about just what it is that people mean by *intelligence.*

How People Define General Intelligence

The most famous study of experts' concepts of the scope of intelligent behavior was done by the editors of the *Journal of Educational Psychology,* in a symposium titled "Intelligence and its Measurement" in 1921. Fourteen experts gave their views on the nature of intelligence. Some examples of their definitions are as follows.

1. The ability to give responses that are true or factual (E. L. Thorndike).
2. The ability to carry on abstract thinking (L. M. Terman).
3. The ability to learn to adjust oneself to the environment (S. S. Colvin).
4. The ability to adapt oneself to relatively new situations in life (R. Pintner).
5. The capacity for knowledge and knowledge possessed (V. A. C. Henmon).
6. A biological mechanism by which the effects of a complexity of stimuli are brought together and given a somewhat unified effect in behavior (J. Peterson).
7. The ability to inhibit an instinctive adjustment, to redefine the inhibited instinctive adjustment in the light of imaginally experienced trial and error, and to realize the modified instinctive adjustment into overt behavior to the advantage of the individual as a social animal (L. L. Thurstone).
8. The ability to acquire abilities (H. Woodrow).
9. The ability to learn or to profit by experience (W. F. Dearborn).

There have been many, many definitions of intelligence since these were presented in the journal symposium, and an essay has even been written on the nature of definitions of intelligence (Miles, 1957). Certain themes seem to run through the definitions, such as the ability to learn from experience and to adapt to one's environment, but the perception of common themes is probably as much in the eye of the perceivers as in the minds of the experts. Clearly, it would be useful to have a nonarbitrary means of combining the perceptions of the various experts.

A contemporary version of this kind of study, and one that does provide a means of combining the concepts of various experts, was conducted by Sternberg et al. (1981). These investigators had many experts rate many kinds of behavior in terms of how distinctively characteristic each one was of intelligence or how important it was for defining intelligence in an ideally intelligent person. The ratings were factor-analyzed, and the three factors that emerged—verbal intelligence, problem solving, and practical intelligence—were taken as characterizing experts' concepts of intelligence.

If we view intelligence as a cultural concept, then we may use laypersons' views as a way to specify the scope of a theory of intelligence. Consider some examples of such an approach.

Neisser (1978) collected informal data from Cornell undergraduates about their concepts of intelligence. More formal studies have been conducted by Cantor (1978), who asked adult subjects to list attributes of a bright person, and by Bruner et al. (1958), who asked people how often intelligent people display various personality traits. These authors found, for example, that intelligent people are likely to be characterized as clever, deliberate, efficient, and energetic, but not as apathetic, unreliable, dishonest, and dependent.

Siegler and Richards (1982) asked adult subjects to characterize intelligence in children of different ages. These subjects tended to conceive of intelligence as less perceptual-motor and as more cognitive with increasing age. Yussen and Kane (in press) asked children in the first, third, and sixth grades what their concepts of intelligence are. They found that older children's concepts were more differentiated than younger children's; that with increasing age, children increasingly characterized intelligence as an internalized quality; that older children were less likely than younger ones to think there are overt signs of intelligence; and that older children were less global than younger children in the qualities they associated with intelligence.

Wober (1974) investigated concepts of intelligence among members of different tribes in Uganda as well as within different subgroups of the tribes. Wober found differences in concepts of intelligence both within and between tribes. The Baganda, for example, tended to associate intelligence with mental order, whereas the Batoro associated it with some degree of mental turmoil. On semantic-differential scales, Baganda tribespeople thought of intelligence as persistent, hard, and obdurate, whereas the Batoro thought of it as soft, obedient, and yielding.

Serpell (1974, 1976) asked Chewa adults in rural eastern Zambia to rate village children on how well they could perform tasks requiring adaptation in the everyday world. He found that the ratings did not correlate with children's cognitive test scores, even when the tests that were used were adapted to seem culturally appropriate. Serpell concluded that the rural Chewa criteria for judgments of intelligence were not related to Western notions of intelligence.

Super (1982) analyzed concepts of intelligence among the Kokwet of western Kenya. He found that intelligence in children seemed to be conceived differently from intelligence in adults. The word *ngom* was applied to children, and seemed to connote responsibility, highly verbal cognitive quickness, the ability to comprehend complex matters quickly, and good management of interpersonal relations. The word *utat* was applied to adults, and suggested inventiveness, cleverness, and, sometimes, wisdom and unselfishness. A separate word, *kwelat,* was used to signify smartness or sharpness.

Sternberg et al. (1981) found that laypersons' concepts of intelligence are remarkably similar to those of experts. Characteristicness ratings by experts and by laypersons were correlated .96, and importance ratings were correlated .85. The two groups thus seem largely to agree about what behaviors are characteristic of intelligence and important in defining the ideally intelligent person. The views were not identical, however. First, the experts considered motivation to be an important ingredient of "academic" intelligence, whereas no motivational factor emerged in factor analyses of laypersons' ratings. Second, the laypersons seemed to emphasize the social-cultural aspects of intelligence somewhat more than the experts did.

Clearly, definitions of intelligence are just a start toward understanding what intelligence is. Such definitions tend to be vague and highly general. Moreover, there is no guarantee that people's informal notions are veridical representations of their intellectual abilities. Thus, such definitions are probably best seen as telling us "the lay of the land," and need to be followed up by more scientifically derived (formal) theories of the nature of intelligence. Such theories have been provided by both the psychometric tradition and the information-processing tradition in psychology.

Psychometric Theories of the Nature of Human Intelligence

Psychometric theories of intelligence (also called *differential* theories, because they are based on the study of individual differences between people) almost always attempt to understand intelligence in terms of a set of static latent sources of individual differences called *factors*. It is proposed that individual differences in intelligence-test performance can be decomposed into individual differences in these factors, each of which is posited to represent a distinct human ability.

Factors are hypothetical constructs intended to describe the underlying sources of individual differences that give rise to observed individual differences in test scores. To obtain factors, we would first give a set of individuals a large battery of tests; then we would compute the intercorrelations between scores on all possible pairs of tests. Now, our goal would be to reduce the scores on the tests to a smaller number of scores on the *factors* supposed to underlie performance on these tests. We would apply the technique of "factor analysis" to perform this reduction. Tests that tend to correlate highly (for example, vocabulary and reading comprehension) tend to group together into single factors. Tests that are only weakly correlated or uncorrelated tend to group into separate factors. For example, if we were to factor-analyze four tests—vocabulary, reading comprehension, arithmetical problem solving, and arithmetical concepts—we would probably obtain two factors, one of "verbal" ability and the other of "mathematical" ability.

Given that almost all differential theories use factors to understand intelligence, we might wonder how the differential theories differ from one another. The primary differences are in (a) the number of factors posited by the theory and (b) the geometric arrangement of the factors with respect to one another.

Consider how number and geometric arrangement can form the bases for alternative theories of intelligence.

Differences in Number of Factors

Differential theorists differ greatly in the number of factors they suppose to be important for understanding intelligent behavior. Indeed, the number of factors proposed in major theories ranges from 1 to 150.

At the lower end, Spearman (1927) proposed that intelligence comprises two kinds of factors, a general factor and specific factors. The ability represented by the general factor permeates performance on all intellectual tasks; the abilities represented by the specific factors each permeate only a single task, and so are not of much psychological interest. Hence there is just one factor of major psychological interest, the general factor, or *g*, as it has often been called. Spearman made two (not necessarily mutually exclusive) famous proposals about the nature of *g*. First, individual differences in *g* might be understood in terms of differences in the amount of mental energy that individuals could bring to intellectual task performance. Second, individual differences in *g* could be understood in terms of differences in people's abilities to use three "qualitative principles of cognition" (Spearman, 1923): apprehension of experience, eduction of relations, and eduction of correlates. In order to understand what each of these three principles represents, consider an analogy of the form *A* : *B* :: *C*:?; for example, *LAWYER* : *CLIENT* :: *DOCTOR* :?. Apprehension of experience refers to encoding (perceiving and understanding) each term of the analogy. Eduction of relations refers to inferring the relation between the first two analogy terms, here, *LAWYER* and *CLIENT*. Eduction of correlates refers to applying the inferred principle to a new domain, here, applying the rule inferred from *LAWYER* to *DOCTOR* to produce a completion for *DOCTOR* : ?. The best-educated answer to this analogy would presumably be *PATIENT*. Given that analogies directly embody these principles, it is not surprising that Spearman (1923, 1927) and many others subsequently have found such analogies to be among the best available measures of *g*. (See Sternberg, 1977, for a review of relevant literature.)

In a more "middle-of-the-road" position, Thurstone (1938) proposed that intelligence comprises roughly seven "primary mental abilities." Consider the identity of each of these abilities, and how it is commonly measured.

1. *Verbal comprehension* is typically measured by tests of vocabulary (including both synonyms and antonyms) and by tests of reading-comprehension skills.

2. *Verbal fluency* is typically measured by tests that require rapid production of words. For example, the individual might be asked to generate as quickly as possible, and within a limited period of time, as many words as he or she can think of that begin with the letter *d*.

3. *Number* is typically measured by arithmetical word problems in which there is some emphasis on both computation and reasoning, but relatively little emphasis on extent of prior knowledge.

4. *Spatial visualization* is typically measured by tests that require mental manipulation of symbols or geometric designs. For example, the individual might be shown a picture of a geometric design in some degree of angular rotation, followed by a set of pictures in various orientations that either are identical (except for degree of rotation) to the original object or are mirror images of the original object. The individual would have to indicate whether each item is the same as the target or is a mirror image of it.

5. *Memory* is typically measured by a test of recall memory for words or sentences, or by paired-associates recall of names with pictures of people.

6. *Reasoning* is typically measured by tests such as analogies (e.g., *LAWYER* : *CLIENT* :: *DOCTOR* : ?) and series completions (e.g., 2, 4, 7, 11, ?).

7. *Perceptual speed* is typically measured by tests requiring rapid recognition of symbols, for example, rapid crossing out of l's that are embedded in a string of letters.

Pretty much at the upper extreme of number of proposed factors is Guilford (1967; Guilford and Hoepfner, 1971), who at one time proposed that intelligence comprises 120 distinct factors, and has more recently increased this number to 150 (Guilford, 1982). According to Guilford, every mental task involves three ingredients: an operation, a content, and a product. There are five kinds of operations: cognition, memory, divergent production, convergent production, and evaluation. There are five kinds of contents: visual, auditory, symbolic, semantic, and behavioral. And there are six kinds of products: units, classes, relations, systems, transformations, and implications. Since the subcategories are independently defined, they are multiplicative; so there are $5 \times 5 \times 6 = 150$ different mental abilities.

Guilford and his associates have devised tests that measure many of the factors posited by the model. As of 1982, Guilford claims to have demonstrated the existence of 105 of the 150 possible factors. Guilford (1982) has also made clear that, although the 150 factors are logically independent, they can be psychologically dependent in the sense of being intercorrelated. Consider how just a few of these abilities are measured. Cognition of visual relations (called "cognition of figural relations" in the 1967 version of the model) is measured by tests using figure analogies or matrices. Memory for semantic relations is measured by presenting to examinees a series of relationships, such as, "Gold is more valuable than iron," and then testing retention in a multiple-choice format. Evaluation of symbolic units is measured by same-different tests, in which subjects are presented with pairs of numbers or letters that are identical or different in minor details. Subjects are then asked to mark each pair as "same" or "different."

Differences in Geometric Structure of Factors

As was noted earlier, two models that posit the same number of factors—and even the same contents for factors—might still differ because they posit different geometric arrangements of these factors. The four most well-known structures are an unordered arrangement, a cubic arrangement, a hierarchic arrangement, and a radex arrangement.

Unordered arrangements consist of lists of factors, all of which are asserted to be of equal importance. Thurstone's (1938) seven primary mental abilities are a good example of this kind of arrangement. Thurstone suggested simply that intelligence could be understood in terms of these seven factors. They are not ordered in any particular way: any permutation of his list is as valid as any other.

The most well-known "cubic" theorist is Guilford. Guilford (1982) has represented the structure of intellect as a large cube composed of 150 smaller cubes. Each dimension of the cube corresponds to one of the three categories (operation, content, product), and each of the 150 possible combinations of the three categories forms one of the smaller cubes.

Hierarchic arrangements have been popular in the recent and contemporary differential literature on intelligence. According to this view, abilities are not of equal importance. Rather, certain abilities are more global, and hence more important, than others. Spearman's (1927) factorial model, with a general factor and less-important specific factors, might be seen as the original hierarchic model, although it is not clear that Spearman thought of his theory primarily in this way. Holzinger (1938) elaborated on Spearman's point of view by suggesting that there existed group factors intermediate in generality between the general factor and the specific factors. These group factors permeated performance on some class of tasks (and always on more than one task), but were not involved in performance of all mental tasks in a given test battery. Burt (1940) proposed a five-level hierarchic model:

1. Human mind
2. Relations
3. Associations
4. Perceptions
5. Sensations

Vernon (1971) proposed a more sophisticated hierarchic model, suggesting that *g* could be decomposed into two broad group factors, verbal-educational ability and practical-mechanical ability. He further proposed that these broad group factors could be further decomposed into narrower group factors, although this further decomposition is of less interest in his theory.

Finally, Guttman (1965) has proposed a radex structure for intelligence. A radex can be thought of as a circle. Each test found on intelligence-test batteries can be placed somewhere in the circle. Tests nearer the center of the circle measure abilities more "central" to intelligence. The purest measures of intelligence would be at the center of the circle, and the least-pure measures would be at the periphery of the circle. Arrayed around the circle are various kinds of task contents and required processes, for example, verbal tasks, numerical tasks, and geometric-pictorial tasks, among other kinds.

Critique

In sum, differential or psychometric theories of intelligence differ primarily in terms of the number of factors they posit and the geometric arrangements of these factors. On their face, the theories seem quite different. It is not clear that these differences are really as consequential as they initially would seem. Indeed, the amount of agreement between these theories could be seen as substantially greater than the amount of disagreement.

First, the theories share common metatheoretical assumptions. All assume that intelligence can be understood in terms of latent sources of individual differences, or "factors." These factors are believed to provide, in some sense, a "map" of the mind. Because the factors are identified in terms of observed individual differences in mental-test performance, all the theories assume that the primary basis for identifying the dimensions of intelligence ought to be observed individual differences. And the kinds of tests that have been used to measure these individual differences have also been quite similar. All are in the tradition of Binet and Simon (1905, 1908), although they differ in the details of exactly what skills they measure.

Second, the alternative theories are, in many cases, mathematically nearly equivalent. We might wonder how such different factor structures could result when essentially the same mathematical technique, factor analysis, is being applied to roughly comparable sets of subjects who are taking roughly comparable sets of tests. The answer lies largely in the placement of axes in a "factor space." Factors can be represented in a space, with each factor being a dimension in the space. When a factor analysis is performed, the locations of points (tests) in the factor space are fixed, but the locations of the factor axes are not. In other words, it is possible to have many—indeed, infinitely many—orientations of factor axes. It turns out that many of the theories differ from one another primarily in terms of the orientation of the factor axes in the factor space, and hence are (roughly) equivalent mathematically. That is, the different theories say the same things in different ways. Recent cognitive-experimental research suggests that the various factorial theories can all be mapped into a common set of information-processing components of task performance (Sternberg, 1980). In other words, no matter what factor structure is used, the basic processes contributing to the factors are the same.

Third, and finally, some of the differences between theories appear, on closer examination, to be differences of emphasis rather than of substance. For example, Spearman's and Thurstone's theories appear to be radically different. But by the end of his career, Spearman was forced to concede the existence of group factors; indeed, he even collaborated with Holzinger on the development of a theory that encompassed group factors as well as the general and specific ones. Similarly, Thurstone was forced, by the end of his career, to acknowledge the existence of a higher-order general factor that in some sense incorporated the primary mental abilities. The primary evidence for such a higher-order factor is that the primary mental abilities are not statistically independent, but rather are intercorrelated with each other: people who tend to be high in one ability tend to be high in others as well, and people who tend to be low in one ability tend to be low in others as well. When we factor these factors, we obtain a general, higher-order factor. The main difference between Spearman and Thurstone may thus have been in the emphases they placed on higher-order versus lower-order factors. Spearman emphasized the former, Thurstone the latter. Humphreys (1964) and Jensen (1970) have provided excellent accounts of how hierarchic models can be formed that incorporate factors at the level of both Spearman's general factor and Thurstone's primary mental abilities.

There has been a long-term debate over the merits of factor analysis as a means for uncovering the nature of intelligence. (See, e.g., Burt, 1940; Eysenck, 1953, 1967; Humphreys, 1962; Royce, 1963, 1979; Sternberg, 1977, 1979.) I have come to view this debate as misconceived, largely because it really does not make sense to evaluate a methodology independent of its use. If our goal is to isolate global, structural constellations of individual differences in test performance, then factor analysis certainly can be useful. As so often happens with multivariate methods, this method has sometimes been misused (for discussions, see Guilford, 1952; McNemar, 1951; Sternberg, 1977). When a method is misused, we may be tempted to blame the method rather than the misusers. Perhaps too much has been claimed for what factor analysis has told us about intelligence. Perhaps more attention should have been paid to just what questions about intelligence factor analysis can and cannot answer. But the same could be said for many other methods as well. When a method is first applied to the study of a problem, it is quite natural for overly strong claims to be made: the limitations of the method simply have not yet become clear. But over the years, these limitations do become more clear, and it is necessary to pay attention to both strengths and weaknesses of the method as applied to various kinds of problems. At the very least, factor analysis was useful in providing initial structural models.

Information-Processing Theories of the Nature of Human Intelligence

Information-processing or cognitive theories of intelligence all attempt to understand human intelligence in terms of the mental processes that contribute to cognitive task performance. A primary difference between them is in what level of cognitive functioning they emphasize in attempting to explain intelligence. At one extreme, some investigators have tried to understand intelligence in terms of sheer speed of information processing, and have used the simplest tasks they could devise in order to measure pure speed uncontaminated by other variables. At the other extreme, other investigators have studied very complex forms of problem solving, and have deemphasized or discounted speed of functioning in mental processing. In general, speed of processing has been emphasized by investigators studying the simpler forms of information processing, whereas accuracy and strategies in information processing have been emphasized by investigators studying the more complex forms of processing.

Let us consider some of the levels of processing that have been studied. This survey is not intended to be complete, but merely representative of the kinds of work that have been done.

Pure Speed

Proponents of the notion that individual differences in intelligence can be traced back to differences in sheer speed of information processing have tended to use simple reaction-time and related tasks in order to make their point. In a simple reaction-time paradigm, the subject is required simply to make a single overt response as quickly as possible after presentation of a stimulus. This paradigm has been widely used ever since the days of Galton as a measure of intelligence (Berger, 1982; Eysenck, 1982). Although Galton (1883) and Cattell (1890) were strong supporters of the importance of sheer speed in intellectual functioning, the levels of correlation obtained between measures of simple reaction time and various standard measures of intelligence, none of which are perfect in themselves (e.g., IQ test scores, school grades, and the like), have been rather weak. Wissler (1901) obtained correlations close to 0, as did Lemmon (1927–1928). Lunneborg (1977) obtained correlations with eight psychometric measures of intelligence ranging from −.17 to −.42, with a median of −.38. (Negative correlations are expected, because longer reaction times are presumed to be associated with lower levels of intelligent performance.) In my view, the most trustworthy results are those of Jensen (1980, esp. 1982), who has reported correlations for two samples, one in the mid-.20s, the other around .10. Clearly, if there is any relationship at all between measures of pure speed and of psychometrically measured intelligence, the relationship is a weak one.

Choice Speed

A more sophisticated form of the preceding notion is that intelligence derives not from simple speed of processing, but rather from speed in making choices or decisions between simple stimuli. In a typical "choice reaction time" paradigm, the subject is presented with one of two or more possible stimuli, each requiring a different overt response. The subject has to choose the correct response as rapidly as possible after stimulus presentation. Correlations with psychometric measures of intelligence have been higher than those for simple reaction time (Berger, 1982). Lemmon (1927–1928) found a correlation of −.25 between choice reaction time and measured intelligence. Lunneborg (1977) found variable correlations. In one study, correlations ranged from −.28 to −.55, with a median of −.40. In a second study, however, correlations were trivial. Jensen (1982) reported a correlation of −.30 for one sample, but a correlation close to 0 for another. Lally and Nettelbeck (1977) obtained a correlation of −.56, but in a sample with a very wide range of IQs (57–130). The problem with using such an extremely wide range of IQs is that it tends to make even weak predictors of IQ look powerful. For example the ability to eat with a spoon will be correlated with adult IQ if only low-enough IQs are included in the sample.

An interesting finding in the research both of Jensen (1979, 1982) and of Lally and Nettelbeck (1977) is that the correlation between choice reaction time and IQ tends to increase with the number of stimulus-response choices involved in the task. In fact, these investigators found a roughly linear relation between the level of correlation obtained and the binary log of the number of choices (i.e., number of bits) in the task, at least through eight choices (three bits). But the correlations for typical ranges of subject ability nevertheless seem to peak at slightly over the −.40 level. Thus, increasing the number of choices in a test of choice reaction time seems to increase correlation with IQ, but such testing is still a long way from providing a causal account of individual differences in psychometrically measured IQ.

Brand and Deary (1982) have reported some extremely high correlations (around −.80) between IQ and a measure derived from reaction time needed to indicate the longer of two vertical lines. They refer to the time needed to do this task as "inspection time." Although these correlations seem most impressive at first, they were derived from very small samples of subjects, who often differed extremely widely in IQ, ranging from mentally retarded to gifted. Using more typical samples, other investigators, such as Nettelbeck (1982), have obtained the more typical levels of correlations for tests of choice-reaction time (about −.30).

Speed of Lexical Access

Hunt (1978, 1980) has proposed that individual differences in verbal intelligence may be understandable largely in terms of differences between individuals' speed of access to lexical information in long-term memory. In this view, individuals who can access information more quickly can profit more per unit time of presented information, and hence can perform better on a variety of tasks, especially verbal ones. Hunt et al. (1975) initiated a paradigm for testing this theory that uses the Posner and Mitchell (1967) letter-comparison task. Subjects are presented with pairs of letters—such as *AA, Aa,* or *Ab*—that may be the same or different, either physically or in name. For example, *AA* contains two letters that are the same both physically and in name; *Aa* contains two letters that are the same in name only; and *Ab* contains two letters that are the same neither in name nor in physical appearance. The subject's task is to indicate as rapidly as possible whether the two letters are a match. In one type of test condition, subjects must state whether the letters are a physical match; in another, the same subjects must state whether the letters are a name match. The measure of interest is the difference between each subject's average name-match time and physical-match time. This measure is taken to be an index of time of access to lexical information in long-term memory. Physical-match time is subtracted from name-match time in order to obtain a relatively pure measure of lexical-access time that is uncontaminated by sheer speed of responding. Thus, whereas those who study simple reaction time are particularly interested in sheer speed of responding, Hunt and his colleagues do what they can to subtract out this element.

Some investigators have used this paradigm as a basis for understanding individual differences in verbal intelligence (e.g., Hunt et al., 1975; Keating and Bobbitt, 1978; Jackson and McClelland, 1979). Unlike tests of simple reaction time and choice reaction time, the lexical-access task yields a remarkably consistent relationship to measured intelligence: correlations with scores on verbal IQ tests are typically about −.30. Lexical-access time therefore seems to be related at some level to intellectual performance; but again it is obviously, and at best, only one contributor to individual differences in what is measured by standard psychometric IQ tests (which, again, are themselves highly imperfect measures of intelligence, broadly defined). The correlation is too weak for us to make any strong statement about direction of causality.

Speed of Reasoning Processes

Some investigators have emphasized the kinds of higher-order processing involved in reasoning in their attempts to understand intelligence (e.g., Pellegrino and Glaser, 1980, 1982; Sternberg, 1977; Sternberg and Gardner, 1983; Whitely, 1980). Following in the tradition of Spearman's qualitative "principles of cognition," these investigators have sought to understand individual differences in intelligence in terms of individual differences in processing information in tasks such as analogies, series completions, or syllogisms. There have been two main emphases in this work, namely, on performance processes and on executive processes. This work will be summarized now, and more will be said about it later.

Performance processes. Investigators seeking to understand intelligence in terms of performance processes try to discover the processes that individuals use in problem solving, from the time they first see a problem to the time they respond to the problem. Consider, for example, the widely studied analogy item. In a typical theory of analogical reasoning, performance on the analogy item is decomposed into component processes, such as *inferring* the relation between the first two terms of the analogy, *mapping* the higher-order relation that connects the first half of the analogy to the second half, and *applying* the relation inferred in the first half of the analogy to the second half of the problem (Sternberg, 1977). The motivating idea is that individuals' skills in solving these problems derive from their ability to execute these processes (rapidly). Moreover, the processes involved in analogy solution have been shown to be quite general, being used in various kinds of inductive-reasoning problems (Greeno, 1978; Pellegrino and Glaser, 1980; Sternberg and Gardner, 1983). Thus, the components are of interest because they are not task-specific, but rather are relevant for a variety of problem-solving tasks (see also Newell and Simon, 1972, for a similar logic applied to other kinds of complex problems).

How well does the performance-process approach work? For the three components just noted (inference, mapping, application), Sternberg (1977) found a median correlation of −.16 for schematic-picture analogies, and of −.34 for verbal analogies. In a geometric-analogies experiment, only application was reliably estimated for individual subjects, and it showed a median multiple correlation (taking into account error rates as well as latencies) with psychometric test performance of .34. Mulholland et al. (1980), also using geometric-analogy problems but a different breakdown of components, obtained results that were roughly comparable to these. Sternberg and Gardner (1983) obtained much more reliable estimates of the reasoning-process parameters than had Sternberg (1977). They administered to subjects three different tasks (analogies, series completions, and classifications) with three different contents (schematic picture, verbal, and geometric). Correlations between a combined reasoning component (including inference, mapping, and application) and psychometrically measured intelligence were −.70 for analogies, −.50 for series completions, and −.64 for classifications, averaged over contents. Correlations were −.70 for schematic-picture items, −.61 for verbal items, and −.67 for geometric items, averaged over tasks. These correlations were negative because the component score is measured as a reaction time: a shorter reaction time is correlated with better test performance. This approach seems capable of yielding rather high correlations, and thus to hold some promise for understanding individual differences in psychometrically measured intelligence, although again it seems highly unlikely that this approach could provide anything like a full account of intelligence.

Executive processes.   Investigators seeking to understand intelligence in terms of executive processes try to discover the processes by which individuals make decisions, such as (a) what performance components to use in solving various kinds of problems, (b) how to combine the performance components into an overall strategy, (c) how to represent information, or (d) how to trade off speed for accuracy (Brown, 1978; Flavell, 1981; Sternberg, 1980). Sternberg (1980) has proposed that "metacomponents" such as these are highly general for tasks involving intelligent performance, and that they are in large part responsible for the appearance of a general factor in mental-ability tests. On this view, what is "general" across the tests is the execution of the metacomponents of task performance. Because metacomponents are difficult to isolate from task performance, existing data about the relationship between these metacomponents and psychometrically measured intelligence are spotty, at best. The only data of which I am aware are reported in Sternberg (1981). Two metacomponents, global planning and local planning, were isolated from a complex reasoning task. Global planning measures general strategic planning of solution strategy across a range of item types. Local planning measures specific strategic planning for an individual item. It was found that global planning scores correlated .43 with measured intelligence and that local planning scores correlated −.33 with measured intelligence. That is, more intelligent individuals tended to spend relatively more time than others in global planning, but relatively less time than others in local planning. This result is consistent with the notion that more-intelligent individuals are *selectively* more reflective than less intelligent individuals; that is, they tend to engage in more abstract kinds of thinking (see also Baron, 1982).

A Triarchy of Intelligence

In a 1984 article, I have proposed that intelligence ought to be understood in terms of three aspects of human information processing.

The first aspect addresses the question of the mechanisms of intelligent functioning. The mechanisms I propose are (a) metacomponents, or executive processes, such as deciding on the nature of the problem and selecting a strategy for solving the problem, (b) performance components, or nonexecutive process-es, used in actually executing a problem-solving strategy, and (c) knowledge-acquisition components, or the processes used to acquire new information. I have proposed a set of each kind of process that should adequately account for intelligent functioning in most of the intellectual tasks used in the laboratory and on IQ tests.

The second aspect addresses another question: At what point of practice do these mechanisms most involve "intelligent" performance? I suspect that tasks and situations most adequately measure intelligent performance when they are either novel in a person's experience or else so customary that performance on them is becoming automatic and hence essentially subconscious. The com-ponents are therefore best measured either early in a person's experience with a task or else much later, when processing is becoming automatized.

The third aspect addresses the question of the relation between intelli-gence and the external world. I think that intelligent behavior is ultimately behavior that involves adaptation to, selection of, or shaping of people's real-world environments. Adaptation occurs when a person attempts to achieve a "good fit" with the environment he or she is in. Selection occurs when a person decides to find a new environment rather than to adapt to the one he or she is in (such a decision might be motivated by a decision that the present environment is morally reprehensible, or is unsuitable for one's talents or interests, and so on). Shaping of the environment occurs when a person cannot find (select) an environment that seems suitable. In this case, the person makes changes in the environment he or she is in, in order to improve its fit with his or her aptitudes, interests, values, etc., capitalize on his or her strengths, and compensate for his or her weaknesses.

In my 1984 article, I argue that an ideal measurement of intelligence would take into account all three aspects of the proposed triarchy, although few everyday tasks or situations do so. For example, we would like to choose a battery of tasks administered in situations that maximize sampling of all three areas. Typical intelligence tests primarily tap only the first aspect of the triarchy, and hence need supplementation.

Critique

The cognitive theories differ in the "levels of processing" about which they theorize (see Craik and Lockhart, 1972; Sternberg and Salter, 1982) and in the kinds of tasks that serve as foci for information-processing analysis. But just as with the psychometric theories, the cognitive theories are more similar than they might at first appear to be.

First, all the theories assume, at some level, that intelligence can be understood in terms of constituent information-processing components. The unit of analysis is a real-time operation on a particular kind of mental representation. Whereas the differential theories are based on a static structural element, the factor, the cognitive theories are based on a dynamic process element, the component. In the first flush of enthusiasm when cognitive theorizing was introduced into the study of intelligence, cognitive researchers seemed to be claiming, either implicitly or explicitly, that understanding processes was more important than understanding factors (see, e.g., Hunt et al., 1973; Sternberg, 1977). This claim was misguided. The two kinds of elements address different questions—one about structure, the other about process—and ultimately can be used to help understand each other (Sternberg, 1980). Arguments about which kind of element is more basic (e.g., Carroll, 1980) are, in my opinion, fruitless, because we have no empirical means for answering this question, nor is it even clear what the question "really" means.

Second, the theories all emphasize speed of processing, whereas psychometric theorizing and testing emphasize accuracy. Not all cognitive theorists, of course, emphasize speed in their theorizing (see, e.g., Baron, 1982; Newell and Simon, 1972; Simon, 1976), but this emphasis has been predominant in cognitive research. On the one hand, this emphasis may reflect genuine beliefs about the psychology of human intelligence. On the other hand, it may reflect the heavy use by cognitive researchers of reaction-time methodologies, in which case methods may be dictating theory (at least in part) rather than the other way around. Even attempts to understand both speed and accuracy of processing simultaneously (e.g., Mulholland et al., 1980; Sternberg, 1977, 1980) have been based on tasks with relatively low error rates, in which speed rather than accuracy has been the more important variable being studied.

Third, and finally, the theories draw their empirical support from performance on tasks that are easily prepared (one might even say "canned") for use in the laboratory. On the one hand, the difference between a simple reaction-time task and an analogies task can be seen as quite large indeed. On the other hand, compared with the kinds of tasks people must perform in everyday life, the difference can be seen as rather small. People no more go around solving testlike analogies (except on tests) than they go around pressing buttons in response to lights or sounds. Although such tasks are not unheard of in the everyday world, they are not typical of the kinds of things people normally do in their lives. The same, of course, can be said for most of the tasks that have been used in differential theorizing, although these tasks have on the average been somewhat more abstract than those in the cognitive literature. If we want to understand intelligence in terms of performance on extremely basic (and, some might say, impoverished) tasks, then tests using such tasks are fine. But it is not immediately obvious that performance in real-world settings can be reduced to components of task performance on very simple tasks.

Relations Between Psychometric and Information-Processing Theories

It is tempting to regard information-processing theories as a replacement for psychometric theories. Indeed, they are replacements *if* our goal is to understand the processes of intelligence that underlie tests and, to some extent, real-world performance. But it is sometimes a mistake to throw away the results from all approaches that happen not to conform to one's own, and I believe this to be true of the situation here. To a large extent, psychometric and information-processing theories are intermappable. The psychometric theories address primarily the question of what structural constellations of processes, contents, representations, and the like give rise to stable patterns of individual differences. The information-processing theories actually attempt to identify the individual processes, contents, and representations. The latter approach is thus useful for a molecular analysis of how tasks are solved. The former approach is useful for discovering how these processes, contents, and representations group together to form relatively stable sources of individual differences. Thurstone (1947) proposed that factorial analyses of human abilities were only a beginning, that they needed to be followed by detailed experimental-process analyses of performance on intellectual tasks. From this point of view, with which I agree, information-processing research represents a natural evolution from psychometric research. It does not supersede it so much as build on it. In particular, analyses of information processing provide the kind of fine-grained analysis of human abilities that should follow from the broad, "lay-of-the-land" types of analyses that psychometric theories provided.

Evaluation of Theories

The review of theories presented so far should at least hint both at the questions that theories of intelligence have addressed well and at the questions that these theories have addressed either not well or not at all. Let us consider both classes of questions.

Strengths of Theories

The theories of intelligence have several notable strengths. Consider some of the main ones.

1. *Detailed specification of mental structures and processes.* A particular strength of theories of the kinds considered so far is their fairly detailed specification of the structures and processes that might be involved in intelligent performance. Differential theories address questions of structure, but generally have less to say about process (although there are exceptions; e.g., Guilford, 1967); cognitive theories address questions of process, but generally have less to say about structure (although again there are exceptions; e.g., Anderson, 1976). For building an essentially mechanistic (and molar) model of the mind, these theories have served well.

2. *Beyond operational definitions.* The theories have enabled investigators to go far beyond the trivial operational definition that "Intelligence is what intelligence tests measure" (Boring, 1923; Jensen, 1969). A common misconception about research on intelligence is that there have been two psychometric "schools" of thought: one, tracing back to Galton (1883), is alleged to be theoretically based; the other, tracing back to Binet and Simon (1905), is alleged to be atheoretical (Hunt et al., 1973). This view of the history of intelligence research is, I believe, incorrect. A review of Binet's numerous writings on intelligence (see, e.g., Binet and Simon, 1973) will reveal that Binet was highly theoretical, at least as much so as Galton. The tests that Binet and Simon created were based on a theory of intelligence, even though it sometimes seemed forgotten (or at least lost sight of) by Binet's successors. The same point would apply equally well to the tests of Wechsler: he, too, had a well-developed theory about the nature of intelligence (Wechsler, 1950). In any event, the theories have helped formalize some of Binet's notions, and have provided a fairly specific account of what it is that IQ tests measure. The tendency of test creators and publishers to choose test items primarily or solely on the basis of statistical criteria does not negate the theoretical bases for the kinds of items used; and recently at least some test creators and publishers have been paying careful attention to the theoretical bases for their tests (e.g., Feuerstein, 1979; Kaufman and Kaufman, 1982).

3. *Heuristic value.* The theories have had a good track record in terms of the evolution of the field of intelligence research (see Sternberg and Powell, 1982). A review of the differential literature on intelligence will reveal that there was active theoretical debate and discussion from at least the early 1900s until the 1950s, when research under this paradigm certainly slowed down and perhaps stagnated. By the late 1960s and certainly the early 1970s, the banner of intelligence research had been actively carried forward by cognitive researchers, who have continued the vigorous debate on the nature of intelligence (see, e.g., Eysenck, 1982; Resnick, 1976; Sternberg, 1982b; Sternberg and Detterman, 1979). Although it is never clear what constitutes "progress" in a field of endeavor, there has certainly been very active theory development in recent years in the study of intelligence.

4. *Practical value.* Some theories have proven to be very useful for practical purposes, such as for diagnosis, prediction, and training. For example, Feuerstein's (1979, 1980) theories of mediated learning experience (the experience of the child as mediated to him or her by the mother) and of deficient cognitive functions, as well as his adaptation of Vygotsky's (1979) notion of the zone of potential development (the difference between an individual's latent ability and his or her developed ability), have proven to be very useful in both the assessment and the training of intellectual functions. Cognitive theories of information processing in memory-task performance, particularly those emphasizing executive processing, have been instrumental in increasing the performance of retarded individuals on intellectual tasks (see, e.g., Belmont and Butterfield, 1971; Borkowski and Cavanaugh, 1979; Brown et al., 1977; Campione et al., 1982).

In sum, explicit theories of intelligence have made some notable contributions to our understanding, assessment, and training of intellectual functioning. Today the field of intelligence is one of active research, and there is every reason to believe that the research being done will contribute to the explosion of knowledge about intelligence that has been characteristic of research during the past decade or so.

Weaknesses of Theories

It will come as no surprise that, for all their strengths, the theories and the research that has been done on them tend to share some notable weaknesses. Consider some of the most salient ones.

Difficulty of falsification.   Many of the theories have proven remarkably difficult to falsify, not because of their extraordinary empirical validity, but because of intrinsic characteristics that make falsification difficult or impossible. Nonfalsifiability has long been a bane of differential theories (see Sternberg, 1977). One reason for this problem is that inferential statistics for exploratory factor analysis are not well developed; another reason is that it is exceedingly difficult to compare theories that differ primarily from each other in the form of rotation applied to an initial factor solution: mathematically, the alternative solutions are equivalent. Although various psychological and heuristic criteria have been proposed for discriminating between theories (see, e.g., Carroll, 1980), there has been nothing approaching a consensus about these criteria. Cognitive theories have fared better in some respects, but not in others. For example, investigators such as Hunt et al. (1973) and Sternberg (1977) have correlated parameters of their models against external criteria, such as psychometric tests of intelligence. But what constitutes a "high enough" correlation? Hunt et al. (1973) make very clear that they are quite satisfied with correlations of the order of .3; I made it equally clear (1981) that I am not satisfied with such low correlations. When we move from the question of statistical significance to the question of theoretical or practical significance, the guidelines seem to become fuzzy indeed. And no matter what level of correlation we accept, we are assuming that information-processing components of some kind are an appropriate unit of analysis for understanding intelligence. But this assumption has not been tested, and is probably untestable (see, e.g., Guilford, 1980; Keating, 1980; Royce, 1980). Similarly, the structural assumptions underlying much of the information-processing work—for example, those of the distributive memory model (Hunt, 1971) that has guided Hunt's (1978, 1980) work on intelligence—are also not clearly testable.

Tasks of doubtful relevance to the real world.   The theories are generally based and tested on kinds of tasks whose relevance to the real world is, at best, slight. There seems to be a substantial gap between the kinds of real-world adaptation required for everyday functioning and the kinds of adaptations required for taking tests well (see my 1984 article for further discussion). Although the skills involved in testlike and laboratory tasks may well contribute to real-world functioning, only an extreme reductionist would claim that they are exactly the same skills, and even such a reductionist would probably grant that there is a great difference in the level of processing at which the skills are exercised. Skeptics might claim with some justification that what are purported to be theories of "intelligence" would better be called theories of the ability to perform well on tests. If intelligence is indeed more than IQ tests measure, then we need strong demonstrations that existing theories are relevant for real-world perform-ance, since that relevance is in dispute (see, e.g., McClelland, 1973; Schmidt and Hunter, 1981).

Inattention to the contexts in which intelligent behavior occurs. Similarly, theories in the differential and cognitive traditions have almost never been sensitive to the interface between intelligence and the context in which it is exercised; yet many psychologists, anthropologists, and others have doubted whether we can fully understand intelligence except in relation to the contexts in which it develops and is exercised (see, e.g., Berry, 1974, 1981, 1982; Charles-worth, 1976, 1979; Dewey, 1957; Keating, 1984; Laboratory of Comparative Human Cognition, 1982, 1983; Neisser, 1976, 1978; Sternberg, 1984; Stern-berg and Salter, 1982). I do not believe that the failure to consider contextual variables necessarily renders the differential and cognitive theories wrong, but it does render them incomplete. Consequential intelligence exists in a world that is much broader and more complex than the testing situations and tasks of most psychologists.

Failure to provide an explicit basis for selection of tasks. Often theorists have failed to supply a rationale for the selection of the tasks used to study intelli-gence. Consider each of the differential and cognitive approaches in turn.

The selection of tasks is of utmost importance to the differential psychol-ogist, since the results of a factor analysis (and other forms of correlational analysis) are greatly affected by the choice of variables to be factor-analyzed. Differential psychologists have traditionally used one of two means for deciding what tasks should be included in an assessment battery.

The first means is to sample widely from the universe of available tasks purported to be useful as measures of mental abilities, but this procedure places the burden of task selection on one's predecessors. How did they decide what tasks are useful for measuring mental abilities? If they decided in the same way, we find ourselves led into an infinite regress.

The second means is to choose tasks on the basis of their correlations with other tasks. But what exactly does this mean? If the differential psychologist chooses only tasks that are perfectly intercorrelated with each other (across subjects), then the result will be trivial variation in task makeup, and guarantees a "unifactor" theory of intelligence, since all tests will be measuring exactly the same thing. If the differential psychologist chooses only tasks that are uncorre-lated, then there will be wide variation in task makeup, and there will be as many factors as there are tasks. Reduction of data, one of the ultimate goals of psychology and any other science, will be impossible. So obviously the differential psychologist must choose tasks that have some intermediate degree of correlation with each other. But the rules for specifying an "intermediate" degree of correlation have never been stated; and since such a degree of correlation includes all but three points ($r = -1$, 0, 1), such rules would be needed in order to use this means of task selection intelligently.

Information-processing psychologists have not fared much better in devising means for task selection, as was pointed out by Newell (1973). Information-processing psychology has at times seemed to be the study of specific tasks without ever knowing exactly why those tasks were chosen for study. Sometimes a task is investigated because an empirical phenomenon that arises when subjects perform the task illustrates a theoretical point. For example, the part-whole free-recall paradigm used by Tulving (1966) provided a counterintuitive demonstration of the superiority of organization theory to frequency theory in accounting for increased free recall during successive trials of practice. But what often seems to happen is that, as the years go by, researchers remember the task, but forget why it was theoretically important; and subsequent research becomes a study of the task for its own sake rather than of the task as a vehicle for testing one or more psychological theories (see discussion in Sternberg and Bower, 1974).

To conclude, then, theories of intelligence have progressed well over the years, but they still suffer from areas of weaknesses that need strengthening. I believe that the work described in this book will give you a good sense of just what researchers on human abilities (particularly information-processing researchers) have accomplished, and of what such researchers have yet to accomplish.

References

Anderson, J. R. 1976. *Memory, Language, and Thought.* Hillsdale, N.J.: Erlbaum.

Baron, J. 1982. Personality and intelligence. *In* Sternberg (1982a).

Belmont, J. M., and E. C. Butterfield. 1971. Learning strategies as determinants of memory deficiencies. *Cognitive Psychology,* 2, 411–420.

Berger, M. 1982. The "scientific approach" to intelligence: An overview of its history with special reference to mental speed. *In* Eysenck (1982).

Berry, J. W. 1974. Radical culture relativism and the concept of intelligence. *In* Berry and Dasen (1974).

———. 1981. Cultural systems and cognitive styles. *In* M. Friedman, J. P. Das, and N. O'Connor, eds., *Intelligence and Learning* (New York: Plenum).

———. 1982. Ecological analyses for cross-cultural psychology. *In* N. Warren, ed., *Studies in Cross-Cultural Psychology* (London: Academic Press).

Berry, J. W., and P. R. Dasen, eds. 1974. *Culture and Cognition: Readings in Cross-Cultural Psychology.* London: Methuen.

Binet, A., and T. Simon. 1905. Methods nouvelles pour le diagnostic du niveau intellectual des anormaux. *L'Année psychologique,* 11, 245–336.

———. 1916. *The Development of Intelligence in Children.* Baltimore: Williams & Wilkins. (Reprinted from *L'Année psychologique,* 14, 1908, 1–90.)

————. 1973. *The Development of Intelligence in Children: The Binet-Simon Scale.* New York: Arno Press.

Boring, E. G. 1923. Intelligence as the tests test it. *New Republic,* June 6, 35–37.

Borkowski, J. G., and J. C. Cavanaugh. 1970. Maintenance and generalization of skills and strategies by the retarded. *In* N. R. Ellis, ed., *Handbook of Mental Deficiency* (Hillsdale, N.J.: Erlbaum, 2d ed.).

Brand, C. R., and I. J. Deary. 1982. Intelligence and inspection time. In Eysenck (1982).

Brown, A. L. 1978. Knowing when, where and how to remember: A problem of metacognition. *In* R. Glaser, ed., *Advances in Instructional Psychology: Vol. 1* (Hillsdale, N.J.: Erlbaum).

Brown, A. L., J. C. Campione, and M. D. Murphy. 1977. Maintenance and generalization of trained metamnemonic awareness by educable retarded children: Span estimation. *Journal of Experimental Child Psychology,* 24, 191–211.

Bruner, J. S., D. Shapiro, and R. Tagiuri. 1958. The meaning of traits in isolation and in combination. *In* R. Tagiuri and L. Petrollo, eds., *Person Perception and Interpersonal Behavior* (Stanford, Calif.: Stanford Univ. Press).

Burt, C. R. 1940. *The Factors of the Mind.* London: Univ. of London Press.

Campione, J. C., A. L. Brown, and R. A. Ferrara. 1982. Mental retardation and intelligence. *In* Sternberg (1982a).

Cantor, N. 1978. *Prototypicality and Personality Judgments.* Unpublished doctoral dissertation, Stanford Univ.

Carroll, J. B. 1980. *Individual Difference Relations in Psychometric and Experimental Cognitive Tasks.* Chapel Hill: L. L. Thurstone Psychometric Laboratory, Univ. of North Carolina.

Cattell, J. M. 1890. Mental tests and measurements. *Mind,* 15, 373–380.

Charlesworth, W. R. 1976. Human intelligence as adaptation: An ethological approach. In Resnick (1976).

————. 1979. An ethological approach to studying intelligence. *Human Development,* 22, 212–216.

Colvin, S. S. 1921. Contribution to "Intelligence and its measurement." *Journal of Educational Psychology,* 12, 136–139.

Craik, F. I., and R. G. Lockhart. 1972. Levels of processing: A framework for memory research. *Journal of Verbal Learning and Verbal Behavior,* 11, 671–684.

Dearborn, W. F. 1921. Contribution to "Intelligence and its measurement." *Journal of Educational Psychology,* 12, 210–212.

Dewey, J. 1957. *Human Nature and Conduct.* New York: Modern Library.

Dockrell, W. B., ed. 1970. *The Toronto Symposium on Intelligence.* Toronto: The Ontario Institute for Studies in Education.

Eysenck, H. J. 1953. *Uses and Abuses of Psychology.* Harmondsworth, England: Penguin.

————. 1967. Intelligence assessment: A theoretical and experimental approach. *British Journal of Educational Psychology,* 37, 81–98.

————, ed. 1982. *A Model for Intelligence.* Berlin: Springer-Verlag.

Feuerstein, R. 1979. *The Dynamic Assessment of Retarded Performers: The Learning Potential Assessment Device, Theory, Instruments, and Techniques.* Baltimore, Md.: Univ. Park Press.

————. 1980. *Instrumental Enrichment: An Intervention Program for Cognitive Modifiability.* Baltimore, Md.: Univ. Park Press.

Flavell, J. H. 1981. Cognitive monitoring. *In* W. P. Dickson, ed., *Children's Oral Communication Skills* (New York: Academic Press).

Galton, F. 1983. *Inquiry into Human Faculty and Its Development.* London: Macmillan.

Greeno, J. G. 1978. Natures of problem-solving abilities. *In* W. K. Estes, ed., *Handbook of Learning and Cognitive Processes: Human Information Processing, Vol. 5* (Hillsdale, N.J.: Erlbaum).

Guilford, J. P. 1952. When not to factor analyze. *Psychological Bulletin,* 49, 26–27.

———. 1967. *The Nature of Human Intelligence.* New York: McGraw-Hill.

———. 1980. Components versus factors. *Behavioral and Brain Sciences,* 3, 591–592.

———. 1982. Cognitive psychology's ambiguities: Some suggested remedies. *Psychological Review,* 89, 48–59.

Guilford, J. P., and R. Hoepfner. (1971). *The Analysis of Intelligence.* New York: McGraw-Hill.

Guttman, L. 1965. A factored definition of intelligence. *In* R. R. Eiferman, ed., *Scripta Hierosolymitana, Vol. 14* (Jerusalem: Magnes Press).

Hebb, D. O. 1949. *The Organization of Behavior.* New York: Wiley.

Hendrickson, A. E. 1982. The biological basis of intelligence, Part 1: Theory. *In* Eysenck (1982).

Henmon, V. A. C. 1921. Contribution to "Intelligence and its measurement." *Journal of Educational Psychology,* 12, 195–198.

Holzinger, K. J. 1938. Relationships between three multiple orthogonal factors and four bifactors. *Journal of Educational Psychology,* 29, 513–519.

Humphreys, L. G. 1962. The organization of human abilities. *American Psychologist,* 17, 475–483.

Hunt, E. B. 1971. What kind of computer is man? *Cognitive Psychology,* 2, 57–98.

———. 1978. Mechanics of verbal ability. *Psychological Review,* 85, 109–130.

———. 1980. Intelligence as an information-processing concept. *British Journal of Psychology,* 71, 449–474.

Hunt, E. B., N. Frost, and C. Lunneborg. 1973. Individual differences in cognition: A new approach to intelligence. *In* G. Bower, ed., *The Psychology of Learning and Motivation, Vol. 7* (New York: Academic Press).

Hunt, E., C. Lunneborg, and J. Lewis. 1975. What does it mean to be high verbal? *Cognitive Psychology,* 7, 194–227.

Intelligence and its measurement: A symposium. 1921. *Journal of Educational Psychology,* 12, 123–147, 195–216, 271–275.

Jackson, M. D., and J. L. McClelland. 1979. Processing determinants of reading speed. *Journal of Experimental Psychology: General,* 108, 151–181.

Jensen, A. R. 1969. How much can we boost I.Q. and scholastic achievement? *Harvard Educational Review,* 39, 1–123.

———. 1970. Hierarchical theories of mental ability. *In* Dockrell (1970).

———. 1979. *g*: Outmoded theory or unconquered frontier? *Creative Science & Technology,* 2, 16–29.

———. 1980. *Bias in Mental Testing.* New York: Free Press.

———. 1982. Reaction time and psychometric *g. In* Eysenck (1982).

Kaufman, A. S., and N. L. Kaufman. 1982. *Kaufman Assessment Battery for Children K-ABC.* Circle Pines, Minn.: American Guidance Service.

———. 1980. Thinking processes in adolescence. *In* J. Adelson, ed., *Handbook of Adolescent Psychology* (New York: Wiley).

Keating, D. 1984. The emperor's new clothes: the "new look" in intelligence research. *In* R. J. Sternberg, ed., *Advances in the Psychology of Human Intelligence, Vol. 2* (Hillsdale, N.J.: Erlbaum).

Keating, D. P., and B. L. Bobbitt. 1978. Individual and developmental differences in cognitive processing components of mental ability. *Child Development,* 49, 155–167.

Laboratory of Comparative Human Cognition. 1982. Culture and intelligence. In Sternberg (1982a).

Laboratory of Comparative Human Cognition. 1983. Culture and cognitive development. *In* P. Mussen, series ed., and W. Kessen, volume ed., *Handbook of Child Psychology, Vol. 1* (New York: Wiley).

Lally, M., and T. Nettelbeck. 1977. Intelligence, reaction time, and inspection time. *American Journal of Mental Deficiency,* 82, 273–281.

Lemmon, V. W. 1927–28. The relation of reaction time to measures of intelligence, memory, and learning. *Archives of Psychology,* 15, 5–38.

Lunneborg, C. E. 1977. Choice reaction time: What role in ability measurement? *Applied Psychological Measurement,* 1, 309–330.

McClelland, D. C. 1973. Testing for competence rather than for "intelligence." *American Psychologist,* 28, 1–14.

McNemar, Q. 1951. The factors in factoring behavior. *Psychometrika,* 16, 353–359.

Miles, T. R. 1957. On defining intelligence. *British Journal of Educational Psychology,* 27, 153–165.

Mulholland, T. M., J. W. Pellegrino, and R. Glaser. 1980. Components of geometric analogy solution. *Cognitive Psychology,* 12, 252–284.

Neisser, U. 1976. *Cognition and Reality: Principles and Implications of Cognitive Psychology.* San Francisco: W. H. Freeman and Co.

———. 1978. The concept of intelligence. *Intelligence,* 3, 217–227.

Nettelbeck, T. 1982. Inspection time: An index for intelligence? *Quarterly Journal of Experimental Psychology,* 34A, 299–312.

Newell, A. 1973. Production systems: Models of control structures. *In* W. G. Chase, ed., *Visual Information Processing* (New York: Academic Press).

Newell, A., and H. Simon. 1972. *Human Problem Solving.* Englewood Cliffs, N.J.: Prentice-Hall.

Pellegrino, J. W., and R. Glaser. 1980. Components of inductive reasoning. *In* R. Snow, P. A. Federico, and W. Montague, Eds., *Aptitude, Learning, and Instruction: Cognitive Process Analyses of Aptitude, Vol. 1* (Hillsdale, N.J.: Erlbaum).

———. 1982. Analyzing aptitudes for learning: Inductive reasoning. *In* R. Glaser, ed., *Advances in Instructional Psychology, Vol. 2* (Hillsdale, N.J.: Erlbaum).

Peterson, J. 1921. Contribution to "Intelligence and its measurement." *Journal of Educational Psychology,* 12, 198–201.

Piaget, J. 1972. *The Psychology of Intelligence.* Totowa, N.J.: Littlefield, Adams.

Pinter, R. 1921. Contribution to "Intelligence and its measurement." *Journal of Educational Psychology,* 12, 139–143.

Posner, M. I., and R. F. Mitchell. 1967. Chronometric analysis of classification. *Psychological Review,* 74, 392–409.

Resnick, L. B., ed. 1976. *The Nature of Intelligence.* Hillsdale, N.J.: Erlbaum.

Royce, J. R. 1963. Factors as theoretical constructs. *American Psychologist,* 18, 522–527.

———. 1979. The factor-gene basis of individuality. *In* J. R. Royce and L. P. Mos, eds., *Theoretical Advances in Behavior Genetics* (The Netherlands: Sythoff and Nordhoff).

———. 1980. Factor analysis is alive and well. *American Psychologist,* 35, 390–392.

Schmidt, F. L., and J. E. Hunter. 1981. Development of a general solution to the problem of validity generalization. *Journal of Applied Psychology,* 62, 529–540.

Serpell, R. 1974. Estimates of intelligence in a rural community of Eastern Zambia. *Human Developmental Research Unit Reports,* no. 25. Lusaka: Univ. of Zambia.

———. 1976. Strategies for investigating intelligence in its cultural context. *Quarterly Newsletter of the Laboratory for Comparative Human Development,* pp. 11–15.

Siegler, R. S., and D. D. Richards. 1982. The development of intelligence. *In* Sternberg (1982).

Simon, H. A. 1976. Identifying basic abilities underlying intelligent performance of complex tasks. *In* Resnick (1976).

Spearman, C. 1923. *The Nature of "Intelligence" and the Principles of Cognition.* London: Macmillan.

———. 1927. *The Abilities of Man.* New York: Macmillan.

Sternberg, R. J. 1977. *Intelligence, information processing, and analogical reasoning: The componential analysis of human abilities.* Hillsdale, N.J.: Erlbaum.

———. 1979. The nature of mental abilities. *American Psychologist,* 34, 214–230.

———. 1980. Sketch of a componential subtheory of human intelligence. *Behavioral and Brain Sciences,* 3, 573–614.

———. 1981. Intelligence and nonentrenchment. *Journal of Educational Psychology,* 73, 1–16.

———, ed. 1982a. *Handbook of Human Intelligence.* New York: Cambridge Univ. Press.

———. 1982b. Reasoning, problem solving, and intelligence. *In* Sternberg (1982a).

———. 1984. Toward a triarchic theory of human intelligence. *Behavioral and Brain Sciences.,* 7, 269–287.

Sternberg, R. J., and G. H. Bower. 1974. Transfer in part-whole and whole-part free recall: A comparative evaluation of theories. *Journal of Verbal Learning and Verbal Behavior,* 13, 1–26.

Sternberg, R. J., B. E. Conway, J. L. Ketron, and M. Bernstein. 1981. People's conceptions of intelligence. *Journal of Personality and Social Psychology,* 41, 37–55.

Sternberg, R. J., and D. K. Detterman, eds. 1979. *Human Intelligence: Perspectives on its Theory and Measurement.* Norwood, N.J.: Ablex.

Sternberg, R. J., and M. K. Gardner. 1983. Unities in inductive reasoning. *Journal of Experimental Psychology: General,* 112, 80–116.

Sternberg, R. J., and J. S. Powell. 1982. Theories of intelligence. In Sternberg (1982a).

Sternberg, R. J., and W. Salter. 1982. Conceptions of intelligence. In Sternberg (1982a).

Super, C. M. 1982. Cultural variation in the meaning and uses of children's intelligence. Paper presented at the Sixth International Congress of the International Association of Cross-Cultural Psychology. Aberdeen, Scotland.

Terman, L. M. 1921. Contribution to "Intelligence and its measurement." *Journal of Educational Psychology,* 12, 127–133.

Thorndike, E. P. 1921. Contribution to "Intelligence and its measurement." *Journal of Experimental Psychology,* 12, 124–127.

Thurstone, L. L. 1921. Contribution to "Intelligence and its measurement." *Journal of Educational Psychology,* 12, 201–207.

———. 1938. *Primary Mental Abilities.* Chicago: Univ. of Chicago Press.

———. 1947. *Multiple Factor Analysis.* Chicago: Univ. of Chicago Press.

Tulving, E. 1966. Subjective organization and effects of repetition in multi-trial free-recall learning. *Journal of Verbal Learning and Behavior,* 5, 193–197.

Vernon, P. E. 1971. *The Structure of Human Abilities.* London: Methuen.

Vygotsky, L. S. 1978. *Mind in Society: The Development of Higher Psychological Processes.* Cambridge, Mass.: Harvard Univ. Press.

Wechsler, D. 1950. *The Measurement and Appraisal of Adult Intelligence.* Baltimore, Md.: Williams and Wilkins, 4th ed.

Whitley, S. E. 1980. Latent trait models in the study of intelligence. *Intelligence,* 4, 97–132.

Wissler, C. 1901. The correlation of mental and physical tests. *Psychological Review* (monograph supplement 3), No. 6.

Wober, M. 1974. Towards an understanding of Kiganda concept of intelligence. *In* Berry and Dasen (1974).

Woodrow, H. 1921. Contribution to "Intelligence and its measurement." *Journal of Educational Psychology,* 12, 207–210.

Yussen, S. R., and P. Kane (in press). Children's concepts of intelligence. *In* S. R. Yussen, ed., *The Growth of Insight in Children* (New York: Academic Press).

2

VERBAL ABILITY

Earl Hunt*
University of Washington, Seattle

Suppose that several people were asked to read a newspaper and take an examination on its contents. Some would do well and some would not. Suppose further that the same people listened to a news broadcast and answered questions about it. The people who did well on one test would generally do well on the other. Does this happen merely because some people are interested in current events and some are not? If testing were expanded to include reading and listening about topics ranging from Shakespeare to sports, people who scored well on one test would still tend to do well on another. The reason is simple: people differ in their ability to comprehend language.

*Numerous colleagues have contributed to my thinking about the issues discussed here. While absolving them from any of my own misconceptions or misrepresentations, I would like to thank all those who have been associated with me in the study of verbal intelligence and attention. Special thanks are owed to Philip Dale and Robert Sternberg, whose careful comments on an earlier version of this paper have very much improved it.

This conclusion is hardly surprising. A survey of "the man in the street" (Sternberg et al., 1981) has shown that people believe in the existence of a talent called "verbal intelligence," and believe that this talent is different from the ability to do abstract reasoning ("academic intelligence") and the ability to solve everyday problems ("practical intelligence").

The fact that people believe an ability to exist is certainly not conclusive evidence that it does exist. (Many people believe in psychic communication, but scientists are skeptical.) For verbal intelligence, though, there is objective evidence that the ability exists. Let us look at a simple example of such evidence.

Box 2.1 presents a brief description of some of the tests that are included in a battery used by the state of Washington to evaluate the scholastic aptitude of college-bound high school students. The tests are similar to those used in other scholastic-aptitude batteries. Palmer et al. (in press) calculated the correlations between tests, based on the data from undergraduates enrolled at the University of Washington. Table 2.1 shows the results. The three correlations for the three pairs of Tests 1, 2, and 3, which all tested language use, are higher than any of the correlations between pairs of tests where one involves language use and the other does not. However, there are positive correlations between tests of different aspects of language use and tests that use language to test some other psychological function. The test of quantitative ability is a good example. It presents mathematical and logical problems, described in story form. A correlation between such a test and a verbal factor would be expected if there exists an underlying "verbal comprehension" ability that is tapped, albeit imperfectly, by any test that involves reading.

The fact that the scores on different tests are positively correlated suggests that the different tests are manifestations of a smaller number of underlying abilities. A statistical technique known as factor analysis has been developed to

---

Box 2.1

Description of some of the tests on the Washington Pre-College Test Battery

Test name	Description
1. Reading comprehension	Answer questions about paragraph
2. Vocabulary	Choose synonyms for a word
3. Grammar	Identify correct and poor usage
4. Quantitative skills	Read word problems and decide whether problem can be solved
5. Mechanical reasoning	Examine a diagram and answer questions about it; requires knowledge of physical and mechanical principles
6. Spatial reasoning	Indicate how two-dimensional figures will appear if they are folded through a third dimension
7. Mathematics achievement	A test of high school algebra

Table 2.1
Correlations between results of the tests listed in Box 2.1[a]

Test no.	1	2	3	4	5	6	7
1	1.00	.67	.63	.40	.33	.14	.34
2		1.00	.59	.29	.46	.19	.31
3			1.00	.41	.34	.20	.46
4				1.00	.39	.46	.62
5					1.00	.47	.39
6						1.00	.46
7							1.00

[a]Data adapted from Palmer et al. (in press).

Table 2.2
A factor structure for the tests in Box 2.1, derived from Table 2.1 (by using principal factors solution followed by a varimax rotation). Factor I is clearly identified as a verbal-ability factor.

	Factors		
Test	I	II	III
Reading comprehension	.79	.20	.09
Vocabulary	.75	.09	.34
Grammar	.71	.34	.04
Quantitative skills	.28	.65	.13
Mechanical reasoning	.28	.38	.53
Spatial reasoning	.00	.60	.40
Mathematics	.28	.65	.13

discover how many such abilities ("factors") are required to account for the observed correlations between tests. Factor analysis also provides a table of correlations between each test in a test battery and the factors that are presumed to underlie the battery as a whole.*

Is verbal ability important in our daily lives? The answer to the question is most definitely "yes." People who have high verbal ability seem to know more about our world. In another study in my own laboratory, university students were given three tests of factual knowledge: about the humanities, about social

---

*I will not attempt here to explain how this is done. See the texts by Cohen and Cohen (1975) or Mulaik (1972) for explanations. Three factors are required to account for the data in Table 2.1. Table 2.2 displays the correlations between the factors and the original tests. The first column ("first factor") has relatively high correlations with tests that involve language use. This suggests that one of the abilities underlying the behavior required by the tests in Box 2.1 is an abstract ability to deal with language. It cannot be stressed too strongly that this sort of evidence for a verbal factor has been found over and over again (Nunnally, 1978).

sciences, and about natural sciences. The tests did not require a great deal of reading, and were primarily requests to retrieve facts. The same students were assigned a "verbal-ability" score based on a composite of the tests described in Box 2.1. The correlations between the verbal-ability tests and the tests of knowledge were .42 for the humanities, .57 for the social sciences, and .28 for the natural sciences. That is, the higher the students scored on the tests of verbal ability, the higher they would tend to score on tests of knowledge. Verbal facility is positively correlated with knowledge acquisition.*

Such a finding is hardly surprising, given the importance that language plays in education and communication. We can go one step beyond. Is the fact of verbal ability a predictor of success in nonacademic life? Tests of verbal ability are among the best single predictors of success in school settings. Studies from the 1950s onward have consistently found correlations that range from .40 to .60 between verbal-ability tests and academic achievement (Matarazzo, 1972). The correlations tend to drop in the higher and more specialized educational levels. The tests also predict success outside the academic field. Table 2.3 presents the correlations between soldiers' performance on tests of ability to comprehend written and verbal material and their performance on various military skills. Military skill was evaluated by both field and written performance. The skills involved for armored-vehicle crewman, vehicle repairman, cook, and supply clerk are not those normally considered to be involved in "academic" tasks. Nevertheless, the correlations between the verbal and job-related tasks were only slightly lower than the correlations reported between verbal ability and college grades. As the authors point out, the result is not surprising. In our society, everyone learns a great deal either by reading or by being told (Sticht, 1975).

Language is ubiquitous. Why is it that some deal with verbal communications better than others? To answer this question, a brief discussion of language itself is in order.

*The data described here were collected by myself and Steven Yantis, and have not otherwise been published.

Table 2.3

Correlations between soldiers' job performance and verbal-ability measures[a]

Skill	Correlation with	
	Reading	Listening
Armor-vehicle crewman	.32	.29
Vehicle repairman	.26	.38
Supply clerk	.40	.42
Cook	.34	.28

[a]Data from Sticht (1975).

A Brief Discourse on Language

A certain amount of language comprehension comes easily. The sentence

(1)   *Please hand me the telephone book.*

contains a social convention (it is a request, not an order), implicitly describes a state of the physical world (there exists a telephone book, located out of reach of the speaker), and expresses a desired change in that world. Although (1) is a simple sentence, by human standards, it is far beyond the communication capacities of other animals.

There is a "first principle" of language use that needs to be stressed over and over again: *language is meant to communicate.* People speak and write in order to build mental representations in the minds of listeners and readers. The messages used to build the representations seldom, if ever, contain all the information that the recipient needs. Both sender and receiver rely on assumptions about the knowledge that they share. Consider this jargon-ridden statement:

(2)   *We'll stop the safety blitz by having the tight end flare right.*

This sentence is meaningful to some people, in some contexts. To others it is jibberish, because they do not know enough about American football. For that reason, a speaker would only make statement (2) to a huddle of experts. Meaning is transmitted only if the speaker and comprehender share a great deal of knowledge, and know that they share it.

The remainder of this section will discuss the process of language comprehension somewhat more formally, in order to identify those basic abilities that a person must have to use language at all. Subsequent sections will present evidence for individual differences in various language-related abilities, and consider how these abilities might account for differences in general verbal intelligence. In the simplest case, there may be a direct, linear relation between an underlying ability and a complex skill: the greater the ability, the more proficient the skilled performance. In other cases, the relation may be more complex. A basic ability may be needed to carry out a complex skill, but virtually everyone may have that ability; so the ability will not account for individual differences in the complex skill. (For example, two legs are needed to run, but "number of legs" does not predict the speed of track stars.) The relation between the ability and the skill may be nonlinear. In particular, it may be that the ability must be present in some degree in order to produce adequate performance, but superior ability may not guarantee superior performance in the more complex task. Think again of athletics. Golf playing requires some upper body strength, but unusual arm and shoulder strength does not guarantee superior performance. The study of verbal intelligence can produce examples of all these different types of relations between underlying abilities and skill in verbal comprehension.

Physically, a linguistic message unit is a string of sounds or symbols that stand as tokens for the conceptual words (or morphemes) in the language.

Comprehension cannot proceed unless the physical tokens are associated with their concepts. This process will be called "lexical access." Although lexical access is logically prior to further analysis, lexical access itself depends on context, because the same physical symbol may refer to different conceptual words. Consider the sounds /read/ and /red/, or the several meanings of "check." Assuming that words have been identified, the comprehender must decide whether or not an expression is well formed, and derive its meaning. The rules for identifying well formedness are called *syntactic rules*. They identify the role that each word plays in an expression. This step can be crucial to meaning. Syntax tells us that

(3) *John loves Mary*

is not the same as

(4) *Mary loves John.*

Semantic analysis enables us to decide what a word means in an expression, by combining the meaning of a word with the role it has been assigned by syntactic analysis. Sentence (4) is hardly equivalent to

(5) *John hates Mary,*

but they have the same syntactic structure.

In order to comprehend meaning, a person must be able to perform lexical, syntactic, and semantic analyses. In the lexical-access phase, a word is identified as standing for a bundle of semantic and syntactic features. Thus every word is restricted in the roles it can play. "Mary" is semantically a female person, and syntactically a noun. Furthermore, the syntactic rules require either that a word have attached to it a marker indicating its syntactic role (a grammatical ending or other change, called an *inflection*) or that syntactic roles be introduced in a particular order relative to each other. In English, word order is very important in determining syntactic roles, whereas relatively little use is made of inflection. Finnish represents the other extreme, for it makes little use of word order and a great deal of use of inflections. Most other languages fall in between these extreme cases.

A comprehender can make use of the fact that some syntactic constructions are more common than others. For instance, by recognizing the initial "Mary" or "John" in the immediately preceding examples, the comprehender knows that a noun phrase has been completed and that therefore only a few kinds of other syntactic categories can possibly follow. The comprehender also knows that the next word will probably initiate the predicate. As a result, the more common forms of syntactic construction are easier to understand. Consider the contrast between

(6) *The horse raced past the barn quickly*

and

(7)   *The horse raced past the barn fell.*

Sentence (7) violates the probabilistic rule that the completion of the initial noun phrase in a sentence signals the initiation of the predicate. A much easier construction to comprehend is

(8)   *The horse that was raced past the barn fell,*

where the use of "that" explicitly indicates that the predicate has not yet begun.

Semantics can also be used to establish probabilities of occurrence for upcoming terms. Words are recognized faster if they can be anticipated from the context in which they occur (Tulving and Gold, 1963). Compare the ease of comprehension of

(9)   *Ivan the Terrible was cruel and despotic to his people*

to that of

(10) *Ivan the Terrible was kind and loving to his family.*

Although syntax and semantics can be discussed separately, in practice the processes of syntax and semantics appear to be inseparably intertwined. Semantics makes it possible to disambiguate the syntax of

(11) *John saw the Grand Canyon flying to California*

and to reject a classic example of syntax without semantics,

(12) *Colorless green ideas sleep furiously.*

This does not mean that people cannot distinguish between syntax and semantics; they can. People will agree that (11) has two possible parsings, and, more reluctantly, will admit that there is a sense in which (12) is a well-formed expression. In doing so, people demonstrate a competence that they have, but that they rarely need to use. In normal comprehension, syntactic and semantic analyses are inextricably intertwined.

We now return to an earlier point: linguistic messages are intended to cause their receivers to have thoughts. The messages do not completely specify those thoughts: They arouse them by their interpretation in context. This is called the "pragmatic" aspect of speech. Consider, for instance, the pragmatic aspects of interpreting example (1), the request for the telephone book. It could mean many things, in many settings. More generally, the speaker is assumed to be trying to build a mental representation in the comprehender's mind. This is done by presenting bits of information, one after another. If an expression has several alternative meanings, the comprehender will choose the one that fits best with his or her own current understanding of what is going on.

The division of language processes into lexical, syntactic-semantic, and pragmatic combines views from both a psychological and a linguistic understanding of language. Language can also be viewed from a strictly psychological perspective. Some of the inferences people draw in comprehension are clearly under conscious control, but others are drawn without awareness and often without control. For instance, consider the earlier remark that when people recognize a word, they can then recognize its semantic associates more quickly. This speeding up of a process is not under conscious control. Verbal comprehension depends on a great many such low-level, "automatic" actions. These are particularly important in the lexical-access and syntactic-semantic phases of comprehension. Pragmatic comprehension is more a conscious, deliberate process. Following current usage, we will use the terms *automatic* and *controlled* to refer to the two kinds of processing. (The terms *microprocess* and *macroprocess* are sometimes used.) It is easy to offer extreme examples. Suppose you were listening to a political speech. Recognizing the speaker's words would be an automatic process, but considering the speaker's motives would be a controlled one.

We can now refine the question "What causes verbal ability?" Do individual differences in verbal comprehension result from differences in the lexical, syntactic-semantic, or pragmatic processes? The straightforward way to answer this question would be to develop tasks that isolate the lexical, syntactic-semantic, and pragmatic phases of language, and then correlate performance on each phase, in isolation, with tests of natural-language comprehension. This strategy has been followed in most tests of verbal ability. It works reasonably well, so long as we are considering the automatic processes of language use: lexical and syntactic-semantic processes. The next two sections will present some of the more important findings about individual differences in automatic processes. We will find that some, but not all, of the variation in ability to comprehend paragraphs, speeches, and stories can be predicted from individual variation in automatic process execution. In the closing sections, we will speculate a little about the role of individual differences in the controlled processing and pragmatic aspects of speech comprehension.

A Closer Look at Lexical Access

Lexical access depends on a person's having a word in his or her vocabulary and being able to get at the vocabulary entry rapidly. A person's vocabulary size is one of the best predictors of other aspects of verbal ability. Vocabulary scores alone correlate .85 with full scores on the verbal portion of the Wechsler Adult Intelligence Scale (Matarazzo, 1972).

General verbal intelligence is also correlated with ease of word use. Skilled readers and listeners recognize common words automatically (La Berge and Samuels, 1974). Perhaps the best argument for automaticity is the demonstration that we cannot inhibit lexical access, even if doing so would be to our advantage. This can be shown by the "Stroop phenomenon," in which automatic lexical access interferes with a concurrent perceptual task (Stroop, 1935). An example of the Stroop phenomenon is shown in Figure 2.1. The task is to name the line drawings, disregarding the printed word inside the figure. It takes longer to name the drawing in Figure 2.1(*a*), in which the printed word is a

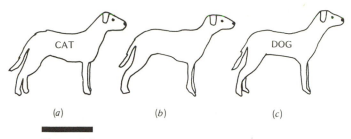

Figure 2.1
Automatic access to words. The figure in (*a*) is harder to name than in (*b*) because of the competition from the overlearned, automatic response to CAT. In (*c*) the figure and the name lead to the same response; so naming is rapid.

"wrong answer," than it takes to name the figure alone, as in Figure 2.1(*b*). If the figure and the printed word converge on the same answer, as in Figure 2.1(*c*), naming is speeded.

Figure 2.2 shows three variants of the "stimulus-matching" task, a procedure used to measure lexical access. In this task, two items are shown, e.g., the pair of words "sink wink." The task is to indicate whether or not the items are the same by some preset criterion. Suppose the criterion is "the items refer to the same word." Then the answer would be "no" for the pair "sink wink", and "yes" for the pair "sink SINK." This is an example of name identity: two physically different written forms are to be considered the same if they are associated with the same word. Other possibilities are to identify pairs of items as "same" if they fall into the same syntactic class (e.g., both nouns) or if they fall into a common semantic category (e.g., DEER and ELK are both animals). It is also possible to go to a lower-order identification, based on purely perceptual characteristics, by specifying that two items are to be considered as "the same" if they are physically identical. In this case, the pair "DEER deer" would be considered to be "different" because the words are set in different type.

Figure 2.3 summarizes a study of stimulus-matching performance in students who had high or low verbal-aptitude scores, as measured by a conventional psychometric test. The criterion for stimulus matching was progressively changed, from physical identity to name identity, and then to semantic-class identity. As can be seen, the relative advantage of the high verbal students over the low verbal students increased as the lexical decision required became more complex (Goldberg et al., 1977).

Figure 2.4 shows an alternative way of measuring lexical access, the *lexical identification* task. A person is shown a letter string, e.g., CARD or CARG. The task is to indicate whether or not the string is a word. Several other procedures for measuring lexical access have also been developed. They correlate highly with each other, indicating that there is a unitary "lexical-access" ability. This ability has a correlation of about .3 with scores on conventional psychometric tests of verbal ability (Hunt et al., 1982; Lansman et al., 1983). That is, there is a modest but consistent trend for people with high verbal ability to perform rapidly in lexical-access tasks. Absolute differences in the time

	*	Warning

(a)

	SINK SINK	Display

	*	Warning

(b)

	SINK sink	Display

	*	Warning

(c)

	SINK wink	Display

Figure 2.2
Stimulus-matching task. The participant watches a screen. A warning signal appears, followed by a pair of terms. The task is to identify the terms as "same" or "different" according to a pre-established criterion. Pair (*a*) contains physically identical pairs; pair (*b*) contains pairs that are physically different but have the same name; and pair (*c*) contains terms that are different by both criteria.

Figure 2.3
"High verbal" students (top 25 percent of the distribution of verbal scores on an intelligence test) make stimulus identification decisions faster than "low verbal" students. The difference between groups increases with the complexity of classification. (Data from Goldberg et al., 1977.)

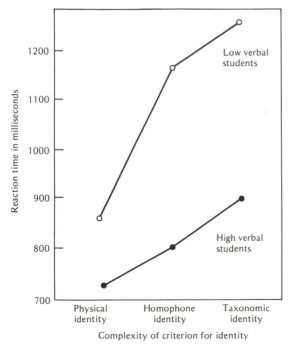

required for lexical access by different sorts of people are rather small. Studies using the stimulus-matching paradigm have led to an estimate that the average college student has a lexical-access time of about 80 milliseconds. Students whose scores on verbal ability tests are in the top 25 percent (for college students) have access times of about 65 milliseconds; students with scores in the bottom 25 percent show access times of 100 milliseconds. Much larger access times have been observed outside the college population, almost all of whose members are of at least average verbal ability (Hunt et al., 1975). Warren and Hunt (1981) estimated access time in mildly mentally retarded individuals to be about 400 milliseconds.

How do differences in lexical access arise? It could be that people with high verbal ability simply read more, and thus have more experience at recognizing words. Although this may be a factor, it does not seem to be the whole story. Jackson (1980) taught college students an artificial alphabet, based on an arbitrary pairing of visual symbols with nonsense syllables. Two symbols were paired with each syllable, making the pairing analogous to the use of uppercase and lowercase letters. Students who were high in reading ability (a good general indicator of verbal ability) performed better at stimulus matching than did poor readers, even when experience with the stimuli was equated.

All the studies cited have dealt with reading, the identification of visually presented words. Would the same picture be obtained if the experiments were conducted with auditory sequences, e.g., recognizing that the spoken sound /card/ is a word but /carg/ is not? Or perhaps recognizing that /dog/ refers to the same concept whether it is spoken by a male or female voice? For some reason, the appropriate studies have not been done.

The vocabulary and lexical-access studies indicate that "high verbal" people know lots of words and are facile at recognizing them. They are also better at acquiring word meanings by observing the context in which words are

---

Figure 2.4
The lexical identification task. The participant watches a screen. A warning signal appears, followed by a letter string. The task is to identify the string as a word, as in (a), or a nonword, as in (b).

	*	Warning
(a)	CARD	Display
	"Yes"	Response

	*	Warning
(b)	CARG	Display
	"No"	Response

used. This is important because most of our vocabulary must be acquired in this way, rather than by explicit definition (Miller, 1981). The process can be illustrated by amplifying on the earlier "Ivan the Terrible" example.

(13)   *The boyars saw Ivan the Terrible as a cruel despot, believing that the new Tsar was trying to abrogate many ancient rights and privileges. The boyars could not move against Ivan because he was loved by the common people, both for his piety and because he used his power to protect them against the boyars' harsh rule.*

What does "boyars" mean? The context in which the term has been used indicates that the boyars must be human, probably medieval Russian. The boyars evidently had political power derived from tradition. Contextual cues come close to correctly defining this term: the boyars were Russian nobles. There is also an internal cue that most readers probably used but did not notice. The terminal "s" and the fact that "boyars" is not capitalized suggest, somewhat tenuously, that "boyars" refers to several people rather than one. These are the only clues to indicate plurality. If the word "Duke" is substituted for "boyars," passage (13) will still be grammatically correct.

Studies dealing with populations as different as grade-school students and college students have shown that people with high general verbal ability are better able to pick up the meaning of words from contextual cues than are students of lower verbal ability (Freyd and Baron, 1982; Sternberg and Powell, 1983; van Daalen-Kapteijns and Elshout-Mohr, 1981). The differences are substantial. The correlation between verbal-aptitude scores and adequacy of definitions was .60 in the Sternberg and Powell study. Although we do not know the exact process of word acquisition, it is probably closely related to lexical access and vocabulary size. In order to discover the meaning of an unknown word, a person must be able to react to the context in which the word appears. For instance, (13) is more comprehensible, and the definition of "boyars" easier to delimit, if the reader knows the definition of the word "abrogate," which also appears in the passage.

The acquisition of word meaning may be closely related to a second process, the anticipation of meaning. What a word does, after all, is to continue the sender's message. There would be no need for the word if the comprehender were able to anticipate it perfectly. A person with high verbal intelligence should be a good anticipator. This idea has been incorporated in *cloze testing,* which is a sort of reversal of word-definition procedures. A person is given the context, and asked to produce a word. An example is

(14)   *Aunt Jane was unhappy because the cat _____ her canary.*

Research with children has shown that this is a good technique for predicting level of verbal ability. Stillman (1982) reports a particularly interesting result. He found that cloze testing predicted verbal-comprehension scores within a group of five- to seven-year-olds, all of whom had already been selected as having unusually high general intelligence scores. (The group average IQ was

136.) The fact that cloze testing could discriminate between people within such a highly gifted group is impressive evidence that sensitivity to the context being built by a message is an important part of verbal ability.

On the other hand, we must not overstate the case. Stanovich (1980) has pointed out that good readers (and, by extension, people who are good at general verbal comprehension) can perform well in situations that require a reaction to context. This does not mean that high-verbal individuals rely on context in the normal process of word identification. In fact, Stanovich suggests that the opposite may be the case. He cites studies indicating that, in normal comprehension, people with good comprehension skills can simply recognize words easily, and have less need to rely on context than do people with poorer verbal skills. We will discuss this point in more depth when we consider the role of attention in verbal comprehension.

What is clear is that the ability to comprehend is associated with possession of a large lexicon and rapid access to it. On the other hand, correlations in the .3 to .4 range are not high enough to begin to account for all individual variations in verbal comprehension. In the next section, we will consider individual differences in the ability to deal with groups of words.

Comprehending Isolated Sentences and Expressions

Most complete speech acts require a reaction to a well-formed expression rather than to words in isolation. A procedure known as the *sentence-verification paradigm* has proven useful in studying such reactions. In sentence-verification studies, the participant is shown a simple sentence or phrase, and then (either simultaneously or within a second or two) is shown a picture. The task is to indicate whether or not the sentence could describe the picture. A frequently used example is

(15) *The plus is above the star*

followed by Figure 2.5(*a*) or 2.5(*b*).

Figure 2.5
Diagrams for the sentence-verification task.

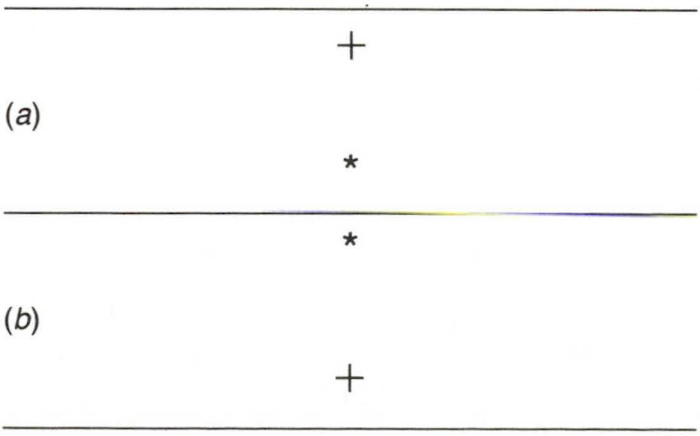

$+$

(*a*)

$*$

$*$

(*b*)

$+$

The time required to verify or reject the sentence as a description of the picture varies with the syntactic complexity of the sentence, even though the sentence is not present when the picture is shown (Clark and Chase, 1972). For instance, it takes longer to verify "plus not below star" than it does to verify "plus above star," and the difference in verification time cannot be accounted for by a difference in reading time.

People differ significantly in the speed with which they verify sentences. In our own laboratory, my colleagues and I have observed individual verification times ranging from 600 to 2400 milliseconds within a single experiment. People who verify sentences rapidly tend to do well on tests of verbal comprehension. The correlations between the time a person takes to verify sentences and his or her score on comprehension examinations lie in the −.40 to −.60 range; the correlations are negative because a shorter verification time corresponds to a larger numerical test score (Baddeley, 1968; Hunt et al., 1975; Lansman, 1978; Lansman et al., 1983). Perhaps most importantly, although the ability to complete sentence verification is statistically related to the ability to do lexical-access tasks, the two are separate abilities. This has been shown in multivariate studies, in which people are asked to do both lexical-access and the sentence-verification tasks. An attempt is then made to predict scores on general verbal-ability tests from performance on the access and verification tasks. The two tasks together are better predictors of the verbal-ability test scores than they would be if they were parallel measures of the same underlying ability (Hunt et al., 1981; Palmer et al., in press).

Why should the ability to analyze simple sentences predict performance in much more complex linguistic tasks? One study suggested that the sentence-verification task evaluates a person's ability to manipulate verbal information in working memory (Carpenter and Just, 1975). To amplify, there is much evidence that human memory is divided into at least two parts: a permanent repository of the information that we have learned; and a much smaller, short-lived "scratch-pad" area that serves as a temporary holding place for information as we attempt to construct representations of the situation that confronts us. Following Baddeley (1976), we will call the scratchpad area *working memory.*

Linguistic analyses suggest that working memory should be heavily used in language comprehension. A few examples show why. English, and many other languages, allow the insertion of relative clauses into a sentence, as in

(16) *My brother, who was a keen amateur photographer, rushed to get his camera.*

The initial noun phrase, "my brother," must be held in memory while the relative clause is analyzed. Passive sentences also introduce a memory demand, as in

(17) *The boy was thrown the ball by the man.*

Here the correct assignment of the role "actor" to "man" and "recipient" to "boy" cannot be completed until after the verb phrase has been analyzed. A third important role of memory is in the resolution of *anaphoric* references to previously introduced terms. In

(18) *John saw Mary and threw the ball to her,*

the pronoun "her" is an anaphoric reference whose semantics can be understood only by equating "her" to the previously introduced term "Mary."

As the examples indicate, the analysis of a single sentence typically requires the manipulation of items in working memory. Experiments in which people are required to do sentence verification in competition with a memory task have shown that the resulting conflict for working-memory resources reduces the efficiency of sentence processing. Figure 2.6 shows the procedure used. Participants first memorize a series of digits, then perform several sentence-verification tasks, and finally repeat back the series of digits. Sentence verification is slowed compared to a control condition in which there is no memory task. Furthermore, memorizing five or six digits produces a greater slowing than memorizing one or two (Baddeley and Hitch, 1974; Lansman, 1978).

The importance of working memory in sentence analysis has been demonstrated more directly by studies of the resolution of anaphoric references. It is well known that the more items a person is holding in working memory, the longer it takes to locate an individual item (S. Sternberg, 1975). Consider the problem of resolving the anaphoric reference IT in

(19) *The nineteenth century was a period in which numerous immigrants came to America. The first wave came from Ireland and Wales. IT closed with a second wave, stemming from Italy and from Poland, Russia, and other Slavic countries.*

as opposed to

(20) *The nineteenth century was a period in which numerous immigrants came to America. First they came from Ireland and Wales. IT closed with a second wave, stemming from Italy and from Poland, Russia, and other Slavic countries.*

In (19) there are two potential referents for IT that must be retrieved, and then one must be selected on the basis of the following text. In (20) there is only one

---

Figure 2.6

| Memorize | 4, 7, 2, 9, 3 |
| Verify | Plus above star |

Plus not below star +

(repeated for five sentences)
Report the digit string.

---

possible referent. In fact, anaphoric references are resolved faster if there are few candidate referents (Ehrlich, 1980; Frederiksen, 1982). Several other techniques for varying the amount of memory processing needed to resolve an anaphoric reference have the same general effect. They slow down the resolution time. Furthermore, the memory-searching process seems to be slower in poor readers than in good readers, since poor readers are disproportionately slowed when a reference is required (Frederiksen, 1982).

Results such as these suggest that people who show good comprehension ability directly in reading and verbal intelligence tests should also do well in tests designed explicitly to measure short-term memory. To some extent this is true. The "traditional" way to measure memory size is by calculating *memory span,* the number of items that a person can repeat, at a fixed error rate. The procedure could be illustrated by eliminating the verification phrases in Figure 2.6. In order to measure memory span, we would keep increasing the number of digits to be memorized until the participant could only answer, say, 75 percent of the items correctly. Thus, if a person could correctly recite six numbers in order, on nine out of twelve trials, the person's memory span would be six. Memory span correlates moderately with total scores on verbal-ability tests (*r* in the .30 to .40 range; Daneman and Carpenter, 1980; Dempster, 1981).

A somewhat finer picture of the relation between memory span and verbal ability can be obtained by looking at the determinants of memory span itself. Unless a person has been trained to deal with the experimental situation, the primary determinants of memory span are lexical access and ability to recall the order in which the items (numbers, letters) are presented (Dempster, 1981). Information about the order of presentation of items clearly must be retained in sentence comprehension. One study in my own laboratory compared the short-term memorizing abilities of college students with high or low verbal-aptitude scores, as measured by a standard psychometric test. We found that all the participants could recall the identity of the items presented reasonably well, but that the "high verbal" students were superior in recalling the order in which the items had been presented (Hunt et al., 1973; see also Schwartz and Weidel, 1978).

An examination of normal text indicates that there are many situations in which a person must hold information in working memory, analyze one or more sentences, and then search working memory for a piece of information needed to remove an ambiguity. How else could one resolve the reference to "them" in the following example?

(21)   *Three men sat in front of the fireplace. It was a dark and stormy night. One of them began to speak.*

Daneman and Carpenter (1980) present evidence that an individual's comprehension ability depends on the dual ability to hold information in memory while analyzing sentences. College students were asked to read sentences and memorize the last word of each sentence. On demand the list of last words was recalled. An example of the procedure would be

(22)   *The bear saw the man.*
       My dog barked at a cat.
       RECALL: man, cat.

Daneman and Carpenter report a correlation of .50 between memory span, as measured in their procedure, and measures of general verbal comprehension. This is somewhat higher than the usually reported correlation between memory span and verbal comprehension. In addition, Daneman and Carpenter found a very high correlation ($r = .80$) between their measure of memory span and their participants' ability to resolve anaphoric references while reading or listening to text.

　　To summarize, people who display high comprehension ability in normal reading and listening situations tend to be quick at analyzing individual sentences in isolation. Their talent is probably not a result of their special knowledge of words or syntactic rules, because both the words used and the syntactic rules studied in sentence verification and similar experiments are very common words and rules. The "high verbal" individual is simply quick at manipulating verbal information. In fact, high verbal people seem able to manipulate information in (auditory) working memory, in general. They tend to have larger memory spans for words and digits, in isolation, and to be adept at holding information in working memory while analyzing simple sentences. Such an ability should be of use in verbal comprehension at a level higher than an analysis of single sentences. The next section will consider how a good working memory should help in constructing a mental picture from a multisentence text.

Comprehending Connected Discourse

　　Suppose a friend were to say to you,

(23)   *I learned a lot about the bars in town yesterday. Do you have an aspirin?*

There is a wealth of implicit information in the two sentences that could never be inferred from lexical, syntactic, and semantic analyses. The sentences together tell more than either does alone. The information is available only to those with background knowledge of bars, aspirin, and, for that matter, your friend. What would you think if the friend worked for the Salvation Army?

　　Example (23) would be understood by applying background knowledge. In other cases, the interpretation depends on the listener's assumptions about the speaker's purpose in communication. When thirty San Francisco merchants were asked the question

(24)   *Do you close before seven?*

only four of them just answered the question. The others provided information about the actual closing time, which is what they assumed the questioner wanted to know (Clark, 1979).

Language comprehension is a game in which the speaker builds mental representations in a comprehender's mind. Although the primary tool the message producer uses is a language, appeals to background information and contextual cues are appropriate. The game forces the message producer to guess the current state of the comprehender's mental representation, in order to choose a message element that will modify it appropriately. From the comprehender's view, the knowledge that each new expression must make sense in context is itself a useful guide to understanding. The last sentence is unambiguous in both of the following examples.

(25) *The pilot and copilot both survived the crash and returned to health. They are flying planes now.*

and

(26) *Mechanics worked all last night to repair the two aircraft the terrorists sabotaged. They are flying planes now.*

Understanding the rules of the verbal-communication game is one of the major goals of modern psycholinguistics.* The current state of knowledge in this field is somewhat frustrating to those whose interest is in individual differences. It has been shown that pragmatic and contextual aspects of speech comprehension are very important as general principles of language use, but little research has been conducted on the differences in the ways that people use pragmatic and contextual cues, or for that matter, on differences in the way that people extract cohesive themes from text. Research on text comprehension has been marked by the development of numerous theories, but there are as yet few data differentiating between competing theories. For these reasons, the remarks that follow are rather speculative.

Consider the following story.

(27) *Tony was hungry. He went to the restaurant and ordered a pizza. When he was finished, he found he had forgotten to take his wallet with him. He was embarrassed.*

The story is understandable only if the reader knows about the economics of restaurants. Schank and Abelson (1977) and their colleagues have suggested that such knowledge is organized into well-learned scenarios, or *scripts,* that describe standard situations. In order to comprehend a message, a receiver must first decide what script is relevant, and then how it is to be modified to fit the situation at hand.

There is a slightly different way of viewing the comprehension process. A text can be viewed as a sequence of connected propositions (Kintsch and Van Dijk, 1978), in which one or two main propositions express the theme. These

---

*We cannot here review this work in detail. If you are interested, see the text by Sanford and Garrod (1981).

can be qualified in complex ways by subpropositions. To illustrate, example (27) could be stated as

(28) *Tony dines out.*

This can be expanded to

(29) *Tony eats (in restaurant) pizza,*

and then

(30) *Tony eats (in restaurant) pizza and pay (cannot),*

and so forth. Comprehension is the process of building up the appropriate propositional structure. The propositional and script views of comprehension are complementary rather than opposed. A script could be thought of as a set of rules that the comprehender uses as a guide in detecting propositional structure.

If scripts are to be used to guide the comprehender, then the comprehender must decide what script is appropriate fairly early in a communication. In fact, people are biased toward assuming that the first one or two sentences of a text indicate the topic, and have difficulty in comprehension if this rule is not followed (Kieras, 1978). Furthermore, and most importantly, the level at which we comprehend a text will depend on the scripts that we recognize as appropriate. This point is not stressed in psycholinguistics, because researchers have tended to study the comprehension of scripts that everybody has. The restaurant script of (27) is a good (and much used) example. The importance of script possession as a determiner of individual differences in comprehension has been studied in quite a different field, the application of expert knowledge.

Many problems in mathematics and the physical sciences are initially stated in words. Figure 2.7 presents an example taken from elementary physics. Ultimately, this problem is solved by manipulating mathematical equations, but first the problem must be comprehended verbally, in order to identify the appropriate mathematical formulation. On the surface, the problem deals with weights held up by a pulley. At a deeper level, the problem deals with balanced forces. In the terminology of scripts, in order to comprehend the problem appropriately, we must connect it to the correct script. The balanced-forces script focuses attention on the key aspects of the problem, whereas a script dealing with pulleys does not. This appears to be one of the differences between novices and experts. When people are asked to sort problems similar to that in Figure 2.7 into sets of "similar" problems, expert physicists sort them by the physical laws involved, whereas novices sort on the basis of surface characteristics (Chi et al., 1982).

Since physicists are generally considered to be intellectually gifted, we could argue that their superior comprehension is due to "greater intelligence" rather than to the possession of appropriate scripts. A less intellectual example of script use can be offered. Students were asked to listen to a radio broadcast of a baseball game, and then were asked questions about it. The students who were

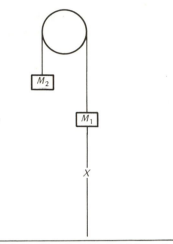

A man of mass M_1 lowers himself to the ground from a height X by holding onto a rope passed over a massless frictionless pulley attached to a block of mass M_2. What is the tension on the rope?

Figure 2.7
Physics word problem used by Chi et al. (1982) in studies of problem solving by experts and novices.

baseball fans showed much greater comprehension than those who were not. Furthermore, it was clear that their comprehension was based on their ability to use their background information ("scripts") about baseball to locate key information in the broadcast (Spilich et al., 1979). The concepts of scripts and of propositional structures seems to apply in quite different domains. One important determinant of a person's ability to understand a verbal message is his or her familiarity with the message topic.

Assume that a comprehender has the appropriate script. In conformity with the rules of the comprehension game, each expression in a message will either establish a new script or, more commonly, modify a previously comprehended proposition in the currently active script. This sequence has been referred to as *Given/New Contract.* In order to maintain coherence, the speaker and listener must agree about what is being modified (the "given") and what the change is (the "new"). Comprehenders and speakers appear to follow regular rules designed to make agreement easy (Clark and Haviland, 1977). To illustrate the process, let us return to the familiar restaurant script.

(31)   *John entered the restaurant. The headwaiter approached him. He was a haughty man with a great appreciation of good food.*

The first sentence establishes a restaurant script and identifies John as playing the role of customer. The second sentence identifies a permissible (but not obligatory) second role in a restaurant script and, by making that role active, transmits a good deal of information about the type of restaurant. The Tony of example

(27) would be very embarrassed in this restaurant. The sentence also changes the focus of the conversation. The active topic is now "the headwaiter" rather than "John." The final sentence contains a proposition that further modifies either "the headwaiter" or "John." It is ambiguous because it states "A male person was haughty . . .," and two male persons have been introduced. Most people, however, will assume that "he" means "headwaiter," because the current topic of conversation is generally accepted as the referent of an anaphora unless another choice is explicitly indicated (Frederiksen, 1982).

Much psychological research has shown that we must distinguish between *working memory* for events that have just occurred, *intermediate memory* for a general picture of the situation, and *permanent memory* for all the information we have (Baddeley, 1976; Hunt, 1972). People apparently keep from one to two sentences worth of information in working memory as they read (Glanzer et al., 1981). Comprehension will obviously be aided if the information currently in working memory includes the topic of the sentence about to be read. In such a case, the referent will be said to be an *explicit focus*. Implicit focusing involves partial activation of concepts related to an explicit focus. Implicit focusing is a matter of degree; some topics that are closely related to the current point in the script will be "waiting in the wings," to continue the script analogy, whereas other topics may be quite distant. In example (31), for instance, the introduction of "the headwaiter" immediately after the customer enters the restaurant is a predictable event. The introduction of, say, "Batman" would have caused a pause in comprehension.

In normal comprehension, the devices for shifting focus work so smoothly that we are aware of them only when they break down. For example:

(32) *John entered the restaurant. The headwaiter approached him. The bar waitress eyed the two of them. He was a haughty man. . . .*

Because we have introduced the bar waitress—not a candidate for the anaphoric referent "he"—continuity of topic has been broken; so it is not at all clear whether "he" refers to the headwaiter or to John. Note how memory must be used in this example. The first two sentences introduce two actors who are potential topics of further sentences or references. Ideally, their names will be held in working memory as the third sentence is analyzed. The situation is analogous to Daneman and Carpenter's (1980) experimental procedure for assessing memory span in the presence of competing verbal tasks.

There are two ways that individual differences in more basic processes could influence the ability to maintain cohesion. Obviously, the comprehender must be sensitive to the rather subtle linguistic rules used to control topicalization and referent resolution. It is not at all clear, though, what form sensitivity should take. Should the good comprehender be more aware of the nuances of linguistic conventions, perhaps even able to verbalize them? Or are people with high verbal aptitude better able to maintain cohesion when there are few linguistic guides? This raises an interesting question. Should a verbally competent person be defined as one who is sensitive to violations of proper usage, or as one who is able to make sense out of bad usage?

Allocating Attention in Comprehension

Comprehending is work. Word recognition, parsing, semantic analysis, reference resolution, and representation building all have to go on at once. Each task requires an effort. Sometimes the effort is so small that we cannot notice it. Who is aware of the process of retrieving meaning when CAT is read? Referents are easy to resolve in

(33) *I saw Mary yesterday. She was coming out of the store.*

but consider the following.

(34) *That guy standing by the store. I saw them come through the door, and he hollered at him like he was going to hit him, then somebody called the cops, but you took forever to come so the guy ran off then he came back when the other guy went away.*

Here understanding requires a conscious effort. Example (34) can be understood, but the text benefits from rereading. Pity the poor police officer, who has to make sense of a spoken version. Should he listen to what the witness is saying, or try to make sense out of what has already been said?

Put in a somewhat more formal way, comprehension requires the execution of two concurrent tasks: surface comprehension of expressions as they are received, and deeper comprehension of the meaning of the message as a whole. Surface comprehension has to take place in real time, because a comprehender must either keep up with a speaker's voice or maintain a steady pace of eye movements in reading. For this reason, surface comprehension has to be given priority; we cannot fit an incoming linguistic message into a representation until we know what the linguistic message is. Such situations, in which there are two concurrent tasks with different priorities, are called *dual-task situations with a primary-secondary task structure*. Several analyses of dual-task execution have been published (Kahneman, 1973; Kerr, 1973; Navon and Gopher, 1979; Norman and Bobrow, 1975; Wickens, 1979). The application of this theory to verbal comprehension is instructive.

A basic concept of dual-task theory is that attention is a finite resource that must be spread over concurrent activities. (There is a strong analogy to electric power.) The theory (e.g., Kahneman, 1973) assumes that attention is allocated to the primary task, and that the secondary task is executed with any resources that are left over. How might this idea apply to verbal comprehension? Two somewhat speculative ideas will be considered.

Earlier a distinction was made between the automatic processes involved in surface comprehension of a message and the processes under conscious control that are used to decide the meaning of the message in context. The automatic processes, primarily lexical-access and syntactic-semantic processes, are rule-governed actions that permit relatively little variation. "CAT" is to be spelled in just one way! Syntactic rules are somewhat more flexible, but the sentence structures that people actually use are certainly more stereotyped than the ideas that the structures may express. Thus the dual-task structure of comprehension can be further described by saying that the primary task of surface comprehension is repetitious, but the secondary task of deep structure comprehension is more unpredictable. Let us again look at the attention literature to consider how people differ in dealing with such situations.

When people are exposed to stereotyped situations over and over again, their actions become automated, and require relatively little, if any, allocation of attentional effort (Schneider and Shiffrin, 1977). As we have seen, verbal comprehension is indeed related to the smooth, rapid execution of automatic processes in isolation. One way of looking at superior execution of conscious-control processes by the verbally intelligent is to say that the high verbal individual has to divert relatively little attentional effort away from conscious processing, which must always be a controlled, attention-demanding task. However, as has often been pointed out, the two levels of processing are not completely independent. Higher-order knowledge of the gist of a text can guide lexical and syntactic processes, as was shown in the previous examples. At this point, Stanovich's (1980) remarks about reading are highly relevant. He pointed out that good readers—for adults, this group is virtually identical to good general comprehenders (Sticht et al., 1974)—seem to make less use of higher-order processes to guide automatic processing, presumably because they do not need to. This permits them to focus their attention on the more difficult level of processing that demands conscious control. Such focusing will be even more effective if the comprehenders have identified scripts that can be applied to identify the points at which special care must be taken in analyzing an incoming message.

If the preceding analysis is correct, any diminution in the total amount of attentional resources available ought to influence comprehension by acting on the attention-demanding pragmatic processes first, because the lower-priority processes should be the first to be deprived of a resource that is in limited supply. There is an anecdotal demonstration of this. We have all had the experience of reading when tired, and suddenly realized that although we have processed words and sentences, we do not have the slightest idea of what the story is about. Somewhat more formal demonstrations of the same idea are provided by studies of the effects of drugs and aging on verbal comprehension.

Taylor (1982) had young adults listen to simple stories, and then answer questions that referred either to information explicitly presented in the text or to information that was presented by inference and hence was extractable only by deep processing. The inferences themselves were simple ones that would normally be drawn as the message was comprehended, rather than constructed from memory in response to a question. Let us consider one of the stories.

(35) *I went to the library this morning and took out three books, two about gardening and one detective story. When I got home I found that I had lost one of the books on gardening. I had stopped at the post office on the way home and I might have left it there. If not, I must have left it on the bus. I went back to the post office, but they said I definitely hadn't left anything there. By then I had no time to go on looking for the book.*

A verbatim question for this passage was

(36) *"What was the missing book about?"*

The answer is specifically stated in the text. An inferential question was

(37) *"Where must I have left the missing book?"*

Although this hardly requires a difficult inference, the answer is not explicit in the passage. Table 2.4 shows how the ability to answer verbatim and inferential questions was affected by the administration of valium, a minor tranquilizer. Inferential questions became more difficult to answer, but verbatim questions did not.

The drug study demonstrates the effects of an internal change in attentional capacity upon the ability to comprehend verbal messages. Can the same point be made by studying verbal comprehension in individuals who differ in their chronic levels of attentional capacity? Studies of adult aging are relevant, because many of the changes in general cognitive ability that are associated with age seem to be due to a reduction in attentional capacity (Hasher and Zacks, 1979). In fact, the drug study just described was modeled after a study of age effects in attention and comprehension (Cohen, 1979). Old and young people listened to the same passages used in the drug study, and answered either inferential or verbatim questions. The speed of presentation of the passages was varied, because rapid presentation of speech should increase the attentional resources needed to allow the listener to keep up with the speaker, and inferential questions should then become even more difficult for the elderly to answer after rapid presentation. Table 2.5 shows the results. The hypothesis was clearly confirmed. (Similar data have been reported by Light et al., 1982.) In a companion study, reading was compared to listening (Cohen, 1981). The elderly found it harder to draw inferences from spoken than from written passages, presumably because they could control the speed of input while reading, but not while listening.

The role of attention allocation in verbal comprehension is only beginning to be explored. Traditionally, research on attention and research on comprehen-

---

Table 2.4
The mean number of questions answered correctly as a function of type (verbatim vs. inferred information) and drug state[a]

Drug state	Verbatim	Inference
Valium, 5 mg	6.16	6.36
Valium, 10 mg	6.53	5.81
Placebo	6.59	6.88

[a]Data from Taylor (1978).

Table 2.5

Percentage of errors in response to inference and verbatim questions, as a function of age, education, and rate of presentation of spoken material[a]

	Question type			
	Inference		Verbatim	
Group	Fast	Slow	Fast	Slow
Old, highly educated	27.8	17.5	10.5	8.7
Young, highly educated	12.5	10.6	7.5	5.5
Old, less educated	60.3	55.9	41.1	38.3
Young, less educated	22.2	20.3	12.9	12.5

[a]From Cohen (1979).

sion have been independent. Indeed, there are very few journals that cover both fields. The remarks here are suggestions for future study, not a presentation of a well-understood topic.

Conclusion: What Happened to Verbal Comprehension?

There is a psychological *dimension of ability* associated with the comprehension of language. However, we cannot think of verbal ability as a dimension of individual variation, analogous to height or weight. Comprehension is a complex process, composed of many subprocesses. These range from the automatic, involuntary acts of lexical identification to the planned strategies people use to extract meaning from lengthy texts. There are individual differences in all the subprocesses. They combine to produce "verbal intelligence."

There is no disagreement between the psychometricians' observation that verbal comprehension behaves, statistically, as if it were a unitary ability and the experimental psychologists' and linguists' contention that verbal comprehension can be broken down into its component processes. The elementary behaviors build on each other. Sentence analysis cannot take place without lexical analysis. Text comprehension depends on sentence comprehension. There is a built-in correlation between performance on a lexical-analysis task and on a sentence-analysis task, and between sentence and paragraph comprehension. In fact, the value of the correlation between a simpler and a more complex task should rise as the complexity of the simpler task rises, because the two tasks will share more and more components.

Although the different components of verbal comprehension are distinct, people who acquire skill in one are likely to acquire skill in another. Whether or not we want to talk about "verbal intelligence" depends very much on the level of discourse. Thinking of people as having (or not having) verbal intelligence is useful up to a point. For a complete understanding of their behavior, we must know how they achieve comprehension.

References

Baddeley, A. D. 1976. *The Psychology of Memory.* New York: Basic Books.

———. 1968. A three-minute reasoning test based on grammatical transformation. *Psychonomic Science,* 10, 341–342.

Baddeley, A. D., and G. Hitch. 1974. Working memory. *In* G. H. Bower, ed., *The Psychology of Learning and Motivation, Vol. 8* (New York: Academic Press).

Carpenter, P. A., and M. A. Just. 1975. Sentence comprehension: A psychologistic processing model of verification. *Psychological Review,* 82, 45–73.

Chi, M. T. H., P. J. Feltovitch, and R. Glaser. 1981. Categorization and representation of physics problems by experts and novices. *Cognitive Science,* 5, 121–152.

Clark, H. H. 1979. Responding to indirect speech acts. *Cognitive Psychology,* 11, 430–477.

Clark, H. H., and W. G. Chase. 1972. On the process of comparing sentences against pictures. *Cognitive Psychology,* 3, 472–517.

Clark, H. H., and S. E. Haviland. 1977. Comprehension and the Given-New Contract. *In* R. O. Freedle, ed., *Discourse Production and Comprehension* (Norwood, N.J.: Ablex).

Cohen, G. 1979. Language comprehension in old age. *Cognitive Psychology,* 11, 412–429.

———. 1981. Inferential reasoning in old age. *Cognition,* 9, 59–72.

Cohen, J., and P. Cohen. 1975. *Applied Multiple Regressional and Correlation Analysis for the Behavioral Sciences.* Hillsdale, N.J.: Erlbaum.

Daneman, M., and P. A. Carpenter. 1980. Individual differences in working memory and reading. *Journal of Verbal Learning and Verbal Behavior,* 19, 450–466.

Dempster, F. N. 1981. Memory span: Sources of individual and developmental differences. *Psychological Bulletin,* 89, 63–100.

Erlich, K. 1980. The comprehension of pronouns. *Quarterly Journal of Experimental Psychology,* 1980, 32, 247–255.

Frederiksen, J. R. 1982. A componential theory of reading skills and their interactions. *In* R. J. Sternberg, ed., *Advances in the Psychology of Human Intelligence, Vol. 1* (Hillsdale, N.J.: Erlbaum).

Freyd, P., and J. Baron. 1982. Individual differences in the acquisition of derivational morphology. *Journal of Verbal Learning and Verbal Behavior,* 21, 282–295.

Glanzer, M., D. Dorfman, and B. Kaplan. 1981. Short term storage in the processing of text. *Journal of Verbal Learning and Verbal Behavior,* 20, 656–670.

Goldberg, R. A., S. Schwartz, and M. Stewart. 1977. Individual differences in cognitive processes. *Journal of Educational Psychology,* 69, 9–14.

Hasher, L., and R. Zacks. 1979. Automatic and effortful processes in memory. *Journal of Experimental Psychology,* 108, 356–388.

Hunt, E. 1971. What kind of computer is man? *Cognitive Psychology,* 2, 57–98.

———. 1978. The mechanics of verbal ability. *Psychological Review,* 85, 109–130.

Hunt, E., J. Davidson, and M. Lansman. 1981. Individual differences in long term memory. *Memory and Cognition,* 9, 599–608.

Hunt, E., N. Frost, and C. Lunneburg. 1973. Individual differences in cognition: A new approach to intelligence. *In* C. Bower, ed., *Advances in Learning and Motivation, Vol. 7* (New York: Academic Press).

Hunt, E., C. Lunneborg, and J. Lewis. 1975. What does it mean to be high verbal? *Cognitive Psychology,* 7, 194–227.

Jackson, M. D. 1980. Further evidence for a relation between memory access and reading ability. *Journal of Verbal Learning and Verbal Behavior,* 19, 683–695.

Kahneman, D. 1973. *Attention and Effort.* Englewood Cliffs, N.J.: Prentice Hall.

Kerr, F. B. 1973. Processing demands during mental operations. *Memory and Cognition,* 1, 401–412.

Kieras, D. E. 1978. Good and bad structure in simple paragraphs: Effects of apparent theme, reading time, and recall. *Journal of Verbal Learning and Verbal Behavior,* 17, 13–28.

Kintsch, W., and T. A. Van Dijk. 1978. Towards a model of text comprehension. *Psychological Review,* 85, 363–394.

LaBerge, D., and S. J. Samuels. 1974. Toward a theory of automatic information processing in reading. *Cognitive Psychology,* 6, 293–323.

Lansman, M. 1978. An Attentional Approach to Individual Differences in Immediate Memory. Ph.D. thesis. Seattle: Univ. of Washington, Dept. of Psychology, June 1978.

Lansman, M., G. Donaldson, E. Hunt, and S. Yantis. 1983. Ability factors and cognitive processes. *Intelligence,* 6, 347–386.

Light, L., E. M. Zelinski, and M. Moore. 1982. Adult age differences in reasoning from new information. *Journal of Experimental Psychology: Learning, Memory, and Cognition,* 435–557.

Matarazzo, J. D. 1972. *Wechsler's Measurement and Appraisal of Adult Intelligence.* Baltimore: Williams and Wilkins, 5th ed.

Miller, G. 1981. *Language and Speech.* San Francisco, Calif.: W. H. Freeman and Co.

Mulaik, S. A. 1972. *The Foundations of Factor Analysis.* New York: McGraw-Hill.

Navon, D., and D. Gopher. 1979. On the economy of human processing system. *Psychological Review,* 86, 214–255.

Norman, D. A., and D. B. Bobrow. 1975. On data limited and resource limited processes. *Cognitive Psychology,* 7, 44–64.

Nunnally, J. 1978. *Psychometric Theory.* New York: McGraw-Hill, 2d ed.

Palmer, J. C., C. M. MacLeod, E. Hunt, and J. Davidson, in press. Information processing correlates of reading: An individual differences analysis. *Journal of Verbal Learning and Verbal Behavior.*

Sanford, A. J., and S. C. Garrod. 1981. *Understanding Written Language.* New York: Wiley.

Schank, R., and R. P. Abelson. 1977. *Scripts, Plans, Goals, and Understanding.* Hillsdale, N.J.: Erlbaum.

Schneider, W., and R. M. Shiffrin. 1977. Controlled and automatic human information processing, I: Detection, search, and attention. *Psychological Review,* 84, 1–66.

Schwartz, S., and T. C. Wiedel. 1978. Individual differences in cognition: Relationship between verbal ability and memory for order. *Intelligence,* 2, 353–370.

Spilich, G. J., G. T. Vesonder, H. L. Chiesi, and J. F. Voss. 1979. Text processing of domain-related information for individuals with high and low domain knowledge. *Journal of Verbal Learning and Verbal Behavior,* 18, 275–290.

Sternberg, R. J., B. E. Conway, J. L. Ketron, and M. Bernstein. 1981. People's conceptions of intelligence. *Journal of Personality and Social Psychology: Attitudes and Social Cognition,* 41, 37–55.

Sternberg, R. J., and J. S. Powell. 1983. Comprehending verbal comprehension. *American Psychologist,* 8, 828–893.

Sternberg, S. 1975. Memory scanning: New findings and current controversies. *Quarterly Journal of Experimental Psychology,* 27, 1–32.

Sticht, T. G., ed. 1975. *Reading for Working: A Functional Literary Anthology.* Alexandria, Va.: Human Resources Research Organization.

Sticht, T. G., L. J. Beck, R. N. Havke, G. M. Keiman, and J. H. James. 1974. *Auding and Reading: A Developmental Model.* Alexandria, Va.: Human Resources Research Organization.

Stillman, C. 1982. Individual Differences in Language and Spatial Abilities among Young Gifted Children. Ph.D. dissertation. Seattle: Univ. of Washington.

Stroop, J. R. 1935. Studies of interference in serial verbal reactions. *Journal of Experimental Psychology,* 18, 643–662.

Taylor, J. 1982. The Effects of Benzodiazepines on Cognition and Performance. Ph.D. thesis. Seattle: Univ. of Washington, Dept. of Psychology, June 1982.

Tulving, E. and Gold, C. 1963. Stimulus information and contextual information as determinants of tachistoscopic recognition of words, *Journal of Experimental Psychology,* 66, 319–327.

Van Daalen-Kapteijns, X., and M. Elshout-Mohr. 1981. The acquisition of word meanings as a cognitive learning process. *Journal of Verbal Learning and Verbal Behavior,* 20, 386–399.

Warren, J., and E. Hunt. 1981. Cognitive processing in children with Prader-Willi syndrome. *In* V. A. Holme, S. J. Sulzbacher, and P. L. Pipes, *Prader-Willi Syndrome.* Baltimore, Md.: Univ. Park Press.

Wickens, C. D. 1979. The structure of attentional resources. *In* R. S. Nickerson, ed., *Attention and Performance, Vol. 8* (Hillsdale, N.J.: Erlbaum).

3

READING ABILITY

Charles A. Perfetti
University of Pittsburgh

The average college student reads about 250 words per minute with some comprehension. But some college-age students read at only half that rate, and others read at nearly twice that rate, at least occasionally. Of course, the range of skill in reading is much greater than the difference between the slow and fast college student reader. Beginning readers, about age six in the United States, also vary greatly in reading ability, but even the best among them does not approach the skill level of even the slow college student. How can we explain the difference between a college student who reads 400 words a minute and one who reads 150 words a minute? How can we explain the difference between an eight-year-old child who can read whole stories with understanding, and one who is still struggling with simple words after two years of instruction in reading? These are the questions to be addressed in this chapter.

To account for reading ability we have to consider its component parts. It is useful to define two general components, *lexical access* and *comprehension.*

Lexical access is the process of "recognizing" a word. It is access to the word in permanent memory, given a printed graphic input. Comprehension is really not a single process, but the result of several processes that operate on texts to produce understanding.

Lexical Access

If we are skilled at reading, we may have the impression that we read words in bunches. We even have the impression that we skip over words, selectively reading only a few words on each line. In fact, most words are accessed one at a time, and very few words are "skipped."

To illustrate this important fact about reading, Figure 3.1 shows a segment of text read by a college student. The number above each word gives the length of time the student's eyes rested on the word, the *eye fixation* time. We can see in Figure 3.1 that not all words are fixated for the same amount of time. Large words are fixated longer than short words, and rare words are fixated longer than common words. And the last word of each sentence is fixated much longer than other words. In Figure 3.1, notice that the words *research* and *produced,* each the final word of its sentence, were fixated for about half a second, much longer than the average fixation. Carpenter and Just (1981) refer to this as *sentence wrapup time.* The reader seems to be pausing to assemble some sentence parts that have been processed but perhaps not fully integrated.*

All these factors that contribute to the duration of an eye fixation are an important part of reading, but only part of it. The reader's purpose in reading will set some general limits on fixation times. Thus, Figure 3.1 shows times for a reader who expects to have to evaluate true-false statements for what he has read. Readers who try to "skim" the text, thus putting emphasis on speed, may show fewer and shorter fixations (Just et al., 1982).

An important fact that has been learned by means of eye camera research of this kind is that although a reader's eyes spend less time on some words than on others, they spend some time on most words. The fact that most words are fixated during normal reading may seem to indicate a very inefficient reading strategy that could be corrected by a speed-reading course. Instead, it reflects another surprising fact about reading: the eye does not pick up much information beyond the word being fixated (Rayner, 1975). The reader does not identify words in the visual periphery. Neither is significant information obtained while the eye is moving. Lexical access initiated by an eye fixation is therefore a central component of reading, occurring four times per second for an average adult reader (240 words per minute). Lexical access is essential to effective reading and is a potential source of reading-ability differences.

How does lexical access work? The starting point is a visual input, a string of letters in the case of English. The processes by which this string of letters

---

*All fixation times include more processing than mere lexical access, especially processes of semantic encoding that activate word meanings needed for the sentence. See Just and Carpenter (1980) for a detailed model.

results in the recognition of a word have been widely investigated, and several theoretical accounts have been suggested (see Baron, 1978, for a review of some of these).

One class of lexical-access theories assumes *interactive processes.* Interactive processing occurs when information at different levels jointly determines some outcome, such as word recognition or lexical access. Interactive processing theories contrast with explanations that are based on strictly "bottom-up" processes. In bottom-up processes, information is passed from low-level processes, such as detection of lines and angles, through intermediate levels, such as letter identification, on to recognition of a word. Bottom-up processes are clearly essential in word recognition and perception generally. They assure that information in the stimulus determines somehow what is recognized. In a

Figure 3.1

Eye-fixation pattern of a college student reading a technical passage. The numbers 1, 2, 3, . . . indicate the sequence of fixations. Thus, number 4 is a regressive fixation, i.e., the result of the reader's gaze going back to the first word. The number below each fixation number is the duration of the fixation. For example, fixation number 7 was on "tools" for 268 milliseconds. The subject read with the expectation of a true-false test. Adapted from Carpenter and Just (1981).

(4)	(11)							
286	466							
(1)	(2)	(3)	(5)	(6)	(7)	(8)		(9)
166	200	167	299	217	268	317		399

Radioisotopes have long been valuable tools in scientific and medical

		(5)					.
		183					
(10)		(1)	(2)	(3)	(4)	(6)	(8)	(7)	(9)
463		317	250	367	416	333	183	450	650

research. Now, however, four nonradioactive isotopes are being produced.

(4)				(8)				
366				183				
(1)	(2)	(3)	(5)	(6)	(7)	(9)	(10)	(11)
250	200	367	400	216	233	317	283	100

They are called "icons" — four isotopes of carbon, oxygen, nitrogen, and

(12)	(13)
683	150

sulfur.

sense, they are what allows a reader to see what really is on the page, rather than some imaginary word.

To illustrate some points about lexical access, Figure 3.2 shows three samples of the word "window." (It also shows the word "pepper." The bottom-most sample was created by deleting (more-or-less randomly) 42 percent of the dots that make up the computer-printed word "window." It is impoverished enough that, in isolation, it is not always recognized as a word. This represents loss of information at a very elementary level, that of the lines and angles that combine to form letters. The middle sample of "window" shows 21 percent of the elementary features deleted. It is much more recognizable as the word "window" because there is much more information at the elementary-feature level, which, in turn, provides more information at the letter level, which, in turn, forces the recognition of "window." The top sample, of course, has all the information possible (within this particular format) and is completely recognizable.

What we see in the "window" example is the dependence of lexical access on bottom-up processes. Distorting the elementary features allows us to notice the contribution of elementary features at a level below the letter. We are ordinarily not very aware of such features. What makes the elementary features theoretically important is that they are recombinable. A vertical line (|) combined in one way with a horizontal line (–) is a "T." In another way, it's an "L." These distinctive features (the lines and angles) have a major role to play in any understanding of the perceptual part of reading (see Gibson and Levin, 1975; LaBerge and Samuels, 1974; Massaro, 1975; Rumelhart, 1977; Estes, 1977).

Interactive Processes

So far we have considered a bottom-up account of lexical access. Information passes from elementary features to letters to words. An interactive model of lexical access is not very different. It simply allows one small change:

Figure 3.2

Three levels of degrading for "pepper" and "window," defined as percent of features deleted. Since lexical access depends in part on these features, recognition decreases with increasing degrading. However, context can compensate for the feature loss. [From Perfetti (in press).]

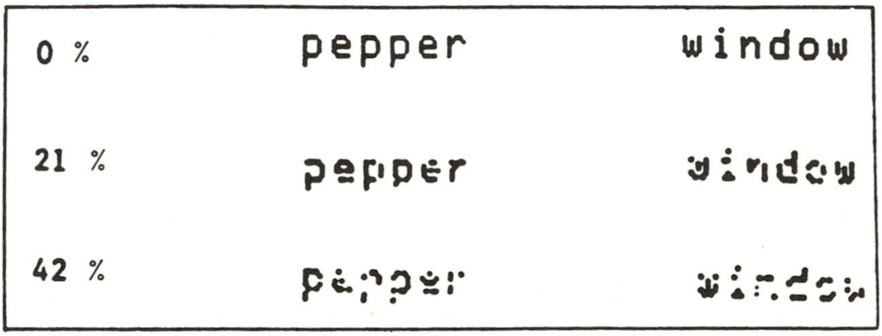

Information can flow in both directions. Thus a *word*, once activated, activates letters, and these can activate letter features. Information passes both from the bottom to the top and from the top to the bottom. This is the central characteristic of the interactive model of Rumelhart (1977).

For this proposal to make sense, it's assumed that each type of information (e.g., features, letters, words) is represented at a different level in memory. There is a word level, a letter level, and a feature level (at least). In the Rumelhart and McClelland theory (McClelland and Rumelhart, 1981; Rumelhart and McClelland, 1981, 1982), information is stored at nodes at these levels, and the nodes are interconnected by activation links. (There are both excitatory and inhibitory links; we will ignore the inhibitory links here for simplification.) The activation links permit excitation to spread from one level to another level, for example, from the letter "w" to words having the letter "w" as a constituent letter. Note that this particular activation pattern is bottom-up, and is not really different from other ways of describing how letter perception mediates word perception. The only interesting difference is that all words beginning with "w" would be given some activation. There is thus competition among nodes at the word level for lexical access. However, although many words are activated, only one will actually be "accessed," and that one will be the one that accumulates the most activation from the letter level. Whereas "w" + "i" will activate "window" and "willow" equally, "w" + "i" + "n" will activate "window" more, and it will eventually be the word accessed.

However, what makes the interactive model *interactive* is that activation goes down from words as well as up to words. For example, suppose the string of letters to be accessed occurs in a text instead of in isolation, as in sentence (1):

(1) *The room was warm and stuffy; so they opened the _____.*

Now suppose that what is actually printed in the blank is the 42 percent degraded stimulus of Figure 3.2. It will be quickly identified as "window," more quickly than if it occurred in isolation or more quickly than if it occurred in sentence (2):

(2) *There were several repair jobs to be done. The first was to fix the _____.*

"Window" is a perfectly sensible completion of sentence (2), but it is not so predictable as in sentence (1). In terms of an interactive activation model, "window" is getting a lot of activation during the processing of sentence (1), considerably less during the processing of sentence (2). This difference in activation is not due to bottom-up activation. The same low-level degraded features are involved in both. Instead, this is activation due to semantic processes that operate even before the visual features of the final word are encountered. This is top-down activation. It interacts with the bottom-up activation in that the *word level* (the level of interest in lexical access) is accumulating activation from both top-down and bottom-up sources. Furthermore, since activation spreads down from the word level as well as up to it, the semantic activation of "window" spreads down to the letters that make up the word. Thus the letters (and features) consistent with the word that is receiving semantic activation become more active, and in turn increase activation for the word "window." At the same time, words consistent with the increasing letter activation are strengthened over other words. In this way, a bit simplified, top-down and bottom-up sources of information combine to produce lexical access.*

The examples that illustrate context effects in word recognition bring in the topic of comprehension. If context is used in word recognition, some comprehension processes have operated on the preceding text.

Comprehension in Reading

Comprehension occurs at many levels during reading. At the lowest level, we can think of accessing the semantic information of a single word as an elementary comprehension event. In the window example, this *semantic encoding* implies that access to the word "window" in memory activates semantic properties of the concept window: that it can be seen through, is often made of glass, etc. This is the link between lexical access and comprehension. At much higher levels of comprehension, the reader glimpses the writer's purpose, anticipates the outcome of some story or argument, etc. To simplify matters, and to focus on the levels of comprehension that have been most important in information processing, we will consider two levels of comprehension beyond semantic encoding. One is based on comprehension of explicit text sentences, the propositional level; the other is comprehension based on knowledge external to the text.

Propositions

Since texts are composed of sentences, the comprehension of sentences is a central component of reading. Propositions are the elementary meaning units of sentences.

To illustrate, in comprehending sentence (1), the reader encodes these propositions:

(a) warm (room)	(The room was warm)
(b) stuffy (room)	(The room was stuffy)
(c) open (they, window)	(They opened the window)
(d) because {[(a) and (b)], (c)}	[They did (c) because of (a) and (b)]

Thus the meaning of the sentence, "The room was warm and stuffy, so they opened the window" comprises four discrete elementary propositions. The key element in a proposition is a predicate, which linguistically can consist of verbs, adjectives, or certain conjunctions. They *predicate* a relationship between two or more concepts within the sentence. Thus, proposition (a) predicates that the room is warm, and proposition (b) predicates that the room is stuffy. Proposition

---

*Actually there are many models that can account for context effects in word recognition, and thus are at least weakly interactive, for example, Morton's (1969) logogen model.

(c) predicates opening as the relationship between "they" and "window." (The fact that it is a past event, i.e., past tense, is ignored here but easily represented.) Proposition (d) is an embedding proposition, in that it represents a relationship between independent propositions. It predicates a *because* relationship between propositions (a) and (b) and proposition (c).

Thus propositions are abstract elementary meaning units that combine in certain ways to make up the meaning of a sentence. A text, i.e., a set of coherently related sentences, can be understood as a list of interrelated propositions. The major theory of text representation based on this assumption is described in Kintsch (1974) and Kintsch and van Dijk (1978).

In terms of information processing, one important thing about propositions is that they are assumed to be the units of processing in *working memory* during text reading (Kintsch and van Dijk, 1978). In an information-processing system, working memory refers to a limited-capacity processing mechanism that performs mental operations (Baddeley and Hitch, 1974; Newell and Simon, 1972). These operations include everything from rehearsing a string of digits, multiplying two-digit numbers, and, for reading, holding propositions in memory and integrating them. The model of Kintsch and van Dijk (1978) assumes that the reader can hold only a few propositions in working memory while reading a new sentence. The propositions of the new sentence must be linked to one of these propositions in working memory. As propositions are assembled and integrated, they can become part of long-term memory. One fact that gives some support to describing reading this way is that the time a reader takes to silently read a short text is a function of the number of propositions it contains, not just the number of words (Kintsch and Keenan, 1973). Comprehension at this level is therefore a matter of encoding word meanings and propositions in working memory, assembling and integrating them, and transferring them to long-term memory. Although readers often fail to retrieve the propositions from long-term memory later, comprehension will nevertheless have occurred.

Of course, there is more to comprehension than encoding elementary propositions. The reader encodes these propositions in the context of knowledge about concepts, general knowledge about the everyday world, and knowledge about the forms of texts. First, we consider comprehension based on general world and conceptual knowledge.

Knowledge-Based Comprehension

In addition to encoding elementary propositions, the reader adds to the sentences of the text by making inferences. These can be considered as propositions that are encoded as part of the reader's text representation. The reader will often "remember" such propositions as being part of the text (e.g., Anderson et al. 1977; Johnson et al., 1973; Sulin and Dooling, 1974). For example, suppose sentence (1), the window sentence, appears in a text preceded by sentence (3):

(3)   *Joe and his infant daughter were waiting for the doctor to get back from lunch.*

(1)   *The room was warm and stuffy; so they opened the window.*

When asked later to recall the text which contained these sentences, the reader may recall for (1) that "Joe opened the window in the office because it was hot and stuffy." Recalling *hot* rather than *warm* is a local text change based on encoded word meaning. However, recalling *Joe* as the window opener instead of *they,* and *office* (a word that was not used) as the location instead of *room,* suggests changes based on inferences. It is significant that such examples, which are very common in recall of texts of all kinds, reflect the retention of meaning at a general level. They reflect a combination of what the reader knows (that people visit doctors in places called "offices") and what he or she readily infers (that an infant is not likely to be an agent in opening a window) with the explicit propositions of the text.

Some of the inferences a reader makes are semantically or logically implied by the text propositions, but others are not. The two inference examples above are in the latter category. Their plausibility is strictly psychological, based on the reader's world knowledge. (In fact, they could well have been in a "waiting room" rather than in an "office.") Had the reader recalled something about the window being *closed* when they entered the room, that would be a semantically forced inference. A window can be said to have been opened only if its initial state was closed.

Although there are different types of inferences, it is probable that these different types are governed by a single comprehension principle: in processing a text, a reader combines explicit propositions with his or her own general knowledge to produce an understanding of the text. This knowledge includes what the reader knows about word meanings, e.g., the relationship between "open" and "close," as well as what he or she knows about how things are in doctors' offices, restaurants, etc. The organized knowledge about such things is often referred to as a *schema* (Bartlett, 1932; Anderson et al., 1978; Rumelhart and Ortony, 1977), a conceptual abstraction containing slots to be filled in with specific details. For example, a schema for window opening would include slots for the manner of opening: by lifting, by pushing, by turning a handle, etc. The core of the schema, its invariant part, has to do with causing a window that is closed to become open. More complex schemata have essentially the same properties. For example, a visit to a doctor includes slots relating to appointments (vs. walking in), receptionists, waiting rooms, nurse's examinations, etc.

One particular schema that has been the object of analysis and research is the restaurant schema or *script* (Schank and Abelson, 1977). A demonstration of how recall of text information depends on the activation of a schema was provided by Anderson et al. (1978) with the help of the restaurant schema. These investigators had subjects read either a passage about having dinner at a fancy restaurant or one about a trip to a supermarket. Common to the two passages were eighteen food items. Would readers of the two passages recall these items equally well? The schema hypothesis predicts otherwise. Although both supermarkets and restaurants contain food items, the restaurant schema organizes them more powerfully. For example, this schema includes an ordering principle for classes of foods (appetizers, soups, salads, entrees, desserts), whereas the supermarket schema does not. This organization should enable more recall of food items than from the less powerfully structured supermarket schema. This is what Anderson et al. (1978) found.

Although a schema may often be useful as a retrieval plan, sometimes the contribution of knowledge is in comprehension itself, especially when the content of a text is very vague (Bransford and Johnson, 1972) or highly metaphorical (Dooling and Lachman, 1971). Here a cue, provided by a story title or something that activates an appropriate schema, allows comprehension of something that would be otherwise incomprehensible.

Discourse Structure

A second major type of knowledge that a reader uses in comprehension is based on the structure of the text. The best-known models of such text structures are *story grammars* (Mandler and Johnson, 1977; Rumelhart, 1975; Stein and Glenn, 1979; Thorndyke, 1977). A story grammar is a rule-based description of regularities in the structure of stories. These regularities provide another example of a schema. Schemata organize what the reader knows about the structure of narratives: that narratives have a setting and an episode as their basic structure; that an episode has a structure consisting of goal striving, conflict, and resolution; that one episode can embed another episode. These are the kinds of central structural relationships that have been captured by the rules of story grammars. Other relationships important for story comprehension are identified in the causal chain of events underlying the story (Omanson, 1982).

How do such structures work in comprehension? Very likely, such structures provide schemata to which the reader can attach specific events and characters of the story. As the reader becomes aware that what is being read is a "story," there is activation of story-appropriate information. For example, having encoded a story *setting,* the reader can anticipate some event that will start things moving *(the initiating event).* This event will cause a psychological reaction in the story protagonist *(internal reaction),* who will try to do something to set things right *(attempt).* Along the way, these attempts may fail (negative *outcome*), and new reactions, attempts, and outcomes ensue. Implicit knowledge of story schemata may be helpful to the reader in anticipating events in a story and in implementing a retrieval plan for recalling the story. Apparently, children at a very young age are able to use story grammars to assist in their reproduction of stories (Stein and Glenn, 1979). Finally, there is some evidence that the structures of a story grammar may play some role when a story is being read. Mandler and Goodman (1980) found that the time needed to read a sentence in a story was related to whether the story structure component to which it belonged was completed. When the component (e.g., attempt) had not yet been completed, reading the sentence was faster than when the sentence ended that component.

Summary

We have discussed the major components of reading. When we read a text, scanning individual words from left to right, most of the words are accessed. Lexical access, the process by which a reader makes contact with information stored with a word in long-term memory, is thus a major component of reading. Access is achieved by means of the interaction of lower-level and higher-level information, including levels of representation corresponding to visual features, letters, and words. Activation spreads among these levels whether initiated by stimulus information or by contextual information. The encoding of word meanings is the major outcome of lexical access, and as enough words are accessed, their encodings are included in the propositions that reflect the elementary meaning units of a text. The basic level of comprehension includes assembling and integrating propositions in working memory. This level is heavily influenced by the reader's knowledge, including knowledge of text forms, of semantic relations, and of schemata for the ordinary world, among other things. Given this sketch, we are ready to address more directly this question: Why are some people better at reading than other people?

Ability Differences

Since reading involves the interaction of different processes and sources of knowledge, there are different ways in which people can vary in reading ability. Also, what we mean by "reading ability" will vary somewhat with the age or skill level of the reader. Among high school and college students, a reader of high ability may be one who reads silently at a high rate with comprehension. We would also expect the high-ability reader to achieve "critical" understanding of the text, to gauge an author's persuasive purpose, to understand extensions or applications of the text, etc. At this level, reading comprehension looks a lot like thinking. Among seven-year-olds in the second grade, a reader of high ability may be one who correctly reads single words out loud, especially long words and rare words. We would expect the high-ability reader to read with comprehension as well, but the emphasis would be on word decoding. At intermediate levels, third grade and beyond, comprehension increasingly becomes the main standard of reading ability. We focus here on reading ability as comprehension, but we know that lexical access is part of this process.

Let us therefore take the ability to read rapidly and easily with comprehension as the ability we wish to understand. Differences in this ability can arise from several sources within an information-processing framework. Readers can differ in their knowledge-based comprehension, and in their lexical-access abilities. The high-ability reader is strong in all these abilities, and the low-ability reader may be weak in any or all of them.

Knowledge-Based Approaches to Ability

Since comprehension in reading is the hallmark of mature reading ability, it is natural to expect knowledge and knowledge application to be important ability factors. It is axiomatic that a reader understands what is read only in relationship to what he or she already knows. Indeed, a clever experiment by Anderson et al. (1977) demonstrated that a passage written with two possible interpretations was understood in two very different ways, depending on the background of the reader. The passage told the story of "Rocky" who "got up from the mat," planned "his escape," "considered his situation," and, after "getting angry," finally prepared "to make his move." What is this passage about? Students from a weight-lifting class tended to understand this as a story about a wrestling match; others tended to understand this as a story about a planned prison escape. (Presumably, wrestling students would have been even more disposed to the wrestling interpretation than weight lifters.)

This finding demonstrates that what we understand depends on our experience when passages are written to be ambiguous. However, even passages that seem unambiguous to the writer will be comprehended in terms of the reader's knowledge. To the extent that two readers do not have identical knowledge, they cannot have identical representations of a passage which depends on that knowledge. Voss and his associates (Chiesi et al., 1979; Spilich et al., 1979) assessed how much college students knew about baseball, and then had them listen to a half-inning account of a fictitious game. When subjects later recalled this brief account, subjects high in baseball knowledge recalled more than subjects low in baseball knowledge. More interesting, high-knowledge subjects had a qualitatively different representation of the half-inning. Their recalls included more information about the events that were significant for the game itself, i.e., the events related to the sequences of actions that make up the essential structure of the game. Low-knowledge subjects recalled somewhat more of the information not relevant to the essential game structure. That is, in general, the subjects were not very different at remembering the score and that certain batters got hits and others made outs. However, a high-knowledge subject was more likely to remember that Ioto's single to right sent Saguchi from first to third with the tying run. A low-knowledge subject was more likely to remember the attendance, or what time the team plane would depart after the game.

An important thing to notice is that in neither the "Rocky" nor the baseball demonstration is there an issue of reading ability per se. Subjects, at least in the baseball studies, were equated on general reading ability. What is demonstrated is that individual differences in knowledge lead to individual differences in comprehension. The application of individual differences in knowledge to reading ability is an extension of this principle. Individuals who are high in reading ability tend to have more useful knowledge, or at least apply it more readily, than readers of low ability.

This conclusion is certainly correct as far as it goes. However, it merely implies that individuals will become better readers if we can fill their heads with more knowledge. In fact, there are several, more specific ways in which the knowledge-based approach can be applied to reading ability. Spiro (1980) has outlined some distinct ways in which the availability of schemata (or knowledge structures) can be understood to affect reading ability. First, the individual needs to acquire enough schemata, of enough generality, that they can be applied to many different texts *(schema acquisition)*. Second, the individual must be able to apply the right knowledge structure to the right situation *(schema selection)*. Third, the reader often needs to modify the application of a schema during reading, to "fill in" his or her general idea of what a text is about *(schema instantiation and refinement)*, and even to change schemata or combine them when necessary.

When we consider schemata in this way, as structures that the reader not only needs to "have" but also must be able to use appropriately, we realize that *application* of knowledge is critical in reading. It is likely that readers differ in skill at applying the right schema to the right situation. Individuals do differ in their ability to assess their own knowledge, skills of *metacognition.* For example, children often fail in various problem-solving tasks at the metacognitive level (Brown, 1978). That is, they fail to recognize an increase in difficulty level or to plan ahead or to monitor the outcomes of their performance.

Similar metacognitive processes need to be applied to a text. The reader must have a sense of what is central to the text content and what is less important. Is this a skill that low-ability readers lack? It's not clear. In one study (Smiley et al., 1977), skilled readers' recall of stories reflected the importance of the text content (as rated by judges) more than did the recall of less-skilled readers. However, when the texts of the Smiley et al. (1977) are analyzed by a theory that distinguishes only two levels of importance within a text (Omanson, 1982), recall of less-skilled readers included important content as much as did recall of more-skilled readers. In a study with adult readers, Omanson and Malamut (1980) found that high- and low-ability adults equally differentiated central from noncentral content in the recalls. Beck et al. (1982) found the same result with third-grade readers. Presumably, further research will illuminate this issue. For now, we can say that awareness of the role of a given unit (e.g., a sentence) in the overall structure of a text is an important factor in reading. However, even low-ability readers have *some* of this awareness.

Proposition-Processing Factors in Ability

A second major component in reading is the assembling and integrating of propositions in working memory. Another approach to understanding reading ability is therefore to suggest that differences in working memory are central. Since assembling propositions is partly a matter of lexical access and semantic encoding, the working-memory approach suggests at least two general possibilities for ability differences. (1) Relative to high-ability readers, low-ability readers may have effective lexical access but ineffective or limited working memories. (2) They may have ineffective lexical access, causing the appearance of a memory problem. Notice that both these explanations predict that low-ability readers will have less working-memory capacity than high-ability readers. The difference is that one explanation attributes the memory problem to the word level, whereas the other attributes it to the functioning of working memory itself.

Why would working memory matter for reading? Recall that in reading, the content of the text is encoded by the reader as a set of propositions. We saw in the "window" example that a single eleven-word sentence could contain four propositions. Three ordinary sentences could have a dozen propositions for a reader to assemble and integrate. When the reader is trying to comprehend these propositions, working memory is at work! It can't do everything at once, and its finite capacity is a potential bottleneck in comprehension.

Do low-ability readers have less memory capacity than high-ability readers? Apparently they do. Among children, high-ability readers remember *verbatim* words at least from the sentence being read and the preceding sentence better than do low-ability readers (Goldman et al., 1980; Perfetti and Lesgold, 1977). This conclusion comes from a continuous reading task in which subjects were occasionally tested for their memory of words they had just read. Most of the time, both high- and low-ability readers could remember verbatim the last three words or so they had read, even though they could not know that a test was coming. However, high-ability readers could usually remember verbatim six to ten words from the sentence they were currently reading. Low-ability readers could not remember this many words.

One interesting fact is that the ability to remember words just read depends on whether the words are part of the sentence being read or part of the preceding sentence, rather than just how far back the words were. Thus, high-ability readers can usually remember the tenth word back if it's in the sentence they're reading, but not if they are currently reading the next sentence (Goldman et al., 1980). This is evidence for the assumption that working memory keeps active, if possible, the words needed to assemble and integrate the propositions from the sentence. The end of the sentence means that the integration processes can be completed, and the words are less well-remembered as working memory becomes occupied with assembling the propositions of the next sentence. (Recall the "sentence wrapup" process of Carpenter and Just, 1981, which occurs at the end of a sentence.) As far as we know, both high- and low-ability readers have similar within-sentence processes like this. However, high-ability readers are able to handle more verbal information in memory, both from within the sentence and from the preceding text (Perfetti and Lesgold, 1977). This working-memory difference exists between high-ability and low-ability adult readers as well (Daneman and Carpenter, 1980). Finally, this working-memory factor does not depend on reading. It is a general process-limiting factor for verbal processing, whether by reading or by listening. The memory differences between high- and low-ability children are therefore found when texts are heard as well as read (Perfetti and Goldman, 1976), and high-ability adult readers remember more spoken words (as well as more read words) than do low-ability readers (Daneman and Carpenter, 1980).

Lexical Factors in Ability

The second possible explanation for reading-ability differences at the proposition level is that these differences reflect lexical factors. Low-ability readers may be less effective at accessing the lexicon. Specifically, they could be slower at accessing the word in memory from a print input, or they could be slower at encoding the semantic information (stored with the word) needed for comprehension. Of course, speed of processing aside, there is also the consequence of inaccurate word-recognition. This is obviously a problem for many younger readers.

We can return now to one of our initial ability questions: Why do some people read fast with more comprehension, but others read slowly with less comprehension? Jackson and McClelland (1979) separated college students according to their "effective reading speed," essentially a measure of their words per minute weighted by their comprehension. These fast and slow readers performed a number of simple information-processing tasks. The tasks included same/different decisions for pairs of letters, for pairs of words (same meaning or different), and for nonletter patterns, among other tasks. (For example, subjects performed visual searches for letters through displays of different sizes, and they also had their auditory memory tested.) Based on subjects' performance on their tasks, Jackson and McClelland (1979) concluded that a major factor that correlated with reading speed was speed of memory retrieval. This process is the activation of any symbol in long-term memory from a visual input. Thus, the name of the letter B is activated when the visual shape (B, b) is perceived. Such memory retrieval is a basic process of accessing symbols associated with visual inputs. Being fast at this process is a major contributor to being a fast reader, according to Jackson and McClelland (1979; also Jackson, 1980).* It is easy to see why this might be. During reading, symbol activation processes occur over and over at the word and subword level.

A second major contributor to reading speed of college students was identified by Jackson and McClelland (1979): students with high effective reading speed are also good at listening comprehension. Presumably this is a factor independent of visual symbol activation or name retrieval. However, to be sure about this, we would have to have auditory tasks analogous to some of Jackson and McClelland's (1979) visual tasks. It could be that a very general memory-activation process is involved. In any case, the conclusion that reading ability is closely related to general language comprehension is well established for children (Berger and Perfetti, 1977; Curtis, 1980; Perfetti and Goldman, 1976) as well as for adults (Daneman and Carpenter, 1980; Jackson and McClelland, 1979).

There is at least one process we can therefore identify at the lexical level that could partly explain differences in reading speed: the speed at which a symbol is activated in memory, given a visual input such as a letter. A related factor has been identified by the research of Frederiksen (1978) on high school readers. In his studies, high-ability readers were distinguished from low-ability readers by their skill at multiple-letter encoding (among other things). This

---

*Among adults, this processing ability does not seem to depend on whether the symbol is linguistic. For example, geometric forms produce processing differences (Jackson, 1980). However, among children, reading-ability differences may depend more on *linguistic* symbol activation. This is because their speed of linguistic processing has not reached the limits set by general speed of memory retrieval (Perfetti, in press).

means that in recognizing a word, such as "window," the high-ability reader might have an advantage in encoding "win," "ind," "dow," or other subword patterns within the word, or in encoding the entire six-letter string.

Does all this mean that what the high-ability reader is good at is perceiving letters? Absolutely not. It's clear from the research (Frederiksen, 1978, and Jackson and McClelland, 1979, among others) that low-ability readers perceive letters as well as high-ability readers. Differences are found only when some coding operation is involved, or when a response must be made to several letters at once. Notice that both of these processes are central to lexical access during reading. The essential processing feature seems to be speed of activation in long-term memory of the units needed for lexical access.

It is possible that these units include patterns of English orthography, that is, the structure of English spelling that allows "spr" to be a letter sequence to begin a word such as "spruce" or "sprout," but not to end a word (or, more generally, the structure that permits the sequence "plone" to be possible—a "pseudoword"—and makes some other sequence of those same letters, e.g., "nlpeo," impossible). If the process of lexical access included activation of letter sequences, then the ability to activate such sequences could be a major ability factor. A reader who implicitly knows that "plo" is possible and that "nlp" is not, might be able to use this information to advantage in lexical access. Evidence on this possibility is suggestive, but rather meager (Massaro and Taylor, 1980).

In summary, processes of lexical access contribute to reading ability. These processes seem to include, at minimum, the activation of letter codes in memory (but not mere letter perception), at least for adult readers. They may also include units that reflect permissible strings of letters based on orthographic structure.

Verbal Efficiency Theory

The processes of lexical access seem to suggest an explanation of why one reader may be faster than another. After all, as processes of letter activation are speeded up, lexical access is speeded up, and this adds up to a reader who can read more words per minute. Rapid lexical access affects not just speed, but also comprehension, according to the verbal efficiency theory (Perfetti and Lesgold, 1977, 1979; also Perfetti and Roth, 1981).

This theory suggests that the quality of comprehension will be affected by the efficiency of the reader's lexical access and working memory. In discussing working memory previously, we noted that problems could arise either because of an ineffective lexical access that affects working memory or because of intrinsic memory problems. To see these possibilities, imagine a reader who encounters the following text.

1. *Radiosotopes have long been valuable tools in scientific and medical research.*
2. *Now, however, four nonradioactive isotopes are being produced.*
3. *They are called "icons": four isotopes of carbon, oxygen, nitrogen, and sulfur.*

4. *Each icon has one more neutron in its nucleus than the number found in carbon (12), oxygen (16), nitrogen (14), and sulfur (32).*
5. *The odd neutron gives the isotopes a distinctive magnetic characteristic.*

This text includes the text fragment shown in Figure 3.1. It is repeated here with numbered sentences to illustrate a text that the average adult reader might find a bit difficult. Verbal efficiency theory is usually applied to children's reading, but the problems facing a child of low ability can be seen more readily by an adult when he or she faces a more difficult text. In such a text, awareness of demands on lexical access and working memory is increased. For example, a reader who doesn't have a memory entry for "radioisotopes" is in immediate difficulty. He might spend some time *parsing* the letter string into "radio" + "isotopes" or even "radio" + "x." Succeeding words in the text are more accessible. However, it's easy to see that at least some readers would be slowed down by "nonradioactive" (sentence 2), "icons" (sentence 3), "nucleus" (sentence 4), etc. Even more common words—e.g., "scientific" and "research" (sentence 1) or "being" and "produced" (sentence 2)—have to be semantically encoded and combined in working memory. Typically, several words have to be activated at once for comprehension. This is seen in sentence 4, when the reader must hold some representation of "one more" at least until the end of the sentence because the basic interpretation of "one more" depends on it.

Try this simple comprehension test: Sentence 5 begins with the phrase "The odd neutron." What odd neutron? In order to semantically encode this phrase, the reader must map it onto the entire sentence (4), including its relation to "icon" (it's "icons" that have "odd neutrons") and its semantic antecedent in "one more neutron . . . than" (which is what "odd" refers to).

Verbal efficiency theory says that any reader's comprehension will be at risk when lexical processes make demands on working memory. The resources of working memory are needed for integrating sentence meanings, and any process that competes for these resources is a potential source of difficulty. At the extreme, a reader who must labor over the words at the end of a sentence can be expected to have forgotten the words from the beginning of the sentence, thus making necessary associations difficult to establish. These connections can be made by more work on the sentence, but there are limits to this. Eventually, the reader is forced to settle for a semantic encoding of the text that is incomplete or otherwise of low quality.

Children who are learning to read are especially vulnerable to the kind of problem just described. Indeed, it's only by use of a difficult text (as in the above example) that we can mimic this problem for adults. In part, this is because children, after they have learned to decode words, are still in the process of "overlearning." There is some amount of time and practice necessary to become an expert in lexical access, that is, to be able to recognize most words without effort. In learning to read, these access processes require significant effort. However, as experience increases, the effort decreases. One theory is that early in reading *attention* is directed at the basic graphic level of the word, i.e., its letters and their sound correlates (phonemes). With experience, these lower-

level properties are processed without attention, allowing higher-level properties of meaning to be the focus of the reader's attention (LaBerge and Samuels,
1974). This change with practice is sometimes referred to as "automatization."
But whether these lexical processes really become automatic (or attention-free)
is not critical. What is critical is that they become efficiently executed, producing more semantic product for less effort.

Let's return to the assumption that lexical access is an interactive affair, not
simply the accumulation of lower-level information. If so, then the statement
that high-ability readers are faster at lexical access than low-ability readers is
incomplete. Are they faster at using bottom-up information or at using top-down
information in lexical access? Suppose that the word "window" can occur in
various states of feature disturbance of the sort illustrated in Figure 3.2. It takes
longer to identify "window" with 42 percent of its features deleted than with 21
percent deleted, which in turn takes longer than with its features 100 percent
intact. Some studies of Perfetti and Roth (1981) show that, among children,
low-ability readers are more affected by degrading than are high-ability readers.
For example, high-ability readers identified normal undegraded words about
150 milliseconds faster than did low-ability readers, over a variety of context
conditions. With 21 percent degrading, the ability difference increased to about
300 milliseconds. This is due not to perceptual differences, but rather to differences in lexical-access abilities, perhaps based on orthographic knowledge.

There is perhaps no more reliable result in the area of children's reading
ability than word-identification differences. Higher-ability readers are faster at
identifying words than low-ability readers, and they are less affected by bottom-
up factors such as degrading (Perfetti and Roth, 1981) or word length (Perfetti
and Hogaboam, 1975), or whether the word is real or a pseudoword (Hogaboam
and Perfetti, 1978).

Higher-ability readers are also less affected by context. Perfetti and Roth
(1981) varied the quality of contexts such as the two window examples described earlier. Recall that, in one case, the word "window" is highly predictable
(what do you raise in a room when it's hot and stuffy?); in the other case, it's not
as predictable. (What could need fixing around the house? Almost anything.)
When a word was in a highly predictable context, low-ability readers were
nearly as fast as high-ability readers at identifying the word, even when the word
was degraded. In the less-predictable contexts and when the word was without
context, the high-ability reader was much faster.

There were also some anomalous contexts in one of the studies of Perfetti
and Roth (1981). To illustrate for "window," an anomalous context might be
this:

(4)   *There was something wrong with the car. Joe raised the hood and tried to
        adjust the* _____ .

"Window" is not merely unpredictable in this context, but actually counter-
indicated by the context. The top-down information leads the reader to expect
something related to a car engine, and he or she is surprised when bottom-up
information sends data incompatible with this expectation. The important result

is that such surprises slow down word identification of low-ability readers more than that of high-ability readers. The lexical processes of the low-ability reader may be therefore more dependent on context than are those of the high-ability reader.

This dependence may be in part a way of compensating for less-proficient lower-level word-recognition skills. This explanation of ability differences has been called the *interactive-compensatory theory* by Stanovich (1980). According to Stanovich (1980, 1981) and Perfetti and Roth (1981), the critical skill that the high-ability reader has is *context-free* word-recognition ability. The autonomous nature of this ability allows the skilled reader to process words efficiently regardless of context.

Phonologically Based Processes

We have discussed lexical processes in reading without any reference to speech processes. That's partly because the role such processes play in reading is subject to widely different interpretations. There are two general possibilities for implicit speech processes in *silent* reading. One is that lexical access occurs *after* a print stimulus is transformed into a speech equivalent. For example, the letters "c-a-t" are mentally transformed to the speech sounds /kæt/, and this speech form is what allows access to the word-concept "cat." This process obviously is critical in the acquisition of reading skill, but does not necessarily occur in highly skilled reading (Coltheart, 1978; see also Katz and Feldman, 1981, for a different but related view). For skilled adults, it is possible that speech processes do not occur as part of lexical access or, more likely, that they occur as part of it, but not as an intermediate stage between print and meaning. Perfetti and McCutchen (1982) propose that speech sounds are automatically activated as part of lexical access. Their role would be to aid the comprehension work of working memory, helping the reader keep track of exact words, rather than of vague meanings, for a few seconds. As we have seen, this is something skilled readers are much better at than less-skilled readers.

In any case, one hypothesis about reading ability is that high-ability readers use speech information more than do low-ability readers. One form of this hypothesis is that skilled readers use phonological codes in language processes more than do less-skilled readers (Barron, 1978, 1981). Another form of this hypothesis emphasizes the greater reliance of skilled readers on phonological codes in memory (Liberman et al., 1977; Mann et al., 1980). This reliance is reflected in the fact that, under certain conditions, high-ability readers are especially prone to errors in remembering rhyme materials (Liberman et al., 1977; Mann et al., 1980), reducing the memory advantage they otherwise have over low-ability readers.

It's not clear exactly how to understand a phonological factor of this sort, especially how it would operate in normal reading, as distinct from memory tasks (for a further discussion of this, see Perfetti and McCutchen, 1982). One possibility, consistent with the verbal efficiency theory, is that words read by low-ability readers are activated slowly (inefficiently) and result in low-quality phonological codes that are vulnerable to memory loss by succeeding coding operations.

Reading Disability

At the extreme low end of the reading ability continuum, there are individuals of many different sorts. The terms *dyslexia* and *specific reading disability* are typically reserved for those who have very low reading ability but have general intelligence within the normal range (at least as measured by IQ tests that minimize reading demands). Typically, the dyslexic is two or more grades below the reading norm. This kind of reading disability, one not completely dependent on general intelligence, also may occur to some extent among adults.

The classic view of dyslexia has been that it is a perceptual processing deficit with a basis in cerebral organization (Orton, 1925). More recently, disability researchers have emphasized multiple subtypes of dyslexia based on specific deficits including verbal deficits (Johnson and Myklebust, 1967). However, there appears to be considerable evidence against a perceptual-deficit explanation, and some evidence for a verbal-deficit explanation (Vellutino, 1979).

Can the reading problem of the dyslexic be understood in terms of the processing factors of lexical access and comprehension that affect reading ability in general? The answer seems to be "yes," although exactly which processes are responsible for reading disability is a complex and controversial matter (Morrison, 1980; Valtin, 1978–1979; Vellutino, 1979). In fact, much of the research on the lexical, phonological, and memory processes of less-skilled readers has used definitions of reading skill that approximate the criteria of disability (e.g., Liberman et al., 1977; Perfetti and Lesgold, 1977). The conclusion that less-skilled readers have processing problems associated with decoding and verbal memory may be generally, if cautiously, applied to dyslexic children.

Indeed, Vellutino (1979) has suggested that the general mechanisms of verbal processing, especially including those common to decoding, linguistic knowledge, and verbal memory, are the major processing problems in dyslexia. Certain research does seem to suggest that some disabled readers have memory problems that do not depend on linguistically codable material (Morrison et al., 1977). However, even this research weighs against a perceptual processing explanation. We are increasingly led to think of disability as a processing problem that involves the activation and use of information in memory. Linguistic information may be especially, although not exclusively, vulnerable to these problems.

Summary and Conclusions

Reading ability depends on the contribution of several processes in interaction. Lexical processes are those that result in recognition of words and encoding of word meanings. These processes are governed by the interactions of low-level information (e.g., letters) and high-level information (e.g., semantic context). Working-memory processes include those that operate on words and other sentence units to encode propositions, the basic units of meaning, and to integrate those propositions within and across sentences. All these processes are highly influenced by the knowledge of the reader.

Individual differences in reading ability occur in all these areas. In general, some approaches to reading ability have emphasized knowledge-based factors; others have emphasized lexical and memory factors. For example, schema theory emphasizes that comprehension ability depends on activation of appropriate knowledge structures during reading. It reminds us that word-level skills are not sufficient for comprehension. Verbal efficiency theory emphasizes that word-level processes need to occur with minimal effort, so that working memory can be devoted to comprehension work. It emphasizes that aside from his or her other knowledge, the skilled reader is efficient at context-free identification of words. Low-ability readers are more dependent on context because of less-efficient verbal skills. This ability in recognizing words and grasping their meanings depends on rapid symbol activation in memory, and possibly on linguistic processes concerning letter patterns (orthography) and phonology, at least among children. Specific reading disability, or dyslexia, may be understood partly in terms of the same verbal-processing factors that account for general reading ability.

References

Anderson, R. C., R. E. Reynolds, D. L. Schallert, and T. E. Goetz. 1977. Frameworks for comprehending discourse. *American Educational Research Journal,* 14, 367–381.

Anderson, R. C., R. J. Spiro, and M. C. Anderson. 1978. Schemata as scaffolding for the representation of information in discourse. *American Educational Research Journal,* 15, 433–440.

Baddeley, A. D., and G. T. Hitch. 1974. Working memory. *In* G. A. Bower, ed., *The Psychology of Learning and Motivation, Vol. 8* (New York: Academic Press), pp. 47–89.

Baron, J. 1978. The word-superiority effect: Perceptual learning from reading. *In* W. K. Estes, ed., *Handbook of Learning and Cognitive Processes, Vol. 6* (Hillsdale, N.J.: Erlbaum), pp. 131–166.

Barron, R. W. 1978. Reading skill and phonological coding in lexical access. *In* M. M. Gruneberg, R. N. Sykes, and P. E. Morris, eds., *Practical Aspects of Memory* (London: Academic Press), pp. 468–475.

———. 1981. Reading skill and reading strategies. *In* Lesgold and Perfetti (1981), pp. 299–327.

Bartlett, F. C. 1932. *Remembering: A Study in Experimental and Social Psychology.* New York: Cambridge Univ. Press.

Beck, I. L., R. C. Omanson, and M. G. McKeown. 1982. An instructional redesign of reading lessons: Effects on comprehension. *Reading Research Quarterly,* 17, 462–481.

Berger, N. S., and C. A. Perfetti. 1977. Reading skill and memory for spoken and written discourse. *Journal of Reading Behavior,* 9, 7–16.

Bransford, J. D., and M. K. Johnson. 1972. Contextual prerequisites for understanding: Some investigations of comprehension and recall. *Journal of Verbal Learning and Verbal Behavior,* 11, 717–726.

Brown, A. L. 1978. Knowing when, where, and how to remember: A problem of metacognition. *In* R. Glaser, ed., *Advances in Instructional Psychology* (Hillsdale, N.J.: Erlbaum), pp. 77–165.

Carpenter, P. A., and M. A. Just. 1981. Cognitive processes in reading: Models based on readers' eye fixations. *In* Lesgold and Perfetti (1981), pp. 177–213.

Chiesi, H. L., G. J. Spilich, and J. F. Voss. 1979. Acquisition of domain-related information in relation to high and low domain knowledge. *Journal of Verbal Learning and Verbal Behavior,* 18, 257–274.

Coltheart, M. 1978. Lexical access in simple reading tasks. *In* G. Underwood, ed., *Strategies of Information Processing* (London: Academic Press), pp. 151–216.

Curtis, M. E. 1980. Development of components of reading skill. *Journal of Educational Psychology,* 72, 656–669.

Daneman, M., and P. A. Carpenter. 1980. Individual differences in working memory and reading. *Journal of Verbal Learning and Verbal Behavior,* 19, 450–466.

Dooling, D. J., and R. Lachman. 1971. Effects of comprehension on retention of prose. *Journal of Educational Psychology,* 88, 216–222.

Estes, W. K. 1977. On the interaction of perception and memory in reading. *In* D. LaBerge and S. J. Samuels, eds., *Basic Processes in Reading: Perception and Comprehension* (Hillsdale, N.J.: Erlbaum), pp. 1–25.

Frederiksen, J. R. 1978. Assessment of perceptual, decoding, and lexical skills and their relation to reading proficiency. *In* A. M. Lesgold, J. W. Pellegrino, S. D. Fokkema, and R. Glaser, eds., *Cognitive Psychology and Instruction* (New York: Plenum), pp. 153–169.

Gibson, E. J., and H. Levin. 1975. *The Psychology of Reading.* Cambridge, Mass.: M.I.T. Press.

Goldman, S. R., T. W. Hogaboam, L. C. Bell, and C. A. Perfetti. 1980. Short-term retention of discourse during reading. *Journal of Educational Psychology,* 72, 647–655.

Hogaboam, T., and C. A. Perfetti. 1978. Reading skill and the role of verbal experience in decoding. *Journal of Educational Psychology,* 70, 717–729.

Jackson, M. 1980. Further evidence for a relationship between memory access and reading ability. *Journal of Verbal Learning and Verbal Behavior,* 19, 683–694.

Jackson, M. D., and J. L. McClelland. 1979. Processing determinants of reading speed. *Journal of Experimental Psychology: General,* 108, 151–181.

Johnson, D., and H. Myklebust. 1967. *Learning Disabilities: Educational Principles and Practices.* New York: Grune and Stratton.

Johnson, M. K., J. D. Bransford, and S. K. Soloman. 1973. Memory for tacit implications of sentences. *Journal of Experimental Psychology,* 98, 203–205.

Just, M. A., and P. A. Carpenter. 1980. A theory of reading: From eye fixations to comprehension. *Psychological Review,* 87, 329–354.

Just, M. A., P. A. Carpenter, and M. Masson. 1982. *What Eye Fixations Tell Us About Speed Reading and Skimming.* Pittsburgh: Carnegie Mellon Univ. Tech. Report.

Katz, L., and L. B. Feldman. 1981. Linguistic coding in word recognition: Comparisons between a deep and a shallow orthography. *In* Lesgold and Perfetti (1981), pp. 85–106.

Kintsch, W. 1974. *The Representation of Meaning in Memory.* Hillsdale, N.J.: Erlbaum.

Kintsch, W., and J. M. Keenan. 1973. Reading rate as a function of the number of propositions in the base structure of sentences. *Cognitive Psychology,* 5, 257–274.

Kintsch, W., and T. A. van Dijk. 1978. Toward a model of text comprehension and production. *Psychological Review,* 85, 33–394.

LaBerge, D., and S. J. Samuels. 1974. Toward a theory of automatic information processing in reading. *Cognitive Psychology,* 6, 293–323.

Lesgold, A. M., and C. A. Perfetti, eds., 1981. *Interactive Processes in Reading.* Hillsdale, N.J.: Erlbaum.

Liberman, I. Y., D. Shankweiler, A. M. Liberman, C. Fowler, and F. W. Fischer. 1977. Phonetic segmentation and recoding in the beginning reader. *In* A. S. Reber and D. L. Scarborough, eds., *Towards a Psychology of Reading, The Proceedings of the CUNY Conference* (New York: Wiley), pp. 207–225.

Mandler, J. M., and M. Goodman. 1980. On the psychological validity of story structure. Paper presented at the annual meeting of the Psychonomic Society, St. Louis, November, 1980.

Mandler, J. M., and N. S. Johnson. 1977. Remembrance of things parsed: Story structure and recall. *Cognitive Psychology,* 9, 111–151.

Mann, V. A., I. Y. Liberman, and D. Shankweiler. 1980. Children's memory for sentences and word strings in relation to reading ability. *Memory and Cognition,* 8, 329–335.

Massaro, D. W. 1979. *Understanding Language: An Information-Processing Analysis of Speech Perception, Reading, and Psycholinguistics.* New York: Academic Press.

Massaro, D. W., and G. A. Taylor. 1980. Reading ability and the utilization of orthographic structure in reading. *Journal of Educational Psychology,* 72, 730–742.

McClelland, J. L., and D. E. Rumelhart. 1981. An interactive activation model of context effects in letter perception, part 1: An account of basic findings. *Psychological Review,* 88, 375–407.

Morrison, F. J. 1980. Reading disability: Toward a reconceptualization. Paper presented at the annual meeting of the Psychonomic Society, St. Louis, November 1980.

Morrison, F. J., B. Giordani, and J. Nagy. 1977. Reading disability: An information processing analysis. *Science,* 196, 77–79.

Morton, J. 1969. Interaction of information in word recognition. *Psychological Review,* 76, 165–178.

Newell, A., and H. A. Simon. 1972. *Human Problem Solving.* Englewood Cliffs, N.J.: Prentice-Hall.

Omanson, R. C. 1982. An analysis of narratives. *Discourse Processes,* 5, 195–224.

Omanson, R. C., and S. R. Malamut. 1980. The effects of supportive and distracting content on the recall of central content. Paper presented at the annual meeting of the Psychonomic Society, St. Louis, November 1980.

Orton, S. T. 1925. Word-blindness in school children. *Archives of Neurology and Psychiatry,* 14, 581–615.

Perfetti, C. A. In press. *Reading Ability.* New York: Oxford Univ. Press.

Perfetti, C. A., and S. Goldman. 1976. Discourse memory and reading comprehension skill. *Journal of Verbal Learning and Verbal Behavior,* 14, 33–42.

Perfetti, C. A., and T. Hogaboam. 1975. The relationship between single word decoding and reading comprehension skill. *Journal of Educational Psychology,* 67, 461–469.

Perfetti, C. A., and A. M. Lesgold. 1977. Discourse comprehension and sources of individual differences. *In* M. A. Just and P. A. Carpenter, eds., *Cognitive Processes in Comprehension* (Hillsdale, N.J.: Erlbaum), pp. 141–183.

———. 1979. Coding and comprehension in skilled reading and implications for reading instruction. *In* L. B. Resnick and P. A. Weaver, eds., *Theory and Practice of Early Reading, Vol. 1* (Hillsdale, N.J.: Erlbaum), pp. 57–84.

Perfetti, C. A., and D. McCutchen. 1984. Speech processes in reading. *In* N. Lass, ed., *Advances in Speech and Language, Vol. 7* (New York: Academic Press).

Perfetti, C. A., and S. Roth. 1981. Some of the interactive processes in reading and their role in reading skill. *In* Lesgold and Perfetti (1981), pp. 269–297.

Rayner, K. 1975. The perceptual span and peripheral cues in reading. *Cognitive Psychology, 7*, 65–81.

Rumelhart, D. E. 1975. Notes on a schema for stories. *In* D. Bobrow and A. Collins, eds., *Representation and Understanding: Studies in Cognitive Science* (New York: Academic Press), pp. 211–236.

Rumelhart, D. E. 1977. Toward an interactive model of reading. *In* S. Dornic, ed., *Attention and Performance, VI* (Hillsdale, N.J.: Erlbaum), pp. 573–603.

Rumelhart, D. E., and J. L. McClelland. 1981. Interactive processing through spreading activation. *In* Lesgold and Perfetti (1981), pp. 37–60.

———. 1982. An interactive activation model of context effects in letter perception, part 2: The contextual enhancement effect and some tests and extensions of the model. *Psychological Review, 89*, 60–94.

Rumelhart, D. E., and A. Ortony. 1977. The representation of knowledge in memory. *In* R. C. Anderson, R. J. Spiro, and W. E. Montague, eds., *Schooling and the Acquisition of Knowledge* (Hillsdale, N.J.: Erlbaum), pp. 99–136.

Schank, R. C., and R. Abelson. 1977. *Scripts, Plans, Goals, and Understanding.* Hillsdale, N.J.: Erlbaum.

Smiley, S. S., D. D. Oakley, D. Worthen, J. C. Campione, and A. L. Brown. 1977. Recall of thematically relevant material by adolescent good and poor readers as a function of written and oral presentation. *Journal of Educational Psychology, 69*, 881–887.

Spilich, G. J., G. T. Vesonder, H. L. Chiesi, and J. F. Voss. 1979. Text-processing of domain-related information for individuals with high and low domain knowledge. *Journal of Verbal Learning and Verbal Behavior, 18*, 275–290.

Spiro, R. J. 1980. Constructive processes in prose comprehension and recall. *In* R. J. Spiro, B. C. Bruce, and W. F. Brewer, eds., *Theoretical Issues in Reading Comprehension* (Hillsdale, N.J.: Erlbaum), pp. 245–278.

Stanovich, K. E. 1980. Toward an interactive-compensatory model of individual differences in the development of reading fluency. *Reading Research Quarterly, 16*, 32–71.

Stanovich, K. E. 1981. Attentional and automatic context effects in reading. *In* Lesgold and Perfetti (1981), pp. 241–267.

Stein, N. L., and C. G. Glenn. 1979. An analysis of story comprehension in elementary school children. *In* R. O. Freedle, ed., *Advances in Discourse Processes, Vol. 2* (Hillsdale, N.J.: Erlbaum), pp. 53–120.

Sulin, R. A., and D. J. Dooling. 1974. Intrusion of a thematic idea in retention of prose. *Journal of Experimental Psychology, 103*, 255–262.

Thorndyke, P. 1977. Cognitive structures in comprehension and memory of narrative discourse. *Cognitive Psychology, 9*, 77–110.

Valtin, R. Dyslexia: 1978–79. Deficit in reading or deficit in research? *Reading Research Quarterly, 14*, 201–221.

Vellutino, F. R. 1979. *Dyslexia: Theory and Research.* Cambridge, Mass.: M.I.T. Press.

4

SECOND-
LANGUAGE
ABILITIES

John B. Carroll
University of North Carolina, Chapel Hill

Around the world, most children have little or no difficulty learning to speak and understand whatever language happens to be their mother tongue. Up to about age six or seven, they also have little difficulty in learning a second or even a third language if that language is commonly used in their immediate environment, such as their home or on the playground. They can become, as it were, native speakers of several languages at once. But as they grow older, it becomes increasingly harder for them to learn a second language in a "natural" way. If, for example, the family of an eight-year-old child moves to a foreign country where a different language is used, the child will take longer to learn the second language from playmates who speak that language, or from classmates at school. It is somewhat of a mystery why there is a decline with age in the ability to learn a second language "naturally."

When we speak of second-language abilities, we are usually speaking of the abilities required by older children and adults to learn a second language in some relatively formal learning situation—usually, a course of training in the second language at school, or the like. In such situations, people appear to differ immensely in talent for second-language learning. A few fortunate individuals learn a second language quite easily and rapidly, but most people seem to have much difficulty, and take a long time to acquire anything like native-language proficiency. And there appear to be some people who have so little aptitude for second-language learning that they never approach real success even if they are highly motivated and give serious effort to learning.

Of particular interest is the fact that it is unusual (though not impossible) for people to learn to speak a second language without an "accent," even if they do acquire the ability to speak and understand the language fluently.

These common observations prompt us to think that there is something that we can call *second-language aptitude.* But since second-language aptitude seems to be complex, it would be more accurate to suppose that there are several special abilities that make some people better able than others to learn second languages. This chapter considers what these abilities may be, given that much research has been undertaken on the subject (Carroll, 1962, 1981; Diller, 1981; Pimsleur et al., 1962).

First, we will consider the concept of aptitude and how aptitudes can be identified and measured. Second, we will discuss various ways of learning second languages, and how different aptitudes might play a role in these. Third, we should also consider what factors other than aptitudes might play a role in second-language learning. Fourth, we will look at some of the research on second-language aptitudes and what this research suggests about the nature of those aptitudes. (In the main, this research has been performed with a psychometric rather than an information-processing approach, but it is interesting to speculate about what an information-processing approach might have to say about these aptitudes.) Finally, we will consider whether second-language aptitudes can be improved, and what might be done to help people with low or below-average second-language aptitudes.

The Concept of Aptitude

Writers on aptitude have offered many, somewhat different definitions of the concept. Some think of it very broadly, defining it as comprising any and all characteristics of individuals that predispose them to learn something either well and rapidly or less well and more slowly. Some psychologists therefore include interest and motivation in the concept of aptitude. They might say, for example, that a person with a high motivation to learn a second language would thereby tend to have better aptitude. Although interest and motivation might often be important in successful learning, let us take here a somewhat narrower view, and think of aptitude largely in terms of *constitutional* attributes of the individual (characteristics "built in" to the individual's brain and nervous system) that make for higher or lower degrees of success in learning. According to this view, an aptitude might be at least in part innate, or it could have developed over a long period as a result of the individual's experiences and activities. In any case, aptitudes are regarded as being relatively enduring. Although it may be possible to improve an individual's aptitudes by special instruction or training, this is not easily done, and there seem to be limits to how far aptitudes can be changed.

In theory, we could observe the operation of aptitudes by taking a group of people who are similarly motivated to learn and exposing them to identical learning conditions. Some would learn well and rapidly, others more slowly or less well. We could *infer* that they differ in some underlying characteristics that cause them to differ in learning success. On a more practical level, however, suppose that we could obtain some information on their various characteristics *before* they begin the learning experience, and show that this information does indeed rather accurately forecast each student's learning success. We could then say that the information we could get on people's characteristics before the learning experience constitutes information on their "aptitudes" for that learning. This is precisely the basis on which most research on second-language aptitudes has been conducted. The research is particularly convincing when a single set of characteristics can be shown to forecast a specific type of learning, and that such characteristics are not significantly changed by the learning.

A major problem in aptitude research is to discover exactly what kind of information we need to get, or can get, in order to predict success in learning. Before we take up this problem, however, we need to consider the task of learning a second language.

Learning a Second Language

The second languages a person might learn differ enormously. Some are fairly similar to the person's native language. For example, German is fairly similar to English in many respects, and French is fairly similar to Italian. A speaker of English will find it somewhat easier to learn German than French, but a speaker of French will find it easier to learn Italian than English. For speakers of English, some languages are quite difficult to learn because of their dissimilarity to English; for example, Russian, Arabic, Hebrew, and Japanese would be more difficult to learn than some other languages, because their phonetic and grammatical systems are more different. In addition, all these languages have writing systems that present difficulties,* particularly that of Japanese.

The point is that languages do differ somewhat in difficulty, and this has to be taken into account in predicting how long someone might take to learn a given language, regardless of his or her own second-language aptitudes. Research suggests, however, that all languages require more or less the same aptitudes to learn. Aptitude seems to interact with language only in the sense that a person with a given degree of aptitude may take longer to learn some languages, because of their relative difficulty, than others. Table 4.1 is an extract

---

*Actually, the Cyrillic alphabet of Russian, or the alphabets of Arabic and Hebrew, constitute only an initial problem for a person who starts out with a knowledge of only the Roman alphabet used in English. With sufficient aptitude for second-language learning, a person can learn most foreign language writing systems in a relatively short time. Only "character" languages like Chinese, Japanese, and Korean present special difficulties.

from a chart prepared by the U.S. Foreign Service Institute to indicate this relation. This table assumes instruction at the rate of four to six hours per day (plus the same number of hours of drill and study), and shows how many months will be needed, by persons of high and of average language aptitude, to learn different languages to a standard described as:

> Fluency and accuracy in speaking with sufficient vocabulary to meet any ordinary requirements which do not involve the speaker in a technical subject outside his own specialty; ability to read newspapers and documents with limited reference to a dictionary.

People can have different goals in learning a second language. Surveys have shown that most American college students are more interested in learning to speak and understand a second language than in learning to read the language. Yet some students are mostly interested in learning to read books, magazines, and newspapers in a second language, and their interest in speaking the language is minimal. These different interests are sometimes reflected in different types of language courses. Before World War II, most school courses

---

Table 4.1
Time requirements for second-language learning[a]

Language categories			Training required[b] for people with:	
			High aptitude	Average aptitude
A. Italian French Spanish Portuguese	Rumanian German Swedish Norwegian	Danish Dutch	6 months	9 months
B. Russian Lithuanian Bulgarian Persian Indonesian	Estonian Finnish Polish Hungarian Czech	Greek Turkish Hindi Serbo-Croatian	12 months	15 months
C. Arabic Vietnamese	Cambodian Burmese	Thai	15 months	18 months
D. Chinese[c]	Japanese[c]	Korean[c]	18 months	24 months

[a]Extracted from a chart prepared by the Foreign Service Institute, U.S. Department of State.

[b]Training required to meet standards S3 and R3, minimum professional levels of speaking and reading abilities, at the rate of four to six hours of instruction per day, plus another four to six hours of individual drill and study per day, plus three months in part-time training and using the language, preferably in an area abroad where the language is widely used.

[c]This group of languages requires a substantial increase in time because of the difficulty of the writing system. If reading proficiency is not needed, these languages can be included in Category C.

were oriented primarily toward reading and translating, as are some instruction-al programs even today. Such courses have often been taught by the so-called *grammar and translation method,* whereby a student learns the rules of the grammar and then tries to read and translate texts. In contrast, many courses today are taught by the *audiolingual method.* In this method, the emphasis is on learning to understand and speak the language, and there is less emphasis on grammatical rules. The student is expected to acquire these rules in a more or less natural manner by practicing sentences with different grammatical struc-tures. In the *cognitive code* approach, the emphasis is on giving learners awareness and understanding of the semantic rules governing different types of grammatical structure, and the circumstances in which different words and sentence structures are most effective in communication. Occasionally an *im-mersion method* may be used, in which all or nearly all instruction is carried on in the second language; just as a child learns the mother tongue, the student is expected to acquire the language by the process of trying to speak and under-stand it in natural communication situations.

To some extent, these different ways of learning second languages may require slightly different combinations or profiles of second-language aptitudes. Courses taught by the grammar and translation method put more demand on ordinary intellectual abilities; courses that emphasize the spoken language make more demands on special language-learning aptitudes. But surprisingly, the same aptitudes are required, on the whole, regardless of the methods and goals of different types of language-learning courses.

Whatever the ease or difficulty of a language, it usually takes a long and devoted effort to learn it to a really useful degree of mastery. In the U.S. government, five-point scales of speaking and reading proficiency have been established: *1* represents the proficiency of a tourist who can just barely "get along" in a foreign country by speaking the language; *3* represents the minimal professional level expected of a foreign-service officer; and *5* represents the proficiency of a native speaker, rarely if ever attained by a non-native. In intensive, full-time instruction such as that conducted by the Defense Language Institute, the average person will take nine to twelve months to attain a *3*-level proficiency in most of the languages taught. This would be the equivalent of at least five or six years of the usual type of college and university language course. Languages cannot be learned overnight, even in immersion courses, contrary to the impressions created by advertisements of commercial language schools. A one-month Berlitz-type course does well to produce a *1*-level proficiency on the government scale.

Why are languages difficult to learn? Because they are very complex and extensive systems of meaning symbolization. Their vocabularies consist of thousands of words, and even though most of the words a person encounters are from a relatively small vocabulary of high-frequency words, it is the rarer, low-frequency words that often become critical in comprehension. The sound units ("phonemes") of which those words are composed are frequently quite different from the sound units in a person's native tongue, and in fact the whole sound system of a second language is organized differently. Similarly, the grammatical system of a second language is described by a complex set of rules that differ in many ways from those of the native language. For example, where English uses word order to convey grammatical meanings, a language like Russian depends very little on word order, and much more on grammatical inflections signaled by prefixes, suffixes, and the like. Learning the vocabulary, the sound system, and the grammar of a second language constitute somewhat distinct tasks, and apparently these tasks require somewhat different aptitudes.

Success in second-language learning depends on many factors, not only aptitudes. Motivation and interest are important to the extent that they enable learners to devote sufficient time and effort to the task. Often the *kind* of motivation may be important. Gardner and Lambert (1972), for example, distinguish *instrumental* motives from *integrative* motives. The former are motives to learn a language in order to achieve certain life goals, such as job and career success; the latter are motives to learn a language in order better to know and communicate with speakers of other languages. These motives may play somewhat different roles in language learning. People with integrative motives, for example, tend to acquire better pronunciation and fluency.

The type of instruction may also have an important role. A cognitive-code approach may for some people produce better results than a grammar/translation method or an audiolingual method. Above all, the learner must have good native or near-native speakers of the foreign language to imitate and converse with, if good pronunciation and fluency are to be attained.

Identifying Second-Language Aptitudes

Given this analysis of the task of learning a second language, two main approaches have been employed in seeking to identify what characteristics are predictive of later success (or lack of success) in learning.

The first approach is to try out tests and measurements of well-known cognitive abilities, on the assumption that some of these abilities may be relevant to second-language learning. In the early days of research on second-language aptitudes, standard intelligence tests were found to forecast learning success reasonably well (Henmon et al., 1929), possibly because, in second-language courses then taught, the grammar/translation method was frequently used, in conjunction with an emphasis on learning to read and translate written texts (as opposed to acquiring skills in speaking and understanding the spoken language). Standard intelligence tests predicted success in learning a "dead" language like Latin just as well as they predicted success in learning modern languages. In more recent research, however, tests of reasoning and memory abilities have been used, along with an effort to identify any special abilities that might be pertinent to second-language learning as taught by modern methods. In selecting such abilities, the researcher considers the particular aspects of the learning task to which an ability might apply. For example, tests of associative-memory ability might be expected to be pertinent to how well a student will learn a large number of vocabulary items and their meanings. A student who does well on a simple test of paired-associate memory might be expected to find the learning of a large foreign-language vocabulary easier than a student who has trouble with such a simple test.

The second main approach to identifying relevant aptitudes is the *work-sample* method. A researcher tries to design simple learning situations that resemble, as much as possible, aspects of the second-language learning process. Students who can learn to perform these simple tests easily and accurately might also be expected to do well in the actual learning of a second language. For example, one task that has been found rather successful as a predictor is one in which the student must learn words for numbers (1, 2, 3, 10, 20, 30, 100, 200, 300, for example) in a real or made-up foreign language, and, after a brief learning and practice period, must respond to rapidly spoken expressions for numbers like 312 or 203 by writing down the corresponding digits. Even success in this relatively simple task may depend on several abilities: an ability to recognize the sounds of the number words; an ability to remember the numbers they correspond to; and an ability to maintain sufficient attention to these stimuli and their sequencing to transcribe them into digits accurately. Presumably, such abilities would also be involved in learning to understand rapidly spoken sentences in the second language.

Actually, there may not be much difference between these two main approaches, because the tasks presented in many types of standard ability tests may also constitute work samples of the eventual learning task. But the distinction may be a practical one for guiding research.

Although researchers try to use whatever principles and findings of psychology they believe to be relevant, as well as whatever intuition and insight they may have into the requirements of the second-language learning task, the actual development of a successful battery of aptitude measures is to some extent a matter of trial and error. Some types of tasks that might logically seem promising may turn out not to "work." For example, in one series of experiments (Carroll, 1962), several carefully contrived tests were developed to measure the ability to discriminate between foreign language sounds (for example, between the initial "p" as pronounced in English *pan* and the quite different initial "p" as pronounced in French *pain,* "bread"). It turned out that these tests did not work well; that is, they failed to predict success in learning the sounds of a foreign language. The tests were relatively unreliable, and did not differentiate students adequately. Further, the tasks were of about the same difficulty for all students— either quite easy, of medium difficulty, or hard, depending on what pairs of sounds were used. It appears that there is not just one ability to discriminate between foreign language sounds, but perhaps many such abilities, or perhaps none, in the sense that most individuals have about the same capacity to learn to discriminate between sounds in foreign languages. In any case, these tests of sound-discrimination ability were dropped from further consideration as possible components of that aptitude battery.

To illustrate what kinds of information can be gained from trying out possible aptitude measurements, let us look at the results obtained in a series of experiments conducted some years ago in an unusually favorable environment (Carroll, 1962, 1981). These tests were given at the start of what the U.S. Air

Force called a "trial course" for selecting foreign-language trainees from among airmen who had volunteered for such training. The trial course consisted of a five-day intensive training in Mandarin Chinese. Recruits who passed this course (and usually only about 25 percent of them did) were promised eight months of further intensive training at a university (in Russian, Chinese, or some other language of military interest), and eventual assignment to duties in the military services in which they would use their language training. They were highly motivated to pass the trial course, because doing so promised to release them from the "kitchen police" and other unpleasant duties of their regular assignments.

From the standpoint of the researchers, this was a favorable situation in which to try out experimental tests, because the recruits were highly motivated to do as well as possible both on the tests and in the trial course, and the results of the trial course would be almost immediately available as a basis for evaluating the tests as aptitude measurements. It was not necessary, as it is in many test-validity studies, to wait months or even years to obtain the *criterion data,* that is, the actual learning or performance success of the subjects in the training course.

In two successive trial courses of this type, four-hour batteries of experimental tests were given on a Monday morning, and the scores could be compared with trial-course outcomes by Friday afternoon of the same week. The results exceeded expectations: we could derive a battery score that agreed better than 80 percent with trial-course pass/fail outcomes. Furthermore, this score had correlations with instructors' grades on the order of $r = .80$. On the basis of such findings, the Air Force eventually dropped the rather expensive and logistically difficult practice of giving trial courses, and instead began using aptitude tests to select persons for language training.

Of most interest to the researchers was to find what kinds of tests were most effective in predicting trial-course success, and to try to infer what kinds of abilities they tested. Although nearly all the tests showed at least some positive correlation with course outcomes (either the pass/fail criterion or instructors' grades), some were much more effective than others. Also, the intercorrelations of the tests had to be considered, because some tests were merely redundant with others, in the sense that they contributed no new information beyond what other tests contributed.

Boiling down the information from some 20 to 25 test scores, we found that four types of tests were most effective, in the sense that they made significant and independent contributions to the prediction of success in the trial course, as follows.

Phonetic Coding Ability

The first type were those that tested the ability to learn, recognize, and remember correspondences between particular sounds of a language and printed symbolizations of those sounds, as in a phonetic transcription. The best of these tests was one called *Phonetic Script.* In it, sequences of syllables (many of them nonsense syllables with no meaning in English) were presented from a tape recording while the subject looked at phonetic transcriptions of these syllables such as

/ siyk sayk seyk sik /.

(For purposes of the illustration, imagine that these are nonsense syllables, pronounced like the English words *seek, psych, sake, sick,* respectively.) The problem for the person taking the test is to quickly learn how the sounds correspond to the phonetic representations of them. After a group of these items had been presented, the examinee would have to go back and underline the particular syllable heard in a test phase on each item. For example, if the syllable *psych* were presented, the correct response would be to underline "sayk" rather than, say, "siyk" or "sik," which some examinees might think to be the proper transcription of *psych.*

Similar tests seemed to tap some underlying ability that we eventually decided to call *phonetic coding ability.* For example, some of the tests presented the phonetic transcriptions in a foreign-language alphabet like Devanagari (used in Hindi) or Mongolian; the examinee's problem was to find out and remember what sounds, as presented in syllables spoken on a tape recording, corresponded to the characters of the foreign alphabet. Scores on these tests correlated highly with those on the *Phonetic Script* test. Still another test that seemed to measure this same ability was one that had previously been used in assessing aptitude to learn stenography. In it, the student was to recognize what English words were represented by abbreviated spellings such as *grttud* ("gratitude"), *komn* ("common"), and *vlntr* ("volunteer"). Although not so directly interpretable as a measure of an ability to recognize sound-symbol correspondences, it nevertheless dealt with such correspondences as they might function in learning words in a foreign language. In fact, all these tests appeared to tap a special ability required in learning the sounds of a foreign language. For example, in learning Chinese a student has to learn to distinguish syllables with different *tone* or pitch contours, as represented (at least in one transcription) by the different diacritical marks in *mā, má, mǎ, mà.* More basically, a student has to mentally *code* the sounds of any foreign language phonetically in order to use them distinctively, just as in learning the non-English sounds in French *vu* ("seen") and *voeu* ("vow"). Apparently, the ability to do this mental phonetic coding is tapped even with tests that use only English sounds.

Grammatical Sensitivity

The second category consisted of tests of the ability to recognize the grammatical functions of words and other components of sentences. One such test, called *Words in Sentences,* essentially tested the ability to solve grammatical analogies. Each item in it consists of a "key" sentence in which a particular word or phrase is marked by underlining, and another sentence (or group of sentences) that contains five words or phrases marked as possible choices. The examinee's problem is to choose the word or phrase in the second sentence that has the *same grammatical function* as the marked word or phrase has in the "key" sentence. Here is a sample item:

He gave <u>her</u> a book to read.
She taught <u>Henrietta's</u> <u>son</u> to swim to <u>his</u> <u>mother</u>
            A   B   C   D
whenever she called <u>him</u>.
                         E

The right answer is *B* because *her,* in the key sentence, and *son,* in the second sentence, are both indirect objects of their verbs. (At least, *B* would be the best choice among those offered; some linguists might hesitate to call "son" exactly an indirect object.) Subjects can respond correctly, however, without knowing grammatical terminology, by using their sensitivity to grammatical functions. Obviously this ability could be expected to be relevant to learning the grammatical structure of a second language. Apparently many people have little grammatical sensitivity of this kind, even after they have had some formal training in English grammar (and perhaps their failure to learn grammatical analysis is attributable to poor basic ability). At the same time, many people with little exposure to instruction in English grammar can solve such grammatical analogies quite readily.

Rote Learning Ability

The third type were tests of the ability to form quick associations between arbitrarily paired items, and to remember these associations. As Chapter 5 by Campione et al. points out, associative-memory ability is one of the well-recognized factors of cognitive ability. The tests of it that have been included in second-language-aptitude batteries have usually been adapted to address the way in which associative memory might operate in second-language learning. Such was true of two tests used in the research described earlier (Carroll, 1962). One was the *Number Learning* test, mentioned previously, in which the subject learned names of numbers in a made-up language, and then had to transcribe spoken number words into written digits on hearing them presented rapidly. The other was a standard Paired-Associates test in which the examinees study a list of nonsense words (described as words in "Kurdish"), with their assigned English meanings. After brief practice, the examinee answers a series of multiple-choice questions requiring choice of the correct meaning of each nonsense word. Scores on both these tests made significant contributions to the prediction of second-language success in the trial course, apparently because part of the student's task in learning Chinese was to learn seemingly arbitrary associations between Chinese words and their meanings.

Inductive Language-Learning Ability

The last group consisted of tests of the ability to infer rules governing stimulus material. This is another of the well-recognized factors of cognitive ability, usually identified as the *Inductive Factor*. Tests of this ability were made "face valid" for testing second-language aptitude, by presenting materials in an artificial language. This followed the lead of a number of artificial language tests that had been included in standard scholastic aptitude tests and second-language aptitude batteries. However, one of the tests was presented in printed format, but another was developed as an elaborate audiovisual presentation of the rudiments of a made-up "American Indian" language called "Tem-Tem" (Sapon, 1955). For example, on visual presentation of a series of slides depicting either one horse, two horses, or a group of horses, with associated auditory presentation of words corresponding to the pictures, the student was expected to infer that this language contained a "dual" number, besides the familiar singular and plural, signaled by a certain suffix whenever *two* things were being referred to. Other series of pictures and associated heard phrases were designed to give the examinee the opportunity to infer rules concerning the word order of subject, verb, and object. After a series of brief lessons in Tem-Tem, the student was tested on what had been learned, by being required to choose the one picture, from a series of four, correctly described by a heard sentence. No explanations of grammatical rules were given; the examinee was expected to draw his or her own conclusions from the pictures seen and the phrases heard. Students making high scores on this test tended to be those who passed the trial course.

To summarize, from this and many other field trials of potential aptitude tests, we could identify four distinct types of second-language abilities:

1. Phonetic coding ability: an ability to identify distinct sounds, to form associations between those sounds and symbols representing them, and to retain these associations.

2. Grammatical sensitivity: the ability to recognize the grammatical functions of words (or other linguistic elements) in sentence structures.

3. Rote learning ability for foreign-language materials; the ability to learn associations between foreign-language words and their meanings rapidly and efficiently, and to retain these associations.

4. Inductive language-learning ability: the ability to infer the rules governing a set of language materials, given samples of language materials that would permit such inferences.

In addition, it appeared that persons with good general verbal intelligence, as indexed by scores on vocabulary tests, are better second-language learners. However, high vocabulary in a person's own native language is not necessary or critical in learning a second language. It is therefore not to be recognized as a distinct second-language ability.

Second-Language Aptitude Batteries

Currently, for testing students at high-school, college, and adult levels, there are two widely used second-language aptitude batteries, the *Modern Language Aptitude Test,* MLAT (Carroll and Sapon, 1959) and the *Pimsleur Language Aptitude Battery,* PLAB (Pimsleur, 1966). (The MLAT also exists in a form specially designed for children in grades 3–6.) There is also a Defense

Language Aptitude Battery (DLAB) used by the U.S. Defense Department. This is similar in many respects to the MLAT and the PLAB, and measures some of the same abilities that they test (Petersen and Al-Haik, 1976).

Each of these batteries contains a group of separate tests whose scores, when combined, tend to be moderately to highly predictive of success in second-language learning. Each battery has been based on extensive research to identify second-language learning abilities and ways to measure them before the learner begins study of a second language.

The MLAT contains five tests that measure different aspects of at least three of the four second-language learning abilities mentioned previously.

Number Learning requires the examinee to learn the names of numbers in a made-up language (e.g., "kek" = 1, "mam" = 10, "kekji" = 100) and then to transcribe heard number expressions (e.g., *kekji mam* [= 110]), given at a fairly fast rate on a tape-recording, into two- or three-digit numbers. It apparently measures one aspect of the rote-memory component of second-language apti-tude, and in addition may tap an attentional factor that has not yet been clearly identified in research.

Phonetic Script presents series of spoken syllables, along with their tran-scriptions in a phonetic script. The examinee must observe and learn the associations between the sounds composing these syllables and their transcrip-tions. (A sample item was given earlier, page 91.) It seems to be a direct measure of the "phonetic coding ability" aspect of second-language aptitude.

Spelling Clues is a highly speeded test that also appears to measure phonetic coding ability, but in a different way from the *Phonetic Script* test. In essence, it is a vocabulary test in which the examinee must find the word that most closely conveys the meaning of a word spelled in a disguised way, such as *grttud* ("gratitude"), *komn* ("common"), or *vlntr* ("volunteer"). Here is a sample item the reader may try:

> *nvrmnt*
>   1. *a type of nerve fiber*
>   2. *the surface of a road*
>   3. *what surrounds a place*
>   4. *a kind of mental illness*

Individuals who can recognize the "misspelled" words rapidly and find their meanings among the choices offered tend to be better second-language learners. In addition to phonetic coding ability, this test also measures vocabulary and speed components of second-language abilities. (The correct answer to the sample item is 3, "environment".)

Words in Sentences is a test of grammatical sensitivity. It is a grammatical analogies test in which the examinee has to find the word or phrase in a series of choices offered that has the same grammatical function as one identified in a key sentence. (A sample item was given on page 92.)

Paired Associates is a test of rote-learning or associative memory. It re-quires the examinee to study a series of nonsense words, like those in a foreign language, with their meanings in English, then be tested on his or her memory of these meanings.

Normally, the MLAT test is administered by means of a tape recording. The tape recording is definitely required by the first two subtests, Number Learning and Phonetic Script; the last three subtests are purely paper-and-pencil tests, and can be administered without use of a tape recording. When the test is administered without use of a tape recorder, the total score is based on only the last three subtests (designated as the "short form" of the test).

The Pimsleur Language Aptitude Battery (Pimsleur, 1966) contains six parts, but only the last four of them are actual ability tests. It is designed particularly for students in junior high school. In Part 1, students give data from which their grade-point averages may be computed, and in Part 2, they give an indication of their interest in learning foreign languages. Part 3 is a straightforward English vocabulary test, since Pimsleur found that vocabulary was a reasonably good predictor of second-language learning success. Part 4 is a Language Analysis test; from a series of foreign language sentences and their English translations, students have to figure out enough of the grammar of the foreign language to infer how sentences may be correctly formed in the foreign language. They are then tested on what they have been able to infer, by being asked to evaluate translations of English sentences. This part probably measures both the grammatical sensitivity and the inductive learning components of second-language aptitude. Part 5 tests the student's ability to differentiate pitch contours in a tonal language like Chinese, and to recognize the difference between nasal and nonnasal vowels in a language like French. Part 6 requires students to identify proper spellings of tape-recorded nonsense words, e.g. /tarpdel/ (heard on the tape-recording) spelled as *tarpdel* rather than *tarpled, trapled,* or *trapdel.* Parts 5 and 6 of the PLAB probably measure the "phonetic coding ability" that is also measured by the *Phonetic Script* and *Spelling Clues* subtests of the MLAT. The PLAB is administered by means of a tape recording, since many of the stimuli are auditory.

Total scores on each of these batteries are obtained by combining scores on the separate parts. Since the subtests are not perfectly correlated, each subtest contributes a distinct piece of information about the student's second-language aptitude. Students who appear to be highest in aptitude are those who attain high scores on all of the subtests. Students who obtain average total scores may have different profiles of scores on the subtests: either average on all subtests, or high on some and low on others. Students with the latter sort of profile may be able to compensate for low aptitude in some aspects of second-language abilities by being high in others. Nevertheless, it is the total score that is generally most indicative of a student's probable success in a second-language course, other things like motivation and type and quality of instruction being equal. One way of presenting the magnitude of this relationship is to show an expectancy chart like that in Figure 4.1, plotted from data given in the manual of the MLAT (Carroll and Sapon, 1959).

Suppose an examinee has a total score of 95 on the MLAT. This score is a little below average for adults; the highest possible score is 192. From the expectancy chart we can find that this student has about a 68 percent chance of being in the top *two-thirds* of a typical intensive foreign-language course, that is, of being a "passing" student, but only about a 23 percent chance of being in the top *one-third* of such a class. Of course, these figures need to be compared with a person's chances of being in the top two-thirds or top third if we had no information on language ability (they are 67 percent and 33 percent, respectively). But chances of being in the top two-thirds or in the top third can be read off the chart for other MLAT scores. Obviously, people with very low scores have little chance of success, whereas people with high scores have excellent chances.

Data on the predictive validity of aptitude tests are also often given in terms of a correlation coefficient between the aptitude scores and measures of success. The data of Figure 4.1 correspond to a validity coefficient of about .51, and are based on 957 adults studying in intensive language courses in the Foreign Service Institute of the U.S. Department of State, the U.S. Army, and the U.S. Air Force. Similar expectancy charts could be presented to illustrate the effectiveness of the MLAT or the PLAB for predicting success in high-school and college second-language courses. On the average, the validity coefficients for such courses are comparable to the .51 cited for the adult sample, but they may vary rather widely, say from .20 to .80, depending on the type of sample, the type of instruction, and other factors. Such data suggest that second-language abilities are at least one important factor on which success depends.

Figure 4.1
Expectancy chart showing an individual's chances of being in the top two-thirds or the top one-third in final grades in intensive foreign-language training, as a function of total score on the MLAT.

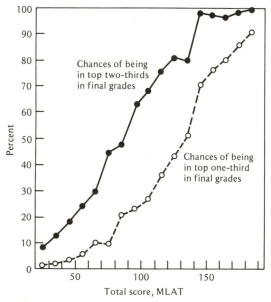

Second-Language Ability and Intelligence

Because of the nature of the tasks set on second-language aptitude tests, it is almost inevitable that there would be at least a moderate correlation between second-language aptitude scores and intelligence. The magnitude of this correlation will depend on various factors, such as the range of abilities in the group studied. In a group of 793 Canadian adult public servants, the correlation between MLAT total score and total score on the Thurstone and Thurstone Primary Mental Abilities battery was found to be .67 (Wesche et al., 1982). Correlations in the range of .40 to .70 are found for high-school and college samples. However, second-language aptitude tests measure certain abilities, such as phonetic coding and rote memory, that are not tested by intelligence tests, and thus make a unique contribution to the prediction of second-language learning success over and above what can be contributed by intelligence tests alone. Validities of second-language aptitude tests in predicting second-language learning success are generally significantly higher than those of intelligence tests.

Second-Language Aptitude and Age

Although average test scores on second-language aptitude tests increase slightly with age, there is little good evidence about the relation of second-language aptitude to this variable. What evidence exists suggests that adults (except possibly some of middle age and beyond) are on the average somewhat better and faster learners of second languages, in school learning situations, than children of school age, contrary to widely held beliefs. On the other hand, with good instruction and models, children below the age of puberty are apparently likely to acquire a better pronunciation of a second language than adults. Final answers to the age/aptitude question await more extensive research (McLaughlin, 1978).

Second-Language Aptitude and Sex

There is very little solid research evidence on sex-related differences in second-language learning abilities. Females tend to make slightly higher average scores on second-language aptitude tests than males, and they are on the average slightly more successful than males in second-language learning. There is no evidence, however, that aptitude tests are differentially valid for males and females, or that they are in any way biased in favor of either sex. That is, a score on an aptitude test has the same meaning, for predicting success in language learning, for both men and women.

Second-Language Abilities from an Information-Processing Perspective

Little research has been done on the information-processing aspects of the second-language abilities that have been identified by psychometric techniques. What can be said here is offered only as speculative, and must be accepted with great caution until further evidence is available (Carroll, 1981).

Phonetic coding ability appears to concern a special type of auditory image: of speech sounds, and combinations or sequences of such sounds. It has to do with the individual's ability to form such images, treat them as distinct, and preserve their form in both short-term and long-term memory. These images seem to be used in various ways, for example, in guiding the production of speech sounds in a second language and in discriminating between different speech sounds as heard in a second language. It has been found that individuals who are poor in phonetic coding ability are likely to have difficulty with the following task. If they are auditorily presented with a nonsense syllable or word, then asked to do some interfering task such as counting backward for ten seconds, they will probably not recall the nonsense stimulus accurately when asked to do so. Also, individuals low on this ability are not as good mimickers of foreign-language words and phrases as are individuals who score high in phonetic coding ability on aptitude tests. Although these tasks involve only short-term memory, appropriate phonetic images or codes of second-language sounds and words must be stored in long-term memory for use in speaking or understanding a foreign language.

As far as we can tell thus far, grammatical sensitivity has to do with awareness of grammatical concepts (such as distinctions between parts of speech, grammatical cases, or differences in word order) and the ability to observe the grammatical functions of language elements, either in one's native language or in a second language that is being learned. Although children can acquire their native language without becoming aware of such grammatical concepts, many do somehow become aware of them, whether by native intelligence or by instruction and training. The ability to become aware of the role of such grammatical concepts in a second language is apparently helpful, though perhaps not strictly necessary, in learning a second language. Insofar as the *Words in Sentences* subtest of the MLAT is a measure of this ability, it not only tests for the presence of appropriate grammatical concepts in long-term memory, but also requires some of the components of inductive reasoning ability in solving the grammatical analogies that are presented.

Rote-learning ability for foreign-language words and meanings calls on an ability to form associations in short-term memory, possibly with the help of mediators found in long-term memory. In actual use during second-language learning, this ability also calls for appropriate rehearsal and other strategies for insuring that the associations formed are placed in long-term memory.

Inductive language-learning ability depends on the capacity to observe relevant relationships between elements in language materials in order to infer the rules that govern these materials. It is probably related to the "fluid intelligence" measured by many intelligence-test tasks. At the same time, it may involve search of long-term memory for relevant hypotheses that can be tested as possible types of rules. For example, a person who is aware that grammatical case is often signaled by suffixes is more likely to perceive the role of such suffixes than is a person who lacks such awareness.

The Modifiability of Second-Language Abilities

What research has thus far been done suggests that second-language abilities are hard to modify. Second-language training itself does little to modify them, contrary to the beliefs of some people who report that learning one language helps in learning still another. Although there may be some transfer of skills from one language to another, the idea that language training increases language *aptitude* is probably false. People who already have high aptitude for second-language learning are the ones who are more likely to learn more languages; people with low aptitude are less likely to try learning many languages beyond a second.

Aptitude tests given at the start of training and then again at the end of training generally show little change. Strenuous efforts to train specific second-language abilities, such as phonetic coding ability, have been relatively unsuccessful, and even if some improvement in ability can be produced by training, it does not seem to carry over to second-language learning.

Given these rather unpleasant facts, what are we to say to the individual who tests at a relatively low level on a second-language aptitude test, but still wants to learn a second language?

First, such a person should be told that a low aptitude score does not mean that he or she *cannot* learn a second language. It may mean, however, that the learning is likely to take more time than it would for the person of average or high aptitude. Aptitude can be taken as an indicator of *rate of learning.* The person of low aptitude will probably have to spend more time and effort, and go more slowly in the learning, than the person of average or high aptitude. If possible, the person should seek a course of instruction in which he or she can pace the learning at a rate that is comfortable, taking more time than normal to cover a given unit of instruction, and to practice and review it properly.

Second, it would be appropriate for a person of low second-language aptitude to seek a type of instruction that is adapted to his or her pattern of abilities. For example, persons who are low on phonetic coding ability are probably more effectively placed in courses that emphasize learning rules of grammar and analyzing sentences more than imitating and practicing foreign-language words and sentences. Relatively high ability in grammatical sensitivity and inductive learning ability would be required in this approach.

In contrast, people who are higher in phonetic coding and rote-memory abilities than in grammatical sensitivity or inductive ability seem to do better in a *functional approach,* in which they practice language patterns in definite situations, with role-playing, conversations, and the use of contextual cues like "props" (actual objects being talked about).

In a program described by Wesche (1981), the Canadian government found it effective to use second-language aptitude profiles to classify students into different types of language courses in its massive programs of French and English teaching for government employees required to learn these languages. Some of her suggestions might profitably be employed in devising language-training programs for other types of students on the basis of their aptitude profiles.

A Final Word

The emphasis in this chapter has been on the role of aptitudes in the prediction of success in second-language learning. It has been suggested that success in learning a second language is at least in part dependent on the extent to which the student possesses certain abilities that are important in facilitating such learning. Two of these abilities, inductive reasoning ability and associative-memory ability, are probably not very specific to second language learning, since they are useful in other types of learning. Other abilities, however, such as phonetic coding ability and grammatical sensitivity, appear to be rather specific to second-language learning.

Regardless of its role in second-language learning, each of these abilities represents an interesting dimension of cognitive capacity. Further research would be needed to elucidate the nature of these abilities, the cognitive process-es that are involved in the tasks that reveal and measure them, the way they grow or decline over the life span, and the degree to which they can be improved by training and other experiences. Because of the well-defined nature of the task of learning a second-language and the generally close involvement of second-language abilities in that task, the study of these abilities is potentially one of the more profitable areas in which progress can be made toward a better under-standing of cognitive abilities and their role in learning and behavior in general.

References and Suggested Readings

Carroll, J. B. 1962. The prediction of success in intensive foreign language training. *In* R. Glaser ed., *Training Research and Education* (Pittsburgh, Pa.: Univ. of Pittsburgh Press), pp. 87–136.

Carroll, J. B. Twenty-five years of research on foreign language aptitude. *In* Diller (1981), pp. 83–118.

Carroll, J. B., and S. M. Sapon. 1959. *Modern Language Aptitude Test, Form A*. New York: The Psychological Corporation.

Diller, K. C., ed. 1981. *Individual Differences and Universals in Language Learning Aptitude*. Rowley, Mass.: Newbury House.

Gardner, R. C., and W. E. Lambert. 1972. *Attitudes and Motivation in Second-Language Learning*. Rowley, Mass.: Newbury House.

Henmon, V. A. C., J. E. Bohan, and C. C. Brigham. 1929. *Prognosis Tests in the Modern Foreign Languages*. New York: Macmillan.

McLaughlin, B. 1978. *Second-Language Acquisition in Childhood*. Hillsdale, N.J.: Erlbaum.

Petersen, C. R., and A. R. Al-Haik. 1976. The development of the Defense Language Aptitude Battery (DLAB). *Educational and Psychological Measurement, 36*, 369–380.

Pimsleur, P. 1966. *The Pimsleur Language Aptitude Battery*. New York: Harcourt Brace Jovanovich.

Pimsleur, P., R. P. Stockwell, and A. L. Comrey. 1962. Foreign language learning ability. *Journal of Educational Psychology,* 53, 15–26.

Sapon, S. M. 1955. A work sample test for foreign language prognosis. *Journal of Psychology,* 39, 97–104.

Wesche, M. B. 1981. Language aptitude measures in streaming, matching students with methods, and diagnosis of learning problems. *In* Diller (1981), pp. 119–154.

Wesche, M. B., H. Edwards, and W. Wells. 1982. Foreign language aptitude and intelligence. *Applied Psycholinguistics,* 3, 127–140.

5

INDIVIDUAL DIFFERENCES IN LEARNING AND MEMORY

Joseph C. Campione
Ann L. Brown
Nancy R. Bryant
University of Illinois, Champaign

Flexible use of the information we have learned is an important ingredient of intelligent performance. In this chapter, we will discuss research aimed at establishing the existence and importance of individual differences in the ability to acquire, retain, and use information (to learn, remember, and transfer). There is a long and interesting history to this debate, and we will trace the research chronologically in an attempt to show how psychologists' theories and studies have changed since the early 1900s, and how ideas about individual differences in intelligence and school achievement have been correspondingly altered.

Learning and memory performance have traditionally been regarded as important indices of intelligence, and many of the items found on typical IQ tests were originally designed to be either somewhat indirect estimates of learning

Preparation of this manuscript and portions of the research reported therein were supported by Grants HD-05951 and HD-15808 from the National Institute of Child Health and Human Development.

efficiency (tests of vocabulary and general knowledge, for example) or somewhat more direct estimates of memory ability (digit span, the maximum length of a number series a person can remember). The underlying idea was that intelligence comprises several extremely general skills, or faculties, specification of which could define what intelligence was and how individuals could be expected to differ in it. Simply stated, the idea was that people might differ in the speed of their learning (fast or slow) and in the strength of their memories (weak or strong); of course, things turned out to be much more complex than this.

It was (and is) certainly true that intelligence tests could serve a useful function in discriminating children who were likely to experience school-related problems from those who were not (that was the charge Binet was given when he was asked to develop the initial tests). That the tests proved to be successful did not explain *why* they were. As a result, there has been a large amount of research attempting to explain what intelligence is, or what such tests assess, in terms of basic psychological processes. The work on learning and memory represents one specific and enduring approach to that complex problem. And as we shall see, experimental evidence establishing the importance of learning and memory processes has turned out to be much more difficult to obtain than many had thought. It is the twists and turns in the general arguments that make the history particularly interesting.

In the first section we will describe some early work concerned with investigating the relation between learning ability and transfer propensity (the ability to make flexible use of learned rules or principles), on the one hand, and measures of ability (most notably intelligence) on the other. Here the results were largely negative, and we will discuss the reasons why. The second section will be concerned with research that began in the middle 1960s on the sources of individual (developmental or comparative) differences in memory performance. This increase in interest in memory phenomena was accompanied by a corresponding decrease in interest in learning mechanisms. In the final section we will return to a discussion of what current psychological research tells us about variations in learning, retention, and transfer efficiency as indices of individual differences.

Intelligence and Learning: Early Approaches

Statements about the relation between intelligence and the ability to learn have been controversial since the inception of the testing movement. Many early theorists made the claim that intelligence *was* the ability to learn (Peterson, 1925). For example, at a 1921 conference concerned with definitions of what intelligence tests actually measured, Buckingham (1921) claimed directly that "intelligence is the ability to learn," as did Dearborn (1921), who said, "intelligence is the capacity to learn and profit by experience."

Similarly, textbooks of the 1920s made the same claim, e.g., Carrol (1928), "an individual possesses intelligence insofar as he can learn;" and Ellis (1929), "intelligence means capacity for learning." The further claim that there should be a close relation between learning as measured in the laboratory and on IQ tests was also common. It seemed obvious that if reasonable amounts of data were collected from learning situations and from intelligence tests, these sources would turn out to have been measuring essentially the same things.

The stronger claim that the *best* indices of intelligence would be those that actually measured learning directly was also prevalent in the 1920s. For example, Dearborn (1921) argued that "measurement of the actual process of learning would furnish the best test of intelligence," and Thorndike stated that, "estimates of it (intelligence) are, or at least should be, estimates of the ability to learn. To be able to learn harder things, or to be able to learn the same things more quickly, would then be the single basis of evaluation" (Thorndike, 1926, pp. 17–18). In short, Woodrow, who was to attack this position, complained that, "statements identifying learning ability with intelligence are found so frequently that a careless reader might form the opinion that such identification is beyond dispute" (Woodrow, 1946, p. 149).

Some Negative Results

By 1946, Woodrow felt confident enough in the contrasting position to claim that "intelligence, far from being identical with the amount of improvement shown by practice, has practically nothing to do with the matter" (Woodrow, 1946, p. 151). Despite Woodrow's careful definition of learning as the "amount of improvement shown by practice," his work (and that of others) led to the generally accepted position that learning and intelligence were not strongly related, a position that was to hold for at least another twenty years (see Gagne, 1967, for expressions of this position). What caused this turnabout?

A consideration of Woodrow's own empirical work will help us trace the history of the total acceptance and then rejection of the learning-intelligence link. We will illustrate with two sets of experiments he conducted, one with retarded and nonretarded children and one with college students. In 1917, Woodrow published two papers concerning the learning (Woodrow, 1917a) and transfer (Woodrow, 1917b) performance of normal and retarded students matched for a mental age of nine years. He found absolutely no differences in learning or transfer between the two groups. When working with college students of differing abilities, Woodrow (1938a, 1938b) again failed to find a link between learning ability and intelligence.

To interpret these studies, it is important to consider some procedural features in more detail. The learning problems given to the normal and retarded children consisted of a geometric-form sorting task where the students were required to sort five forms (stars, circles, etc.) into different boxes. The students sorted 500 of these a day for 13 days. The main metric of learning was the increase with time in the number of forms sorted (the error rates were very low). Transfer tests consisted of two new sorting tasks (lengths of sticks and colored pegs) and two cancellation tasks (crossing out certain letters and geometric forms).

Let us turn next to the tasks used by Woodrow when examining learning in adults. The tasks practiced (apparently randomly selected) included backward writing, reproduction of spot patterns, horizontal adding, canceling letters, estimating lengths, and speed in making "gates" (making four horizontal lines and one diagonal slash in each square of a page divided into 1000 squares).

Woodrow's tasks, and those of others working at the same time, reflected the prevailing conception of learning as "improvement shown by practice," as very general skill or faculty indeed. As such, it did not seem to matter what type of task that improvement was on. There was no detailed process analysis of *what* was changing with practice. There were no systematic rules shared between learning problems that could be induced during the course of practice, and no principled transfer domain to which such rules could be transferred. Furthermore, the conditions under which learning was to occur were simply those of practice unguided save for knowledge of results. In a very real sense, there was no opportunity for students in these experiments to learn. What were they to learn? What were they to remember? What were they supposed to transfer? Why should people with high general ability sort stars and circles, make gates, etc., any more quickly than those with putatively lower ability?

In short, the tasks do not appear to represent the most fertile ground for seeking a relation between learning transfer and ability. Indeed, Humphreys (1979) claims that speeded sorting and cancellation tasks of the type favored by Woodrow are the least likely to be related to a general factor of intelligence. Humphreys argues that in order to find a general factor among tests, we must look for at least a small element of problem solving.

Positive Evidence

Several factors that entered the picture around 1960 began to change the picture somewhat. First, investigators began taking into account several methodological problems, including both the difficulty or complexity level of the tasks being investigated and the range of ability included in the studies (Zeaman and House, 1967). Also, rather than concentrating purely on the products of performance, researchers devoted more attention to the processes underlying those performances, and so could conduct more detailed investigations of learning phenomena in general and of individual or comparative variation in particular.

These changes were indeed major ones. No longer was learning considered a unitary faculty possessed to varying degrees by different individuals. Instead, it was regarded as a highly complex constellation of many separate processes, any set of which might or might not be relatable to intelligence. Different experimental tasks were regarded as tapping different subprocesses. Given such a view, the fact that intelligence and learning sometimes were, and sometimes were not, related was neither surprising nor embarrassing. The game was to identify principles or specify theories that could account for the overall pattern of relations.

The picture that emerged was that any relation between intelligence and learning would appear only if the tasks used were of appropriate difficulty. If the tasks are too hard, no one will learn; and if they are too easy or if they are cognitively undemanding (as in the case of Woodrow's tasks), everyone will learn readily. In neither case is there enough variability to detect any relation that may exist. Similarly, if the range of ability is too narrow, the same problem results. In situations where a "restriction of range" problem pertains, it is difficult, if not impossible, to evaluate meaningfully the relation between ability measures and performance indices. Zeaman and House (1967) and Estes (1982) have reviewed the literature with these considerations in mind, and have concluded that if the level of difficulty is appropriate and the range of abilities sampled sufficiently large, there is evidence for at least a moderate correlation between intelligence scores and performance on some learning tasks.

For example, although there appears to be no correlation between IQ scores and speed of simple classic or instrumental learning, once learning situations involving some degree of selection and choice are employed, evidence for a learning-ability link does begin to appear (Estes, 1982; Zeaman and House, 1967). Examples of such tasks include complex discrimination learning, some types of verbal learning, and procedures designed to assess learning to learn.

Let us consider first discrimination learning or concept identification tasks. In a prototypic experiment, the subjects would see two objects on each of a series of trials. The objects would differ along a number of dimensions—color, shape, size, number, etc.—and the subject's task would be to choose consistently the one that was correct. What was "correct" would be decided by the experimenter; for example, the correct response might be to always choose the red object regardless of its size, shape, or position. In such experiments, it is possible to manipulate the difficulty level in several ways, e.g., by altering the number of dimensions along which the objects can vary. Given appropriate difficulty levels, comparative differences in learning performance are obtained.

Beyond that, by providing a theoretical framework within which to view the results, we can refine our description of the processes underlying these differences. Zeaman and House (1963) postulated that for subjects to perform such tasks well, they must learn both to attend to the relevant dimension (color, in the preceding example) and to choose the correct value along that dimension (red). They were also able to show analytically that the major determinant of group differences was attentional: the more mature learners were more likely to attend to the relevant dimension in the early phases of the problem. Subsequent analyses (Zeaman, 1978) have also suggested that there are comparative differences in the rates at which those attentional tendencies are learned.

Another area in which differences have been found is the formation of *learning sets,* or in learning to learn (Harlow, 1959). In such experiments, subjects are given a series of two-choice discrimination learning problems to solve; each involves two simple objects, such as an ashtray and a toy car. The trick is that, on each problem, only a few (typically four to six) trials are given. Successive problems feature new stimulus objects, and the question is how many problems does it take before the subjects can solve each new problem as quickly as possible. How long does it take them to learn to learn? Note that on each problem, the first trial involves a guess, but perfect responding is possible from that point on. In a pair of studies, Harter (1965, 1967) found clear relations between IQ and rate of learning to learn, particularly for children with mental ages below nine years. The latter result again indicates the importance of task difficulty. The problems that she used were relatively easy for all the older students in her sample; hence IQ effects were not obtained when their performance was considered (Harter, 1965).

The final set of tasks we will mention here involves verbal-learning situations, the most typical being paired-associates learning. On the first trial of such experiments, subjects see a series of pairs of words. On succeeding trials, one word (the stimulus item) of each pair is presented, and the subject is required to provide the second member (the response item) of that pair. In these and other similar verbal-learning tasks, there is a relation between intelligence and learning efficiency, again subject to the caveats regarding task difficulty and range of ability (Zeaman and House, 1967).

These verbal-learning tasks have also been extensively analyzed theoretically in an attempt to find out why learning differences are obtained. We will return to this issue later (in Section II.B). It is interesting to note that much of this analysis took place in the context of theories of memory, not learning. In the next section, we will describe some of the changes in approach that psychologists introduced in the latter part of the 1960s, and discuss how these changes led to different types of research, which have contributed significantly to our understanding of individual differences in learning.

In summary, after a shaky start, psychologists did succeed in demonstrating at least moderate relations between learning and intelligence. To find those relations, detailed analyses of the processes involved in the experimental tasks were required. In addition, it was necessary to make sure that the tasks were cognitively complex enough and that the range of subject ability included was large enough. Some other factors also seem important for finding relations between intelligence and learning; we will discuss them in the next sections.

Intelligence and Memory Performance

At the end of the 1960s, a major shift away from traditional learning theories followed the advent of what became known as information-processing models. Psychologists in general turned their attention away from learning theories based primarily on empirical work with animals, and toward memory theories based on how human adults process material that they are required to remember. Mainstream experimental psychology was dominated by the influence of a general class of such memory models.

Greatly simplified, the *modal* model consisted of three major components: structural features, control processes, and executive control processes (Atkinson and Shiffrin, 1968). The structural features of these general models are relatively few and simple. They are the invariant components of the system, akin to the hardware of a computer, consisting of such architectural features as short-term memory and long-term memory. Of more interest to our argument are the control processes, similar to the software of the computer system (the programmable parts). These consist of the strategies, tactics, and routines (the programs) that the learner can introduce to make more efficient use of the memory system; the choice of a particular process is up to the learner. Within such frameworks, attention shifted in good part to the learner's activities or strategies (control processes), overseen and managed by a set of executive processes. This aspect of the information-processing models of memory was to have a great impact on the study of individual differences in learning and memory, for the question then became not, "Do people have strong or weak memories in general?" but rather, "Do people differ in the flexibility and ingenuity with which they select and apply strategic processes to help them learn?"

In order to address this question, psychologists interested in individual differences began the search for tasks that demanded greater or lesser strategic intervention for their effective execution. The idea was that the magnitude of the difference between individuals would be small on tasks that did not require elaborate strategies, but that in tasks demanding a great deal of learner ingenuity, the magnitude of individual differences would be much larger (Brown, 1974, 1975). In short, if individual differences are in good part the result of strategic processing, then they will be seen most clearly in situations where strategic intervention is at a premium. In order to test this assumption, it was necessary to devise tasks that varied on a continuum ranging from strategy-free to strategy-intensive.

Strategy-Free Tasks

Human ingenuity is such that strategies may creep somewhat into almost any situation, but there are tasks that do not rely on such activities for effective execution. Some variants of recognition memory provide an example. Faced with literally thousands of distinct simple pictures (tiger, church, rose, violin, etc.), adults show near-perfect accuracy at identifying which ones they have seen previously in the experiment (Nickerson, 1965; Standing et al., 1970). This surprising feat was accomplished without conscious recourse to strategies. In studies with children, the pool of pictures was reduced to merely hundreds to avoid overtaxing their patience, but even so preschool students (Brown and Scott, 1971), as well as mildly (Brown, 1973c) and moderately (Martin, 1970) retarded students, all achieved virtually errorless performance on such tasks.

Recognition memory tasks are not the only ones that can be accomplished by students not known for their strategic activity (see the following) or by adults who are not trying to remember the items. Students are also adept at indicating not only that they have seen an item before, but also, if pairs of old items are presented, which one they have seen more frequently or more recently (Hasher and Zacks, 1979). Performance is not quite as good on such tasks as on simple recognition, but again adults perform them without conscious reliance on obvious strategies. Indeed, students who attempted at first to rehearse, or label, or somehow fix items in memory reported abandoning such activities as futile when faced with a large stack of recurring items (Brown, 1973a). It is also true that the magnitude of the difference between adults and children, and between normal or retarded children, is small or nonexistent on such tasks (Brown,

1973a,–c; Hasher and Zacks, 1979). Because these tasks can be accomplished without much strategic intervention, the magnitude of developmental or comparative differences is small.

This is not to claim, however, that the tasks must be impervious to strategic intervention. In both the recognition and recency tasks, slight modifications can be introduced that increase the payoff for strategy use. For example, if the items to be recognized are not simple distinct pictures, but instead consist of complex visual arrays, developmental and comparative differences do begin to emerge, primarily because the less-mature students fail to scan the original pictures exhaustively (Perlmutter and Myers, 1979). Similarly, if the students must recognize disarranged scenes (Mandler and Robinson, 1978), complex spatial arrays (Mandler and Day, 1975), or recurrent pictures that have elements rearranged or deleted (Dirks and Neisser, 1977), then indeed the recognition task becomes more sensitive to individual differences. For example, Dirks and Neisser (1977) asked adults, normal children, and retarded children to view complex scenes, and then tested them on their recognition of items with elements of the scene deleted or rearranged. There was a sizable improvement in performance as a function of age or ability; young and retarded students performed quite poorly. These differences in performance were attributed to strategic processing. Dirks and Neisser found that the older students were more likely to scan the array systematically, to notice that neighboring items can form meaningful groups, to pay attention to nuances of spatial arrangement, or to formulate verbal descriptions of minor details. To the extent that such deliberate ploys are needed to aid complex recognition, one would expect to find an increase in individual differences.

A similar case can be made for judgments of recency. In such studies, subjects see a series of single pictures. On test trials, they are shown two pictures, each of which had occurred previously, and asked to indicate which member of the pair had occurred more recently. Given a large set of recurrent pictures to tag in terms of their relative recency of occurrence, adults and children perform at the same level. However, if the researcher introduces a means by which the learner can anchor time of occurrence if he or she should choose to do so, then performance differences become more apparent.

We can cite, for example, a study conducted with children. Pictures to be tagged were displayed in a variety of contexts. The least-helpful context provided no potential anchor information, because the items were presented in a single, unmarked stack. The most-helpful context provided anchor information, with the first third of the items being initially viewed in the context of a house, the second third in a garden, and the final third in a road setting, corresponding to the stages of a journey that a toy child took to school in the morning. Younger and older children did not differ when there was no contextual information to aid their decisions about relative recency, such as when the items were presented in an unmarked stack or when they all occurred in the same setting (the house, for example). When context could be harnessed to aid the temporal judgment, for example, when one item had occurred in the first setting (house) and the other in the second (garden), then the older children improved their performance dramatically, but the younger ones did not (Brown, 1973b).

This finding was replicated when the contextual cues were less dramatic; e.g., differently colored backgrounds were provided for items during different time periods. Again, older children made effective use of the additional contextual cue to improve their judgments of relative recency, whereas younger children did not. If, however, the children were trained to use the background cues, age differences again disappeared, for now both the younger and older students were harnessing the background information (Brown et al., 1974).

In summary, there exists a class of tasks where strategic intervention is not necessarily needed for efficient memory; in such situations individual (or developmental or comparative) differences are hard to detect. However, as soon as the tasks are modified in a way that makes strategic intervention useful (e.g., by demanding complex scanning activities or by providing contextual cues that can be used to anchor items in time), then the magnitude of the individual differences increases dramatically. The interpretation of these findings is that it is in the spontaneous introduction of strategies that older children differ from younger ones, and brighter individuals from their less-intelligent peers. This brings us to a consideration of strategy-intensive tasks.

Strategy-Intensive Tasks

By far the most commonly studied memory tasks are those of the strategy-intensive variety. Unlike recognition tasks, where a respectable performance can be achieved without recourse to strategic intervention, strategy-intensive tasks demand the flexible deployment of mnemonic strategies before efficient performance can be achieved. The classic strategy-intensive task is rote-ordered recall of lists of unrelated items, such as letters, digits, words, etc. If the learner is required to reproduce, rather than merely recognize, strings of previously seen items, and if that list is more than seven items long, he or she must introduce some deliberate activity to promote memory. The classic strategy for this situation is rehearsal, for example, trying to remember a telephone number by repeating it over and over until you have the chance to dial illustrates one type of rehearsal.

Much effort was expended in the 1970s examining the role of strategy deployment as a determinant of comparative or developmental differences. Several relevant lines of inquiry converge nicely here to allow a reasonably thorough picture of the relation between strategy generation and ability.

Flavell (1970) provided an early series of studies with young children which demonstrate that children become more likely as they grow older to produce, spontaneously, strategies aimed at facilitating subsequent recall. Flavell and his colleagues also demonstrated that young children could use such strategies even though they did not spontaneously produce them; even simple prompts enabled quite young children to, for example, rehearse to-be-remembered items during a delay interval, (and, as a result) to increase their recall accuracy significantly.

Similarly, work with mildly retarded children has made it clear that they are much less likely to produce a variety of strategies in response to memory tasks than are children of average ability of the same chronological age (Belmont and Butterfield, 1969, 1971; Brown et al., 1973; Ellis, 1970; for reviews, see Brown, 1974, 1978; Borkowski and Cavanaugh, 1979; Campione and Brown, 1977; Campione et al., 1982). Several features of this research are notable, including the regularity, consistency, and generality of the findings, along with the magnitude of the differences in both strategy production and relation between strategy and performance level. We will examine these in turn.

First, we should consider consistency. Apparently, in almost any memory situation where strategic intervention of some type is necessary for adequate performance, retarded children with IQs of around 70 perform extremely poorly (Borkowski and Wanschura, 1974; Brown, 1974, 1978; Campione and Brown, 1977, 1978). This is true whether the strategy required involves rehearsal processes (Belmont and Butterfield, 1971; Brown et al., 1973; Ellis, 1970), capitalizing on the organization inherent in to-be-remembered material (Spitz, 1963), or using a variety of elaboration processes to facilitate learning and recall (Borkowski and Wanschura, 1974; Jensen and Rohwer, 1963; Rohwer, 1973).

How large are the differences in strategy use? Often they are quite dramatic. Consider, for example, the Brown (1972) and Brown et al. (1973) studies. Subjects were required to view briefly a set of four items presented successively, each from a different category, and then answer a question about that set, e.g., "What was the last animal you saw?" Given this task, nonretarded adolescents spontaneously rehearse the set as it is presented, whereas mildly retarded students of the same age tend not to do so. But that is only part of the story. To induce retarded children to rehearse adequately on this simple task required that they be given detailed instructions, along with considerable modeling and practice. In contrast, it was exceedingly difficult to *prevent* their nonretarded peers from rehearsing. Even under conditions designed to prevent rehearsal use, they still managed to "sneak in" some unwanted rehearsal. It takes a lot of work to induce retarded children to employ strategies, and a comparable amount of ingenuity to prevent it in their nonretarded counterparts. The main point is that there is a large intelligence-related difference in the tendency to employ a variety of memory strategies. Although not all nonretarded individuals are consistently strategic in their approach to memory situations, and a few retarded adolescents do produce some strategies spontaneously (Belmont et al., 1981; Brown, 1974), the overall difference is quite striking.

The next issue concerns the size of the difference in performance that results from use or nonuse of a strategy in a given memory task. We can look at this aspect of the data in two ways. We can compare mildly retarded with nonretarded children of the same age in terms of their accuracy when the two groups are allowed to perform in any way they wish, or we can look at the performance of retarded children before and after they are given some instruction in the use of a strategy.

Consider first the retarded-nonretarded comparison. The Brown et al. (1973) example mentioned previously can be used here. The retarded children in that study averaged 58 percent correct when they originally performed on the task. Nonretarded children *could not be compared* on the same task, because they simply never made any errors. To force them to make any errors at all, it was necessary to include a filled retention interval; after the four to-be-remembered items were presented, the students were required to spend time counting backward by threes in Spanish (they were taken from a junior high Spanish class) before they were asked a question about the items. The retarded students, in contrast, were asked the category question immediately after they had seen the four items. Clearly, the groups differed greatly in general performance. Similarly, Belmont and Butterfield (1971) compared retarded and nonretarded students on another, similar short-term memory task. The subjects would see a series of items, say, consonants, presented in succession in a series of windows, one item per window. After the last item was presented, a "probe item" would be presented; this was simply a duplicate of one of the just-seen items. The subjects' task was to indicate the window in which that item had appeared. For example, if the series had been "H, K, B, T, D, F," and if the probe item were a "B," the subject should point to the third window from the left. The retarded students showed little evidence of using rehearsal processes, and averaged 45 percent correct on the probes. The nonretarded students, however, showed clear evidence of rehearsing and averaged 74 percent correct.

In both studies, there were differences between the retarded and nonretarded groups in the use of rehearsal processes and large differences in their memory accuracy. Both studies included conditions in which nonretarded students were prevented from rehearsing, in which their recall accuracy dropped significantly, and in which they showed patterns of responding extremely similar to those of the retarded samples. That is, teaching retarded children to rehearse made their performance similar to that of nonretarded students; whereas preventing the nonretarded from rehearsing led them to resemble the retarded in their levels and patterns of recall. These results reinforce the view that it was the use of the rehearsal strategy that was in good part responsible for the recall differences obtained originally.

We can now consider the performance of retarded children before and after instruction in strategy use. In the Brown et al. (1973) study, retarded children taught to rehearse increased their recall accuracy from 58 to 90 percent, an impressive improvement. A more dramatic example comes from a series of studies conducted by Butterfield et al. (1973) using the same task as Belmont and Butterfield (1971). The retarded adolescents responded correctly to the probe on 36 percent of the trials before any intervention; following detailed instruction in the use of task-appropriate strategies, their accuracy increased to a maximum of more than 80 percent correct, an increment of more than 100 percent, resulting in recall performance slightly higher than that of uninstructed nonretarded adolescents.

Dramatic improvement in performance is not limited to rehearsal tasks. Turnure et al. (1976) investigated the role of elaborative processes in learning and memory. Their subjects were given a 21-item paired associates list to learn. They would see each of 21 pairs of items on a study trial, followed by a test trial on which one of each pair would be presented, and the child would have to recall the other member of the pair. Retarded children around seven years old averaged 2.0 items correct when left to work on their own devices. When they were essentially tricked into employing an elaborative strategy for learning the pairs, by responding to questions about why each item was paired with its mate, they increased to an average of 14.4 items correct, an increase in recall of more than 600 percent.

In these studies, as well as in many others, teaching retarded children to engage in task-appropriate strategic activities results in dramatic increases in their recall accuracy. Similar data can be found by comparing the performance of younger and older grade-school children (for reviews, see Brown, 1975, 1978; Flavell, 1970; Kail and Hagen, 1977; Ornstein and Naus, 1978). However, variation in strategy use is a prime determinant of efficiency even in college students, and the mature application of, for example, a hierarchic organizational strategy vastly increases the recall of college students (Bower et al., 1969).

The interpretation of this impressive body of data is that an extremely important source of individual or comparative differences in associative memory tasks is the tendency and ability to bring to bear the kinds of simple mnemonic strategies necessary for adequate performance. It appears that whenever such strategies are necessary—and they are necessary in the vast majority of school-like learning and memory situations—large individual differences are to be found. In contrast, on the strategy-free tasks, differences are either absent or extremely small.

Learning and Transfer Reconsidered

One method used to evaluate the importance of strategic activities involves instructing students to use them. If we want to assess how important the use of strategies is to memory performance, one good way is to measure the performance of an apparently nonstrategic performer working unaided, and compare it with his or her performance following training in the use of the target strategy. As we have indicated, this approach has been quite informative.

From such studies, moreover, three other equally important findings emerged; and they are closely related to the original notions about individual differences in intelligence. The first was simply that training was necessary at all. Most normal students over the age of seven years begin to employ many of these activities without such training. Indeed, these strategies are *not* taught explicitly in schools. The children tend to acquire them in an almost incidental fashion, i.e., without direct instruction. Second, in order for mildly retarded students to learn to use a particular strategy effectively, they needed surprisingly detailed instruction in each component of the strategy, along with instruction in how to assemble and oversee the whole package. They did not appear to fill in many steps if the experimenter did not train them explicitly. In this sense, retarded students are "slow" to learn. Third, after having learned to use a particular strategy quite well, retarded students are not likely to transfer its use to new, but similar and related, problems. They appear "reluctant" to transfer. That is, the research on memory processes conducted during the late 1960s and 1970s seems to have generated, almost incidentally, data that imply the importance of individual differences in learning and transfer processes, in contrast to the work in the first half of the century, where, paradoxically, the direct intent was to show that learning and transfer processes were closely related to individual differences in intelligence. We will consider these suggestions about learning and transfer in more detail in the next section.

Learning from Incomplete Instruction

Consider first the study by Butterfield et al. (1973) already described. To deal with the six-item lists presented, the retarded adolescents were taught to use a "3-3 active passive" strategy. They were taught to rehearse as a set the first three items (to say "H, K, B" over and over after having seen the third item), and then briefly view the last three items to get the test question quickly. The idea is that rehearsal would help to consolidate the first three items in memory, facilitating subsequent recall, but that no active processing would be necessary on the last three items, which would not have time to "fade" from memory before the test question was presented. It turned out that getting retarded children to use that strategy effectively required that they be taught the active and passive components separately and in detail, be given practice on each, and then be taught explicitly how to coordinate the two components of the overall activity.

The presumption, of course, is that more capable students would have been able to master the strategy with less detailed or complete instruction. Rohwer (1973) has provided just such a comparison of the need for more explicit instruction on the part of less-mature learners. He investigated the use of elaborative processes to facilitate paired-associates learning (e.g., to help them remember a pair of items such as fish-telephone, some people make up a sentence containing the two, "The *fish* is talking on the *telephone*," or form a mental image of a fish talking on a telephone). In his studies, Rohwer provided a variety of "prompts" designed to induce students to use such elaborative schemes. His minimal prompt consisted simply of instructions to learn the pairs of items, with more explicit prompts actually presenting the items in the context of, for example, a sentence. There were also some intermediate prompts. He found that the younger or more delayed the student, the more explicit the prompt (or intervention) needed to bring about improved performance.

Similarly, work on "directed" or "controlled" forgetting also demonstrates that the degree of aid needed differs with subjects. The procedure in such experiments might involve the presentation of a series of digits followed by a test question, as in the Belmont and Butterfield examples mentioned earlier. Each digit is presented on a colored background, with a change in background color serving as a cue that the previous items will not be tested and should be ignored. The number of to-be-forgotten items can vary from zero to four. For example, if the series were "3, 4, 8, 6, 1, 2," and if the first three items were presented on a red background, and the last three on a blue background, the subject would be tested only on the last three items. Specifically, the color change on the fourth item would serve as the cue that the first three items would not be tested. In such cases, adults act as though only three items had been presented; accuracy is as though a three-, rather than six-item list had been viewed. Bray

(1973) showed that retarded adolescents can eliminate interference from irrelevant information if they are given several days of pretraining in which the significance of the *forget-cue* is carefully explained and reviewed. In a subsequent study, Hyatt (1976) found that, whereas both normal and retarded adolescents show substantial interference from the to-be-forgotten information when the significance of the cue to forget is not fully explained, provision of a verbal explanation results in performance increases for both normal and retarded students, although some interference is still present for the retarded group. In order to eliminate all interference for the retarded subjects, experimenters must provide both a verbal explanation and trial-by-trial review (Goodman, 1976); i.e., much more explicit instruction is needed by the retarded group than by the normal adolescents.

There is thus much evidence in the memory literature that retarded children learn less well than nonretarded children of comparable age; indeed, the finding seems fairly robust, which only underscores the contrast with Woodrow's (1946) conclusions discussed in the section on page 106. Why the disagreement? One argument is that the more recent studies assume that learning is an ability to profit from guided instruction, rather than a tendency to improve with simple, unguided practice. In addition, the tasks used by Woodrow and his contemporaries did not tap the same kinds of skills and activities assessed by the more recent instructional studies. Indeed, it can be argued that many of the tasks Woodrow used were chosen precisely because they did not allow the use of clever learning activities; the idea was to look at relatively "pure" learning uncontaminated by such factors. It has also been argued that the more similar the learning environment is to school-learning situations, the more likely it is that intelligence-related individual differences will be found (Campione and Brown, in press). If we regard learning as the ability to profit from incomplete instruction (Resnick and Glaser, 1976), there is strong evidence that this represents a major source of individual variation in intelligence.

Transfer of Training

In many of the instructional studies, researchers have probed for longer-term effects of training. Given that students have learned to use a strategy, will they *maintain* it or *generalize* it? *Maintenance* refers to continued, unprompted use of the activity on the same tasks involved in training, whereas *generalization* refers to the tendency to make use of that activity on different tasks. Little evidence has been found, in a wide variety of studies, that generalized effects of training can be obtained with the retarded unless the instructional package is specifically designed with transfer in mind (e.g., Belmont et al., 1982; Borkowski and Cavanaugh, 1979; Brown, 1974, 1978; Brown and Campione, 1978, 1981; Campione and Brown, 1977, 1978).

One problem with this research, for the purposes of this chapter, is that the work has rarely been truly comparative. Typically, only retarded students have been examined, and it is just assumed that brighter students would show broader transfer. Such an assumption, however, is at least somewhat suspect, since there are many examples available where even mature and selected learners (college students) show a dramatic lack of transfer (Gick and Holyoak, 1980, 1983; Hayes and Simon, 1977; Reed et al., 1974). In order to find out if transfer inefficiency is a particular problem for the young or slow, we need a direct comparison between groups of individuals varying in age or overall ability. It is to such relevant data that we now turn.

Comparative Studies of Transfer

To look more directly at transfer performance, we and our colleagues (Campione et al., 1983; Ferrara, 1982; Ferrara et al., 1981) compared mildly retarded and nonretarded children (Campione et al.), and average and above-average ability children (Ferrara, 1982), in situations assessing their ability to acquire and use inductive reasoning rules. These studies, again in contrast to those of Woodrow, featured interactive learning procedures, in which the student and experimenter worked together to solve a series of problems. These sessions were designed to correspond to the conditions of learning occurring in school settings, and are consistent with a general view of learning espoused by Vygotsky (1978). He argued that much of learning is originally social in nature, shared between a learner and a tutor or "more knowledgeable other" (parent, teacher, mastercraftsman, etc.). Tutors, who are initially very much in control of the learning situation, gradually relinquish that control, with the student eventually coming to perform the target activities independently. The metrics of learning and transfer efficiency in such situations are the amounts of help needed for students to solve designated problems independently.

In the series of studies we conducted, we tried to mimic these natural learning forums in order to capture individual differences in learning and transfer propensity. On each of a series of problems, the students were given a series of hints as needed for solution. These were structured in a general-to-specific, weak-to-strong, sequence to ascertain the *minimum* amount of aid required by each student. The procedure used in evaluating individual differences in learning and transfer performance was situated in contexts involving structured and direct instruction in domains where rules and principles could be acquired.

In the Ferrara (1982) research, groups of children of average and above-average ability were given sets of series-completion problems to solve. As shown in Box 5.1, these consisted of a series of letters followed by some blank spaces, and the children's task was to complete the series. Three alphabetic rules are involved in these problems: *identity (I)*, where a letter is repeated; *next (N)*, where the following letter in the alphabet occurs; and *backward next (B)*, where the preceding letter of the alphabet is the solution. In addition, the *period* refers to the number of letters that occur prior to the appearance of regularities. For example, in the simple problem "A, D, A, D, A, D, _ _" (answer = "A, D"), the period is two, and the relations are both identity; this is termed an *II* problem. In the problem "A, B, A, C, A, D, _ _" (answer = "A, E") the period is again two, and the relations are identity for the first letter and next for the second; this is termed an *IN* problem. In the problem "E, T, D, T, C, T, _ _" (answer = "B, T")

■■■■■
Box 5.1
Examples of learning, maintenance, and transfer items

Problem type	Pattern [a]	Sample problem	Correct answer
Original learning	NN	N, G, O, H, P, I, Q, J, ____	(R, K, S, L)
	NINI	P, Z, U, F, Q, Z, V, F, ____	(R, Z, W, F)

Maintenance (learned pattern types; new instantiations)

Near transfer (learned relations and periodicities, but in new combinations)

	NI	D, V, E, V, F, V, G, V, ____	(H, V, I, V)
	NNNN	V, H, D, P, W, I, E, Q, ____	(X, J, F, R)

Far transfer (new relation, backward-next, or new periodicity, three letters)

	BN	U, C, T, D, S, E, R, F, ____	(Q, G, P, H)
	NBNI	J, P, B, X, K, O, C, X, ____	(L, N, D, X)
	NIN	P, A, D, Q, A, E, R, A, ____	(F, S, A, G)

Very far transfer (backward next as well as next relations and "period" of two letters, but relations must be sought between strings of letters rather than within a string)

Instructions:
Pretend that you are a spy. You want to send the message on top in a secret code that only your friends will understand. Someone has begun coding the message for you on the second line. Try to figure out the secret code and finish coding the message by filling in the blanks with the letters that follow the code.

                S I X S HI P S GONE
                T HY R I HQR _ _ _ _   (H N O D)

---

[a] The letters themselves in the pattern notations refer to the alphabetic relations (i.e., *N* = next, *I* = identity, *B* = backward next). The number of letters in each pattern notation equals the period.

the period remains two, and the relations are backward next followed by identity, or *BI*.

All children learned to solve two types of problems originally, *NN* and *NINI* (see Box 5.1). Note that these involve only two of the three possible relations and two of the three periodicities. Having learned to deal with these problems, the children were then asked to solve three types of transfer problems, differing in terms of the number of transformations made on the original learning problems. *Maintenance* items were simply new exemplars of the *NN* and *NINI* problem types. *Near transfer* items involved the same relations and periods but in novel combinations (e.g., *NI*), and *far transfer* problems included either a new relation (backward next, e.g., *BN*) or a new period (three, e.g., *NIN*).

Above-average children learned more quickly than average-ability children, but here we are more concerned with their transfer performance. On maintenance items, performance was virtually perfect (no help was needed), and the groups did not differ. A similar result was obtained on near transfer. However, on far (and very far) transfer items, large group differences emerged. Even though both groups learned the original principles (relations and periods) to the same criterion, the above-average students transferred more broadly. As the number of differences between the learning and transfer problems increased, so did group differences.

In the study by Campione et al., retarded and nonretarded children were examined. The task was a variant of the Raven Progressive Matrices; it consisted of 3 × 3 matrices of geometric figures following certain transformational patterns across rows or columns. Examples are shown in Figure 5.1. The testee's job is to figure out how the missing figure in the lower-right corner should look.

Initially, the children learned each of the three rules shown in Figure 5.1. The top problem is a rotation problem. In such problems, the leftmost figure in each row is rotated 90° to the right to obtain the figure in the center, and that figure is then rotated another 90° to the right to obtain the rightmost figure. The middle problem in Figure 5.1 is an imposition problem, and the lower problem a subtraction problem. All children learned the rotation problems to a criterion of two consecutive problems with no help from the experimenter; they then learned the imposition problems to the same criterion; and finally the subtraction problems. In subsequent sessions, maintenance and transfer were again assessed. Transfer matrices involved a *combination* of two of the rules learned originally. For example, one such problem would involve rotating the leftmost figure in each row 90° to the right *and* superimposing it on the one in the middle column to generate the rightmost column.

Although in this test the retarded and nonretarded children learned the original problem types equally readily (they needed about the same number of hints), large differences were obtained on transfer. On maintenance items, the nonretarded children performed extremely efficiently, as in the Ferrara et al. study; they needed no help to deal with new examples of the problem types with which they were familiar. The retarded children, however, made errors and needed significantly more help even on the maintenance items. They also needed significantly more help to solve the transfer problems. Hall and Day (1982) have obtained similar results with retarded and nonretarded children using balance-beam problems. The same pattern has also been replicated with samples of children as young as four years old faced with simple versions of the series completion and matrices problems (Bryant, 1982; Bryant et al., 1983) and with the elderly (French, 1979).

These experiments, then, show clear ability-related differences in transfer performance, confirming the impression garnered from the instructional work mentioned in the previous section. The higher the overall ability of the learner, the greater the flexibility shown in the use of the rules acquired in the initial phase of the experiments; higher-ability students do transfer more broadly. Note also that the lower the ability level, the smaller is the change from learning to transfer situations required to bring about some disruption of performance. For example, retarded children began to experience problems on maintenance

Figure 5.1

Examples of the matrices problems employed. The top problem is an example of rotation, the middle one of imposition, and the bottom one of subtraction.

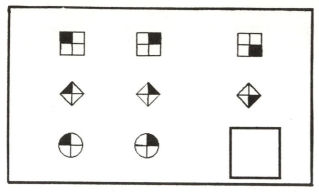

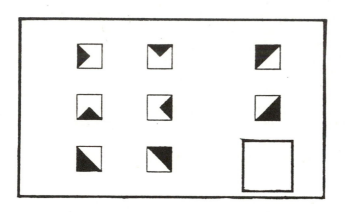

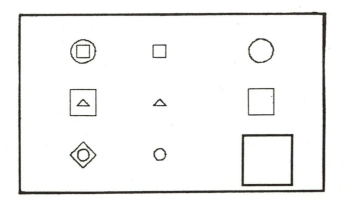

sessions, where they had only to deal with novel examples of familiar items presented in a random order, whereas children of average and above-average ability had no trouble with this modification. For them disruption is not apparent until new problem types are introduced.

Summary and Conclusions

Sizable individual differences in the learning, retention, and transfer of information have been found and related to intellectual variations. The picture is not as simple as had originally been thought, however, since no single, unitary learning or memory faculty of great generality has been revealed. Rather, both learning and memory are complex processes incorporating a wide array of subprocesses, together with procedures for overseeing those subprocesses.

In the areas of both learning and memory, it is now possible to specify where individual differences are or are not likely to be found, and these contrasting cases tell us a great deal about more general sources of individual differences. For example, in the domain of remembering, large individual differences are obtained whenever some form of strategic intervention is required. In strategy-free tasks, such as simple recognition and judgments of recency or frequency, there is little evidence for person-to-person variation. If those tasks are modified to enable or require the use of mnemonic procedures, differences begin to be obtained. And in the more strategy-intensive situations, differences between younger and older, or mildly retarded and nonretarded, children become quite large.

Turning to the learning research, we find several factors that make individual differences more likely to be found. First, the range of subject abilities sampled needs to be wide. Second, individual differences are likely to appear if the tasks involve some degree of cognitive complexity. Finally, modifying the type of learning environment by making the feedback system more akin to that found in school-like settings also increases the likelihood that an ability-learning relation will emerge (Campione and Brown, in press; Cronbach, 1967; Snow and Yalow, 1982).

Individual differences in transfer propensity have also been documented. Even when children of different ability learn rules, principles, or information to the same criterion, the higher-ability students appear much better able to use that information flexibly and to apply it to novel situations. Evidence for this claim has increased recently, mainly because the problems that psychologists have investigated have changed since the 1950s. In the early studies, such as those by Woodrow, it was difficult for subjects to show transfer. Similarly, in the late 1950s to late 1960s, learning was studied mainly in situations where the experimenters arbitrarily designated the correct solutions. Subjects were required to learn arbitrary responses to arbitrary stimuli, and there were no clear ways for them to understand why their "solutions" were correct. There were no principled systems involved. In contrast, in the more recent research involving memory strategies, there is usually a comprehensible reason why rehearsal processes should be used on a specific short-term memory task, and why elaborative approaches are appropriate on another. Subjects who understand these relations can apply that understanding to new problems. Similarly, in the inductive reasoning tasks we reviewed, subjects learn a variety of rules and principles that can be recombined or modified to deal with systematic variations in the nature of the problems presented for solution. Within such systems, higher-ability students transfer more readily and more broadly than those of lower ability.

What could be the underlying reason for these individual differences? Much of the currently available information seems to point to the executive processes of the modal information-processing model sketched earlier. These "executive routines" are charged with overseeing and coordinating the resources (information, strategies, etc.) available to the system. It is by means of such executive processes that learners do the planning, checking, monitoring, sequencing, etc., necessary for adequate performance. Older and brighter children are more likely to carry out these activities efficiently than are lower-ability students. Essentially, higher-ability children profit more from objectively identical learning situations. They profit from incomplete instruction, because they have come to know more about learning itself, and *supplement for themselves* the information afforded. They show better signs of planning; they apportion their efforts appropriately; they monitor their own learning progress; they know how and when to seek advice; etc. (For reviews of this rapidly expanding literature, see Brown, 1978; Brown et al., 1983; Campione et al., 1982; Sternberg and Powell, 1983).

More capable students also prepare for transfer and engage in sophisticated reasoning aimed at accessing and using current knowledge. They prepare for transfer, for example, by regarding "new" problems not as isolated ones, but as instances of a general class (e.g., Scribner and Cole, 1973); they expect what they learn to be relevant elsewhere, and entertain hypotheses about where and when. Simply knowing that transfer is desirable from prior situations to the current one, or from the current one to future ones, is itself part of the battle. Good learners perform thought experiments, seek appropriate analogies, and understand some of the principles involved in learning and reasoning from incomplete knowledge (e.g., Collins et al., 1975). In sum, they supplement incoming information in a number of clever ways to facilitate their own learning, and their understanding of what they are learning. Instruction may be incomplete, but they have the skills to complete it for themselves. We believe the skills involved in such endeavors underlie many of the differences we have described in this chapter.

References

Atkinson, R. C., and R. M. Shiffrin. 1968. Human memory: A proposed system and its control processes. *In* K. W. Spence and J. T. Spence, eds., *The Psychology of Learning and Motivation* (New York: Academic Press).

Belmont, J. M., and E. C. Butterfield. 1969. The relation of short-term memory to development and intelligence. *In* L. P. Lipsitt and H. W. Reese, eds., *Advances in Child Development and Behavior, Vol. 4* (New York: Academic Press).

———. 1971. Learning strategies as determinants of memory performance. *Cognitive Psychology, 2,* 411–420.

Belmont, J. M., E. C. Butterfield, and R. P. Ferretti. 1982. To secure transfer of training, instruct self-management skills. *In* D. K. Detterman and R. J. Sternberg, eds., *How and How Much Can Intelligence Be Increased?* (Norwood, N.J.: Ablex).

Belmont, J. M., R. P. Ferretti, and D. W. Mitchell. 1981. *Memorizing: A test of untrained retarded children's problem solving.* Unpublished manuscript, Univ. of Kansas Medical Center.

Borkowski, J. G., and J. G. Cavanaugh. 1979. Maintenance and generalization of skills and strategies by the retarded. *In* N. R. Ellis, ed., *Handbook of Mental Deficiency: Psychological Theory and Research* (Hillsdale, N.J.: Erlbaum).

Borkowski, J. G., and P. B. Wanschura. 1974. Mediational processes in the retarded. *In* N. R. Ellis, ed., *International Review of Research in Mental Retardation, Vol. 7* (New York: Academic Press).

Bower, G. H., M. C. Clark, A. M. Lesgold, and D. Winzenz. 1969. Hierarchical retrieval schemes in recall of categorized word lists. *Journal of Verbal Learning and Verbal Behavior, 8,* 323–343.

Bray, N. W. 1973. Controlled forgetting in the retarded. *Cognitive Psychology, 5,* 233–248.

Brown, A. L. 1972. A rehearsal deficit in retardates' continuous short-term memory: Keeping track of variables that have few or many states. *Psychonomic Science, 29,* 373–376.

———. 1973a. Judgments of recency for long sequences of pictures: The absence of a developmental trend. *Journal of Experimental Child Psychology, 15,* 473–480.

———. 1973b. Mnemonic elaboration and recency judgments in children. *Cognitive Psychology, 5,* 233–248.

———. 1973c. Temporal and contextual cues as discriminative attributes in retardates' recognition memory. *Journal of Experimental Psychology, 98,* 1–13.

———. 1974. The role of strategic behavior in retardate memory. *In* N. R. Ellis, ed., *International Review of Research in Mental Retardation, Vol. 7* (New York: Academic Press).

———. 1975. The development of memory: Knowing, knowing about knowing, and knowing how to know. *In* H. W. Reese, ed., *Advances in Child Development and Behavior, Vol. 10* (New York: Academic Press).

———. 1978. Knowing when, where, and how to remember: A problem of metacognition. *In* R. Glaser, ed., *Advances in Instructional Psychology, Vol. 1* (Hillsdale, N.J.: Erlbaum).

Brown, A. L., J. D. Bransford, R. A. Ferrara, and J. C. Campione. 1983. Learning, remembering, and understanding. *In* J. H. Flavell and E. M. Markman, eds., *Handbook of Child Psychology, Vol. 1* (New York: Wiley).

Brown, A. L., and J. C. Campione. 1978. Permissible inferences from cognitive training studies in developmental research. *Quarterly Newsletter of the Institute for Comparative Human Behavior, 2,* 46–53.

———. 1981. Inducing flexible thinking: A problem of access. *In* M. Friedman, J. P. Das, and N. O'Connor, eds., *Intelligence and Learning* (New York: Plenum).

Brown, A. L., J. C. Campione, N. W. Bray, and B. L. Wilcox. 1973. Keeping track of changing variables: Effects of rehearsal training and rehearsal prevention in normal and retarded adolescents. *Journal of Experimental Psychology, 101,* 123–131.

Brown, A. L., J. C. Campione, and D. M. Gilliard. 1974. Recency judgments in children: A production deficiency in the use of redundant background cues. *Developmental Psychology, 10,* 303.

Brown, A. L., and M. S. Scott. 1971. Recognition memory for pictures in preschool children. *Journal of Experimental Child Psychology,* 11, 401–412.

Bryant, N. R. 1982. *Preschool children's learning and transfer of matrices problems: A study of proximal development.* Unpublished Master's thesis, Univ. of Illinois.

Bryant, N. R., A. L. Brown, and J. C. Campione. 1983. Preschool children's learning and transfer of matrices problems: Potential for improvement. Paper presented at the Society for Research in Child Development meetings, Detroit, April, 1983.

Buckingham, B. R. 1921. Intelligence and its measurement: A symposium. *Journal of Educational Psychology,* 12, 271–275.

Butterfield, E. C., C. Wambold, and J. M. Belmont. 1973. On the theory and practice of improving short-term memory. *American Journal of Mental Deficiency,* 77, 654–669.

Campione, J. C., and A. L. Brown, 1977. Memory and metamemory development in educable retarded children. *In* R. V. Kail, Jr., and J. W. Hagen, eds., *Perspectives on the Development of Memory and Cognition* (Hillsdale, N.J.: Erlbaum).

———. 1978. Toward a theory of intelligence: Contributions from research with retarded children. *Intelligence,* 2, 279–304.

———. In press. Learning ability and transfer propensity as sources of individual differences in intelligence. *In* P. H. Brooks, C. McCauley, and R. Sperber, eds., *Learning and Cognition in the Mentally Retarded* (Hillsdale, N.J.: Erlbaum).

Campione, J. C., A. L. Brown, and R. A. Ferrara. 1982. Mental retardation and intelligence. *In* R. J. Sternberg, ed., *Handbook of Human Intelligence* (Cambridge: Cambridge Univ. Press).

Campione, J. C., A. L. Brown, R. A. Ferrara, R. S. Jones, and E. Steinberg. 1983. *Differences between Retarded and Nonretarded Children in Transfer Following Equivalent Learning Performance.* Manuscript submitted for publication.

Carrol, R. P. 1928. What is intelligence? *School and Society,* 28, 792.

Collins, A., E. Warnock, N. Aiello, and M. Miller. 1975. Reasoning from incomplete knowledge. *In* D. G. Bobrow and A. Collins, eds., *Representation and Understanding: Studies in Cognitive Science* (New York: Academic Press).

Cronbach, L. J. 1967. How can instruction be adapted to individual differences? *In* R. M. Gagne, ed., *Learning and Individual Differences* (Columbus, Ohio: Merrill).

Dearborn, W. G. 1921. Intelligence and its measurement: A symposium. *Journal of Educational Psychology,* 12, 210–212.

Dirks, J., and U. Neisser. 1977. Memory for objects in real scenes: The development of recognition and recall. *Journal of Experimental Child Psychology,* 23, 315–328.

Ellis, N. R. 1970. Memory processes in retardates and normals. *In* N. R. Ellis, ed., *International Review of Research in Mental Retardation, Vol. 4* (New York: Academic Press).

Ellis, R. S. 1929. *The Psychology of Individual Differences.* New York: Longmans, Green.

Estes, W. K. 1982. Learning, memory, and intelligence. *In* R.J. Sternberg, ed., *Handbook of Human Intelligence* (Cambridge: Cambridge Univ. Press).

Ferrara, R. A. 1982. *Children's learning and transfer of inductive reasoning rules: A study of proximal development.* Unpublished Master's thesis, Univ. of Illinois.

Ferrara, R. A., A. L. Brown, and J. C. Campione. 1981. Children's learning and transfer of inductive reasoning rules: A study of proximal development. Paper presented at the Society for Research in Child Development meetings, Boston, April 1981.

Feuerstein, R. 1980. *Instrumental Enrichment: An Intervention Program for Cognitive Modifiability.* Baltimore: Univ. Park Press.

Flavell, J. H. 1970. Developmental studies of mediated memory. In H. W. Reese and L. P. Lipsitt, eds., *Advances in Child Development and Behavior, Vol. 5* (New York: Academic Press).

French, L. A. 1979. *Cognitive consequences of education: Transfer of training in the elderly.* Unpublished Ph.D. thesis, Univ. of Illinois.

Gagne, R. M., ed., 1967. *Learning and Individual Differences.* Columbus, Ohio: Merrill.

Gick, M. L., and K. J. Holyoak. 1980. Analogical problem solving. *Cognitive Psychology*, 12, 306–355.

———. 1983. Schema induction and analogical transfer. *Cognitive Psychology*, 15, 1–38.

Goodman, M. A. 1976. *Directed forgetting strategies in mentally retarded adolescents.* Unpublished M. A. thesis, Univ. of Cincinatti.

Hall, K. L., and J. D. Day. 1982. A comparison of the zone of proximal development in learning disabled, mentally retarded, and normal children. Paper presented at the American Educational Research Association meetings, New York, March 1982.

Harlow, H. F. 1959. Learning set and error factor theory. In S. Koch, ed., *Psychology: A Study of a Science, Vol. 2* (New York: McGraw-Hill).

Harter, S. 1965. Discrimination learning set in children as a function of IQ and MA. *Journal of Experimental Child Psychology*, 2, 31–43.

———. 1967. Mental age, IQ, and motivational factors in the discrimination learning set performance of normal and retarded children. *Journal of Experimental Child Psychology*, 5, 123–141.

Hasher, L., and R. T. Zacks. 1979. Automatic and effortful processes in memory. *Journal of Experimental Psychology: General*, 108, 356–388.

Hayes, J. R., and H. A. Simon. 1977. Psychological differences among problem isomorphs. In N. J. Castellan, Jr., D. P. Pisoni, and G. R. Potts, eds., *Cognitive Theory, Vol. 2* (Hillsdale, N.J.: Erlbaum).

Humphreys, L. G. 1979. The construct of general intelligence. *Intelligence*, 3, 105–120.

Hyatt, T. 1976. *Directed forgetting in retarded and normal adolescents: The effect of pretraining information.* Unpublished M. A. thesis, Univ. of Cincinatti.

Jensen, A. R., and W. D. Rohwer, Jr. 1963. The effects of verbal mediation on the learning and retention of paired associates by retarded adults. *American Journal of Mental Deficiency*, 68, 80–84.

Kail, R. V., Jr., and J. W. Hagen, eds. 1977. *Perspectives on the Development of Memory and Cognition.* Hillsdale, N.J.: Erlbaum.

Mandler, J. M., and J. D. Day. 1975. Memory for orientation of forms as a function of their meaningfulness and complexity. *Journal of Experimental Child Psychology*, 20, 430–443.

Mandler, J. M., and C. A. Robinson. 1978. Developmental changes in picture recognition. *Journal of Experimental Child Psychology*, 26, 122–136.

Martin, A. L. 1970. *The effect of the novelty-familiarity dimension on discrimination learning by mental retardates.* Unpublished Ph.D. thesis, Univ. of Connecticut.

Nickerson, R. S. 1965. Short-term memory for complex meaningful visual configurations: A demonstration of capacity. *Canadian Journal of Psychology*, 19, 155–160.

Ornstein, P. A., and M. J. Naus. 1978. Rehearsal processes in children's memory. In P. A. Ornstein, ed., *Memory Development in Children* (Hillsdale, N.J.: Erlbaum).

Perlmutter, M., and N. A. Myers. 1979. Development of recall in 2- to 4-year-old children. *Developmental Psychology*, 15, 73–83.

Peterson, S. 1925. *Early Conceptions and Tests of Intelligence.* Yonkers, N.Y.: World Book.

Reed, S. K., G. W. Ernst, and R. Banerji. 1974. The role of analogy in transfer between similar problem states. *Cognitive Psychology,* 5, 436–450.

Resnick, L. B., and R. Glaser. 1976. Problem solving and intelligence. *In* L. B. Resnick, ed., *The Nature of Intelligence* (Hillsdale, N.J.: Erlbaum).

Rohwer, W. D., Jr. 1973. Elaboration and learning in childhood and adolescence. *In* H. W. Reese, ed., *Advances in Child Development and Behavior, Vol. 8* (New York: Academic Press).

Scribner, S., and M. Cole. 1973. Cognitive consequences of formal and informal education. *Science,* 182, 553–559.

Snow, R. E., and E. Yalow. 1982. Education and intelligence. *In* R. J. Sternberg, ed., *Handbook of Human Intelligence* (Cambridge: Cambridge Univ. Press).

Spitz, H. H. 1963. The role of input organization in the learning and memory of mental retardates. *In* N. R. Ellis, ed., *International Review of Research in Mental Retardation, Vol. 2* (New York: Academic Press).

Standing, L., J. Conezio, and R. N. Haber. 1970. Perception and memory for pictures: Single trial learning of 2500 visual stimuli. *Psychonomic Science,* 19, 73–74.

Sternberg, R. J., and J. S. Powell. 1983. The development of intelligence. *In* J. H. Flavell and E. M. Markman, eds., *Carmichael's Manual of Child Psychology, Vol. 1* (New York: Wiley).

Thorndike, E. L. 1926. *Measurement of Intelligence.* New York: Teacher's College Press.

Turnure, J. E., N. Buium, and M. L. Thurlow. 1976. The effectiveness of interrogatives for prompting verbal elaboration productivity in young children. *Child Development,* 47, 851–855.

Vygotsky, L. S. 1978. *Mind in society: The Development of Higher Psychological Processes.* Cambridge, Mass.: Harvard Univ. Press.

Woodrow, H. 1917a. Practice and transference in normal and feeble-minded children, 1: Practice. *Journal of Educational Psychology,* 8, 85–96.

———. 1917b. Practice and transference in normal and feeble-minded children, 2: Transference. *Journal of Educational Psychology,* 8, 151–165.

———. 1938a. The relation between abilities and improvement with practice. *Journal of Educational Psychology,* 29, 215–230.

———. 1938b. The effect of practice on groups of different initial ability. *Journal of Educational Psychology,* 29, 268–278.

———. 1946. The ability to learn. *Psychological Review,* 53, 147–158.

Zeaman, D. 1978. Some relations of intelligence and selective attention. *Intelligence,* 2, 55–73.

Zeaman, D., and B. J. House. 1963. The role of attention in retardate discrimination learning. *In* N. R. Ellis, ed., *Handbook of Mental Deficiency* (New York: McGraw-Hill).

———. 1967. The relation of IQ and learning. *In* R. M. Gagne, ed., *Learning and Individual Differences* (Columbus, Ohio: Merrill).

6

MATHEMATICAL ABILITY

Richard E. Mayer
University of California at Santa Barbara

When confronted with a mathematics problem, some people are able to generate a correct answer, but others are not. For example, consider the following problem, which was given to 70,000 school students as a part of the recent National Assessment of Educational Progress (Carpenter et al., 1980).

> Lemonade costs 95¢ for one 56-ounce bottle. At the school fair, Bob sold cups holding 8 ounces for 20¢ each. How much money did the school make on each bottle?

For this problem, only 11 percent of the 13-year-olds and 29 percent of the 17-year-olds were able to find the correct answer.

Why can some students solve math problems such as the lemonade problem, whereas others cannot? In spite of years of training, why do some people greet mathematics problems with fear and moans and incorrect answers? What do good problem solvers possess that poor problem solvers do not possess?

In short, "What is mathematical ability?" This is the motivating question for this chapter.

Resnick and Ford (1981, p. 3) have provided a rationale for the study of mathematical ability as follows.

> As psychologists concerned specifically with mathematics, our goal is to ask the same questions that experimental and developmental psychologists ask about learning, thinking, and intelligence but to focus these questions [on] a particular subject matter . . . instead of asking ourselves the general question, "How is it that people think?", we ask ourselves, "How do people think about mathematics?" Instead of asking, "How do people's thought processes develop?" we ask, "How does understanding of mathematical concepts develop?" We want to know what mixture of experience and intellect makes this thing called *mathematical ability* happen.

The reasons for studying mathematical ability are both practical and theoretical. On the practical side, studying a subject matter area such as mathematics has direct implications for classroom instruction. On the theoretical side, an understanding of problem solving in a specific domain has implications for issues of human cognition in general.

Two Approaches to Mathematical Ability

In order to find out "What is this thing called mathematical ability?" let's examine some typical problems found on tests of mathematical ability. For example, consider the problems in Box 6.1. Go ahead and answer each problem.

These problems are taken from the mathematics portion of the California Assessment Program (1980), a test given to all third, sixth, and twelfth graders in California public schools. The percentage of correct responses for each problem was 51, 63, 33, 53, 68, and 56. In spite of years of training in mathematics, therefore, many students cannot generate correct answers to basic problems. The development of mathematical ability—a central goal of our schools—seems to be a goal that is not being met. In order to meet it, we need a clearer understanding of the nature of mathematical ability.

There are two basic approaches to the mathematical-ability problem: the psychometric approach and the information-processing approach. The psychometric (or testing) approach defines mathematical ability as "what a math test measures." Thus, mathematical ability is the ability to perform well on tests such as those shown in Box 6.1. However, the psychometric definition is circular. It provides an excellent means for measuring mathematical ability, but it fails to provide an independent description of what is being measured.

In contrast, the information-processing approach is based on task analysis. Any type of mathematics problem can be broken down into information-processing components, i.e., into simple mental operations, skills, and knowledge that are required for problem solution (Sternberg, 1977). Mathematical ability is defined as all the cognitive operations, skills, and knowledge that are components of mathematics tasks. Thus, the information-processing approach

Box 6.1
Some mathematics problems[a]

Grade 3

1. Ron had 7 peanuts. Sue had 2 times as many peanuts as did Ron. How many peanuts did Sue have?
   a. 11
   b. 16
   c. 14
   d. 9

2. There are two rows of children. Each row had 34 children. How many children were there?
   a. 342
   b. 68
   c. 36
   d. 32

Grade 6

3. John has 12 baseball cards. He gives one-third of them to Jim. How many does John have left?
   a. 4
   b. 6
   c. 8
   d. 9

4. Mrs. Jones has $158.62. She makes purchases of $5.25, $49.88, and $10.35. She earns $51.64. How much does she have now?
   a. $172.46
   b. $144.78
   c. $41.50
   d. $13.84

Grade 12

5. An astronaut requires 2.2 pounds of oxygen per day while in space. How many pounds of oxygen are needed for a team of 3 astronauts for 5 days in space?
   a. 13.2
   b. 15.2
   c. 33
   d. 330

6. Three of four students each weighs 60 pounds. What is the weight of the fourth student if the average of weights of all four is 70 pounds?
   a. 100 pounds
   b. 80 pounds
   c. 70 pounds
   d. 65 pounds

[a]From California Assessment Program (1980). Correct answers are: 1, c; 2, b; 3, c; 4, b; 5, c; 6, a.

to the problem of defining math ability overcomes some of the difficulties of the psychometric approach.

An Information-Processing Analysis of Mathematical Ability

As an example of the information-processing approach, let's consider the cognitive processes and knowledge required to solve simple word or story problems. For example, the following problem is typical of word problems found in the elementary grades of school. "John has a nickel. Pete has three more cents than John. How many cents does Pete have?" The information-processing approach asks, "What mental operations and knowledge are needed to solve this problem?"

Mathematical problem solving can be broken down into two major parts (Bobrow, 1968; Hayes, 1981; Mayer, 1983; Wickelgren, 1974): *problem representation,* converting a problem from words into an internal representation; and *problem solution,* applying the legal operators of mathematics to the internal representation in order to arrive at a final answer. For example, representation of the "How many cents?" problem involves translating each sentence from English into some other form, such as an equation, and integrating relevant information into a coherent representation of the problem. Box 6.2 shows that the first two steps are problem translation and problem integration. Solution of the problem involves development and monitoring of a solution plan as well as execution of the solution plan. Box 6.2 refers to these steps as solution planning and solution execution, respectively.

Box 6.2
Steps in mathematical problem solving

Sample problem: John has a nickel. Pete has 3 more cents than John. How many cents does Pete have?

Step	*Examples from sample problem*
Problem representation	
Translation	$J = 5$ $P = 3 + J$
	Pete
Integration	xxxxx xxx $P = 5 + 3$
	John 3 more
Problem solution	
Planning	Start with 5, count-on 3 more.
Execution	"6-7-8" "Pete has 8¢"

Box 6.2 summarizes four steps that are involved in solving problems like the cents problem. What is required to be able to succeed at each step? A careful analysis of this task reveals that each step requires the problem solver to have certain domain-specific knowledge. Box 6.3 shows some of the types of knowledge that may be relevant for representing and solving problems.

1. *Linguistic knowledge* refers to knowledge about the English language, such as how to parse a sentence into parts of speech, or what various words mean.
2. *Factual knowledge* refers to knowledge about the world, such as units of measure.
3. *Schema knowledge* refers to knowledge of problem types, such as the difference between work problems and motion problems.
4. *Strategic knowledge* refers to knowledge of how to develop and monitor a solution plan.
5. *Algorithmic knowledge* refers to a procedure for carrying out a planned operation, such as how to compute in long division.

As shown in Box 6.3, linguistic and factual knowledge are needed in problem translation; schema knowledge is needed in problem integration; strategic knowledge is needed in solution planning; algorithmic knowledge is needed in solution execution.

Mathematical ability for solving word or story problems may be analyzed in terms of the knowledge that a problem solver brings to a mathematical task. For our purposes here, mathematical ability refers to the specific knowledge that

---

Box 6.3
Types of knowledge required for four steps in problem solving

Sample problem: John has a nickel. Pete has 3 more cents than John. How many cents does Pete have?

Step	Knowledge	Examples from sample problem
Problem representation		
Translation	Linguistic	"Pete has 3 more cents than John" means "P = J + 3"
	Factual	A nickel equals 5 cents.
Integration	Schema	This is a "comparison" problem, consisting of two subsets and a superset.
Problem solution		
Planning	Strategic	The goal is to add 3 plus 5.
Execution	Algorithmic	Counting-on procedure.

is required to successfully accomplish each of the four major steps in problem solving. The remainder of this chapter explores what is needed for each of the four steps.

Problem Translation

The first step in representing a problem is to be able to translate each proposition from the problem into an internal representation. In order to translate each proposition in a story or word problem, a problem solver needs some knowledge of language (linguistic knowledge) and some knowledge about the world (factual knowledge). For example, to translate a statement such as, "John has two more dimes than Pete," linguistic knowledge is required to parse the sentence into variables (i.e., John, Pete) and a quantitative relation between them (i.e., two more dimes than); in addition, factual knowledge is required to represent "two dimes" as "20¢." People may differ in their ability to correctly translate problem statements, and these differences may be related to linguistic and factual knowledge.

As an example, let's consider the role of linguistic knowledge in comprehending relational propositions, i.e., propositions which express a quantitative relation between variables. There is ample evidence that students have difficulty in representing relational propositions. In an analysis of factors affecting problem difficulty, for example, Loftus and Suppes (1972) found that the hardest problem in their set was one that contained relational propositions: "Mary is twice as old as Betty was two years ago. Mary is 40 years old. How old is Betty?"

Recent work by Riley et al. (1982) and Greeno (1980) also suggests that children may have difficulty in representing relational propositions. For example, children in primary grades were asked to listen to and immediately repeat problems involving relational propositions, such as: "Joe has three marbles. Tom has five more marbles than Joe. How many marbles does Tom have?" The children tended to make errors in repeating the relation, such as saying, "Joe has three marbles. Tom has five marbles. How many marbles does Tom have?"

Soloway et al. (1982) asked college students to write equations to represent a proposition such as, "There are six times as many students as professors at this university." Approximately one-third of the students produced a wrong equation, such as $6S = P$. Box 6.4 shows how two different students approached the problem. As can be seen, the student who uses a static approach assumes that P stands for "a professor," S stands for "the students for that professor," and = stands for a static association between S and P. In contrast, the student who uses a procedural approach assumes that P stands for "the number of professors," S stands for "the number of students," and the equal sign stands for an active operation that is performed on one number (P) in order to obtain another number (S). Apparently, errors in translation of relational propositions into equations may occur when students view them as static pictures of relations between two variables rather than as a procedural instruction about how to convert one number into another.

In order to test this idea, Soloway et al. (1982) gave the following problem to college students: "At the last company cocktail party, for every six people who

Box 6.4
Two approaches to the students and professors problem[a]

Problem: "There are six times as many students as professors at this university."
Static translation

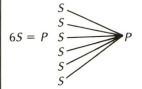

$6S = P$

"There's six times as many students, which means it's six students to one professor and this (points to $6S$) is six times as many students as there are professors (points to P)."

Procedural translation

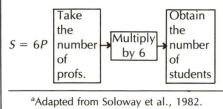

$S = 6P$

"If you want to even out the number of professors, you'd have to have six times as many professors."

[a]Adapted from Soloway et al., 1982.

drank hard liquor, there were eleven people who drank beer." Some students were asked to translate this statement into an equation; the error rate was 55 percent. Other students were asked to translate this statement into a BASIC program; the error rate was cut nearly in half, to 31 percent. Whereas algebraic notation may be ambiguous, it seems that the procedural language of computer programming allows more accurate translations of relational statements.

In a recent series of experiments, Mayer (1982) asked college students to read and recall eight algebra story problems. For example, one problem was as follows.

> A river steamer travels 36 miles downstream in the same time that it travels 24 miles upstream. The steamer's engines drive in still water at a rate of 12 miles per hour more than the rate of the current. Find the rate of the current.

The problems contained three types of propositions: *assignments,* which assigned a value to a variable such as, "The cost of the candy is $1.70 per pound;" *relations,* which expressed a quantitative relation between two variables, such as, "The rate in still water is 12 mph more than the rate of the current;" and *questions,* which asked for a numerical value of a variable, such as, "How much time will it take to empty the tanks?" The results indicated that students made approximately three times as many errors in recalling relational propositions (29 percent errors) than in recalling assignment propositions (9 percent errors). This result is consistent with the idea that students do not know how to represent relational propositions in memory.

Subsequent analyses revealed that three types of errors were made in recalling propositions: *omission errors,* in which the proposition was not recalled at all; *specification errors,* in which a variable in the original proposition was

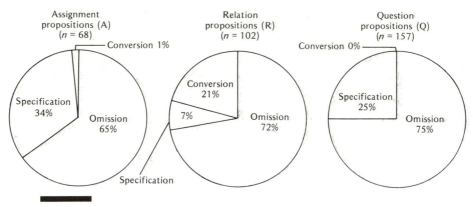

Figure 6.1
Conversion errors occur often for relational propositions but not for assignments. (From Mayer, 1982a.)

changed to a different variable in recall, such as changing "a river steamer travels 36 miles downstream" into "a boat travels 36 mph downstream;" and *conversion errors,* in which the form of the proposition was changed from a relation to an assignment or vice versa, such as changing "the steamer's engines drive in still water at 12 mph more than the rate of the current" into "the speed of the boat in still water is 12 mph." Figure 6.1 shows that many of the relation propositions were converted wrongly, but almost none of the assignments were; of 21 cases of conversion, 20 involved changing a relation into an assignment, and one involved changing an assignment into a relation. These results support the idea that some students may lack appropriate linguistic knowledge for representing relations, and that use of an assignment representation is a default for some relational propositions.

The foregoing review suggests that problem translation (the first component in problem representation) requires specific knowledge of language and facts. In particular, comprehension of relational propositions is required for success in translating some mathematical problems.

Several researchers have shown that children's linguistic knowledge about translation of relational propositions increases with age. For example, Riley et al. (1982) and Greeno (1980) asked children to use wooden blocks to represent such statements as "Joe has five more marbles than Pete." The incidence of correct translations increased from grades K to 3. Similarly, Trabasso and his colleagues (Trabasso, 1977) found that correct encoding of relational facts, such as "The red stick is longer than the blue stick," increases from age 6 to adult. Furthermore, changes in performance in transitive inference tasks involving relational premises depended on children's correct encoding (and memory) of the premises rather than logical reasoning per se.

Problem Integration

The next component in mathematical problem solving is to put the propositions of a story problem together into a coherent representation. In order to integrate or understand the problem, a problem solver needs to have some knowledge of problem types (schema knowledge). For example, the problem solver may note that the cents problem in Boxes 6.2 and 6.3 is a "comparison problem," in which two sets are compared to one another. People may differ in their ability to correctly integrate problems, and these differences may be related to schematic knowledge.

Building an internal representation of a problem requires more than a sentence-by-sentence translation. For example, Paige and Simon (1966) presented impossible problems, such as the following:

> The number of quarters a man has is seven times the number of dimes he has. The value of the dimes exceeds the value of the quarters by two dollars and fifty cents. How many has he of each coin?

Using factual and linguistic knowledge, a person could translate this problem into equations as

$$Q = 7D$$
$$D(.10) = 2.50 + Q(.25)$$

However, a student who tries to relate this problem to past experience with similar problems can recognize that the propositions are self-contradictory: if the man has more quarters than dimes, the dimes cannot be worth more than the quarters. Thus problem representation requires integration as well as translation.

More evidence about how people understand story problems comes from the work of Hinsley et al. (1977). Subjects were given a series of algebra problems from standard textbooks and were asked to arrange them into categories. Subjects were quite able to perform this task with high agreement, yielding 18 different categories: triangle, distance-rate-time, averages, scale conversion, ratio, interest, area, max-min, mixture, river current, probability, number, work, navigation, progressions-1, progressions-2, physics, and exponentials.

Hinsley et al. (1977) also found that subjects were able to categorize problems almost immediately. After hearing the first few words of a problem such as, "A river steamer travels 36 miles downstream . . . ," a student could say, "Hey, that's one of those river current problems." Hayes et al. (1977) and Robinson and Hayes (1978) found that students use their schemas to make accurate judgments about what information is relevant in a problem and what is not. For example, in one study, the following "crop-duster problem" was presented one phrase at a time (Robinson and Hayes, 1978).

> A crop-dusting plane carries 2,000 pounds of Rotenone dusting compound, 250 pounds of high-test fuel, a pilot highly skilled in low-altitude flying, and a duster-machinery operator, the pilot's younger brother. The plane must dust a rectangular tobacco field 0.5 miles wide by 0.6 miles long. The dusting compound must be spread with a density of 200 pounds per 0.001 square mile. Further, the compound must be spread between 6 A.M. and 9 A.M., when there is sufficient light and before the morning dew has evaporated, to assure the adherence of the compound to the plants. The plane can dust a 44-foot-wide strip at one time. The plane flies the length of the field with a 6 m.p.h.

tailwind and back against the same headwind. With the wind, the plane uses fuel at the rate of 80 pounds per hour. The ratio of flying time against the wind to time with the wind is 9:8. The duster operator must try to spread the compound uniformly on the ground despite varying speed. (Question is stated next.)

As each phrase was added to the problem, subjects were asked to judge whether it was necessary for solving the problem (pass one) and then the entire process was repeated (pass two). The results evaluated the proportion of relevancy judgments for four kinds of information: relevant information was judged important on both passes (84 percent on pass 1; 89 percent on pass 2); space and weight information was judged important on pass one (93 percent) but not on pass two (46 percent), since the subject was aware of the question on pass two; and irrelevant information was judged low in importance on both passes (35 and 11 percent, respectively). Apparently subjects can make accurate judgments about the relevance of information in a problem as it is being presented.

When a person uses the wrong schema, many difficulties may arise. For example, consider the "smalltown problem," which is a sort of distance-rate-time problem with irrelevant information about a triangle.

Because of their quiet ways, the inhabitants of Smalltown were especially upset by the terrible New Year's Eve auto accident which claimed the life of one Smalltown resident. The facts were these. Both Smith and Jones were New Year's Eve babies, and each had planned a surprise visit to the other on their mutual birthday. Jones had started out for Smith's house traveling due east on Route 210 just two minutes after Smith had left for Jone's house. Smith was traveling directly south on Route 140. Jones was traveling 30 miles per hour faster than Smith, even though their houses were only five miles apart as the crow flies. Their cars crashed at the right-angle intersection of the two highways. Officer Franklin, who observed the crash, determined that Jones was traveling half again as fast as Smith at the time of the crash. Smith had been driving for just four minutes at the time of the crash. The crash occurred nearer to the house of the dead man than to the house of the survivor. What was the name of the dead man?

When Hinsley et al. (1977) gave this problem to subjects, half of the subjects interpreted it as a "distance-rate-time problem," and half interpreted it as a "triangle problem." For example, subjects who attended to the irrelevant triangle information drew triangles and tried to determine the lengths of the two legs and the hypotenuse. One subject misread "4 minutes" as "4 miles" and assumed this was the length of one of the legs; another subject assumed that "5 miles apart" referred to the length of the hypotenuse. In contrast, other subjects ignored the triangle information and focused on the DRT aspects of the problem. For example, one subject stated: "It looks like a distance problem. So Jones is going east two minutes after Smith is going west. So it might be an overtake problem." Subjects who interpreted the problem as a DRT problem all initially assumed that one driver was going east and the other one was going west. Hinsley et al. (1977) concluded that subjects use either a triangle schema or a DRT schema as a template in understanding the smalltown problem. These schemas influence what the subject looks for, and even encourage systematic mistakes in interpreting the information.

As a follow-up to the work of Hinsley et al. (1977), Mayer (1981) analyzed the algebra story problems found in standard algebra textbooks used in California public schools. The analysis yielded more than 100 basic types of problems. For example, 12 different types of motion problems were found, such as overtake, closure, round trip, speed change, and opposite direction. Some problem types were quire common (occurring with a frequency of 25 or 30 per 1000 problems), whereas others were rare (occurring with a frequency of less than 4 per 1000).

In a recent study (Mayer, 1982a), students were asked to read and then recall a series of eight algebra story problems. The results indicated that students could recall high-frequency versions of problems more easily than low-frequency versions. Figure 6.2 summarizes the strong relation between probability that a problem would be correctly recalled, and the observed frequency in algebra textbooks for 16 problems used in several experiments. An analysis of errors in recall indicated that, of 21 cases in which a problem was recalled as a different kind of problem, 17 cases involved changing a low-frequency version of a problem into a higher-frequency version, and 4 cases could not be classified. Apparently students possess "schemas" for problem types, and use these schemas to mentally represent the problems. When they lack a schema for a given problem type, representation is more likely to be in error.

The foregoing review suggests that problem understanding (the second component in the problem-solving process) requires specific knowledge of problem types. In particular, people's understanding of word and story problems is influenced by whether they have (and can access) an appropriate problem schema.

Figure 6.2

More common problem types are easier to recall. (From Mayer, 1982a.)

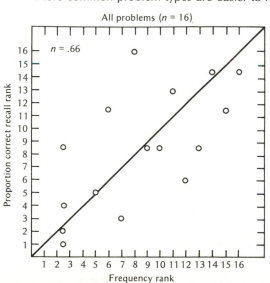

Individual differences in schematic knowledge may be partly related to individual experience with mathematics problems. For example, Greeno and his colleagues (Riley et al., 1982; Greeno, 1980) have identified three types of word problems: *cause/change problems* (such as "Joe has 3 marbles. Tom gives him 5 more marbles. How many marbles does Joe have now?"); *combination problems* (such as "Joe has 3 marbles. Tom has 5 marbles. How many marbles do they have all together?"); and *comparison problems* (such as "Joe has 3 marbles. Tom has 5 more marbles than Joe. How many marbles does Tom have?"). Although all three examples given above require the same computations (3 + 5 = ____), Greeno and his colleagues reported substantial differences in students' performance on different problem types. Children in grades K and 1, who presumably had little experience with word problems, performed well on cause/change problems, but more poorly on some combination and comparison problems. Children in grades 2 and 3 performed better than the younger children on comparison problems. This pattern suggests that children first use a schema for cause/change problems, and try to apply this schema to all problems; with more experience, they develop additional schemas, such as combination and comparison. Errors in comparison problems may therefore occur when people lack the appropriate schema.

Weaver (1982) has distinguished between an "unary operation" view of computation (e.g., 5 + 3 means that you start with five and the operation is "add three"), and a "binary operation" view of computation (e.g., 5 + 3 means "combine three and five"). Box 6.5 gives examples of the two views of computation. As can be seen, the unary view is like Greeno's "cause/change" problem, whereas the binary view is like Greeno's "combine" problems. Fuson (1982) has argued that the unary view tends to be the first to develop in children, even before formal instruction.

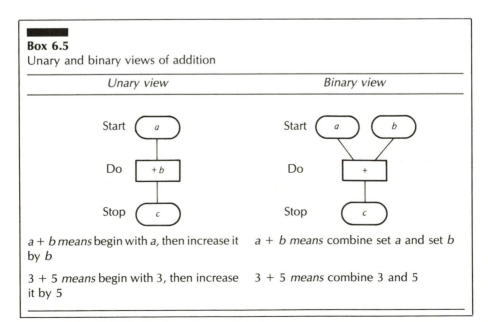

Box 6.5
Unary and binary views of addition

Unary view	*Binary view*

Start   (*a*)   Start   (*a*) (*b*)

Do   [+ *b*]   Do   [+]

Stop   (*c*)   Stop   (*c*)

a + b means begin with *a*, then increase it by *b*   *a + b means* combine set *a* and set *b*

3 + 5 means begin with 3, then increase it by 5   *3 + 5 means* combine 3 and 5

Solution Planning

The next component in mathematical problem solving is to devise a solution plan. In order to devise a plan of attack, a problem solver needs to have some knowledge of problem-solving heuristics (i.e., strategic knowledge). For example, for the cents problem in Box 6.2, the problem solver may decide to use a "counting-on" strategy for computing the answer. People may differ in their ability to correctly devise solution plans, and these differences may be related to strategic knowledge.

Recent experiments by Mayer (1982b, 1978) have suggested that the solution strategy a person uses may depend on how the problem is presented. For example, some subjects were given equations to solve, such as,

$$(8 + 3x)/2 = 3X - 11$$

Other subjects were given the same problem expressed in words:

"Find a number such that, if 8 more than 3 times the number is divided by 2, the result is the same as 11 less than 3 times the number."

By analyzing the pattern of response times for various steps in solving the problems, Mayer (1982b) was able to identify two distinct strategies for solving these problems. The first was the *reduce strategy,* trying to carry out any indicated operations or clearing of parentheses as soon as possible. This strategy was preferred by the subjects who solved problems in word format. Presumably, the word format was so cluttered that subjects needed to reduce the information. Secondly, some used the *isolate strategy,* trying to move all the X's to one side and all the numbers to the other side of the equality. This strategy was preferred by the subjects who solved the problems in equation format. Presumably, the equation format allowed subjects to mentally rearrange the equation. The results indicated that 95 percent of equation-group subjects used the isolate strategy, and 5 percent used the reduce strategy; in contrast, 81 percent of the word-group subjects used the reduce strategy, and 19 percent used the isolate strategy.

In another study (Mayer, 1978), students were asked to learn simultaneous equations, such as,

$$F = 2 \times H$$
$$H = 5 \times R$$
$$R = 4 \times B$$

Other students were asked to learn the same information presented in word format, as follows.

In a certain forest the animals are voting for their leader. The frog gets twice as many votes as the hawk. The hawk gets five times as many votes as the rabbit. The rabbit gets four times as many votes as the bear.

Then, subjects were asked to answer questions concerning the information, such as "Is F greater than R?" (or "Did the frog get more votes than the rabbit?").

A careful analysis of the pattern of errors by type of question revealed again that subjects used two distinct strategies. First, they used the *inference strategy,* trying to solve the equations by substituting one equation into another. For example, for the preceding question, the strategy is to locate the relevant equations, $F = 2 \times H$ and $H = 5 \times R,$ and then to substitute for the common term (H): $F = 2 \times (5 \times R)$, so $F = 10 \times R$; thus F is greater than R. Second, some preferred the *feature strategy,* trying to remember how many times each term was "greater than" or "less than" in the original information. For example, frog wins once and loses zero times, while the hawk wins once and loses once; thus, overall, the frog is greater than the hawk.

The pattern of response times indicated that the inference strategy was used for equation format, whereas the feature strategy was used for word format. Thus, as before, the subjects' choice of strategy is at least partly determined by the presentation format of the problem. This work suggests that people may come to a problem with a variety of potential solution strategies.

Problem-solving strategies for solving algebra story problems are rarely taught explicitly to learners. For example, Simon (1980) has observed that students are drilled on *how* to carry out algebraic operations, such as how to add the same quantity to both sides of an equation, but are rarely taught *when* to carry out the operations. In a recent study, Schoenfeld (1979) attempted to teach five problem-solving strategies to mathematics students. The five strategies were as follows.

1. Draw a diagram if at all possible.
2. If there is an integer parameter, look for an inductive argument.
3. Consider arguing by contradiction or contrapositive.
4. Consider a similar problem with fewer variables.
5. Try to establish subgoals.

In addition, students received practice problems for each of the five strategies. A control group was given the same practice problems, but without any discussion of problem-solving strategies. All subjects were given a pretest and a posttest that involved doing mathematical problems. As expected, there was a great improvement for the trained group (from 20 percent correct on the pretest to 65 percent on the posttest), but no change for the control group (25 percent correct on both tests). Schoenfeld's experiment is promising, because it suggests that some problem-solving strategies can be explicitly taught to learners.

Solution Execution

Solution execution requires that the problem solver be able to carry out operations, such as computation. In order to execute problem solutions, a person needs some knowledge of solution procedures, that is, algorithmic knowledge. For example, the problem solver needs to know that the sum of 3 + 5 is 8. People may differ in their ability to carry out operations, and these differences may be related to algorithmic knowledge.

Computational algorithms depend on the availability of well-practiced subskills in the problem solver. In particular, early computational algorithms tend to make use of the student's experience in counting. For example, Box 6.6 shows three counting models for children's addition algorithms, based on research by Groen and Parkman (1972). Each model shows how a child would solve a single-digit addition problem of the form, $m + n =$ _____. The diamonds represent decisions, and the rectangles represent operations. The three models are as follows.

Counting-all model. Set a counter to 0. Increment it by m and then by n. For 3 + 5, the child recites, "1, 2, 3, 4, 5, 6, 7, 8."

Counting-on model. Set a counter to the first number *(m)*; increment it by *n*. For 3 + 5, the child states, "4, 5, 6, 7, 8."

Min model (for counting-on). Set a counter to the larger of m or n; increment the counter by smaller number of m and n. For 3 + 5, the child states, "6, 7, 8."

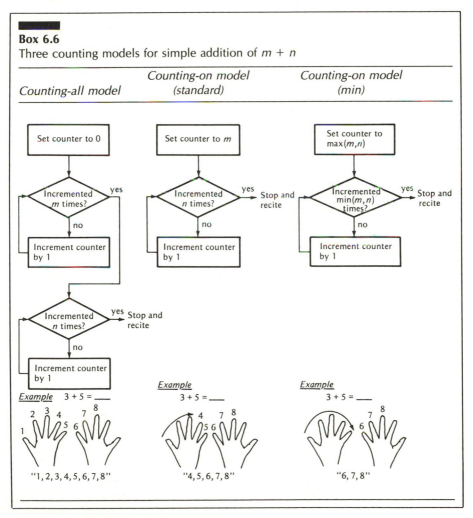

Box 6.6
Three counting models for simple addition of $m + n$

Counting-all model	Counting-on model (standard)	Counting-on model (min)

In order to discover which model children actually use, Groen and Parkman (1972) asked first graders to answer all single-column addition problems (i.e., all problems yielding sums of 9 or less). Each of the three models makes different predictions about differences in response time for different problems, as follows.

Counting-all model.   Response time is a function of $m + n$. For example, $3 + 5$ requires 8 increments, and $5 + 3$ requires 8 increments.

Counting-on model.   Response time is a function of n. For example, $3 + 5$ requires 5 increments; $5 + 3$ requires 3 increments.

Min model.   Response time is a function of the lesser of m and n. For example, $3 + 5$ requires 3 increments; $5 + 3$ requires 3 increments.

Groen and Parkman (1972) found that first graders behaved as predicted by the min model. Fig. 6.3 shows the response time of first graders for problems requiring 0, 1, 2, 3, and 4 increments (based on the min model). For example, according to the min model no increment is required in $0 + 2, 2 + 0, 8 + 0$, and so on; one increment is required in $4 + 1, 1 + 4, 8 + 1$, and so on; two increments are required in $2 + 7, 7 + 2, 5 + 2$, and so on; three increments are required in $3 + 4, 3 + 5, 5 + 3$, and so on; four increments are required in $4 + 5$, and $5 + 4$. As can be seen, response time seems to increase for problems as a function of the minimum of m and n. The other models did not predict the first graders' performance as well.

Apparently, by the first grade, the dominant algorithm for simple addition is to use a counting-on procedure (such as the min model). However, Fuson (1982) has observed that preschool children often use counting-all procedures, with more sophisticated procedures (such as counting-on) developing as children gain more experience in addition problems.

As children acquire more experience with simple addition problems, a new procedure develops: what Fuson (1982) calls "known facts." The new procedure is to memorize by rote the answers for simple addition problems. As can be seen in Fig. 6.3, first graders seem to be very fast on "doubles" such as $2 + 2, 3 + 3$, and so on. Apparently, they have memorized answers for *some* but not all of the addition "facts." Thus, a "known facts" procedure is used for some problems, but a "counting-on" procedure is used for others. By adulthood, the number facts are well memorized and counting algorithms may no longer be needed. In addition, as students acquire more known facts, they can use these to derive answers for related problems (what Fuson calls "derived facts"). For example, for $5 + 7 = $ _____, you can take 1 from the 7 and give it to the 5 so $6 + 6 = 12$. Thus, Fuson suggests a progression in which students move from counting-all to counting-on (basing computation on counting models) to derived facts to known facts (basing computation on memorized answers).

Woods et al. (1975) provide examples of counting algorithms for simple subtraction problems. For example, Box 6.7 shows three models for children's subtraction algorithms for problems of the form, $m - n = $ _____. The three models are as follows.

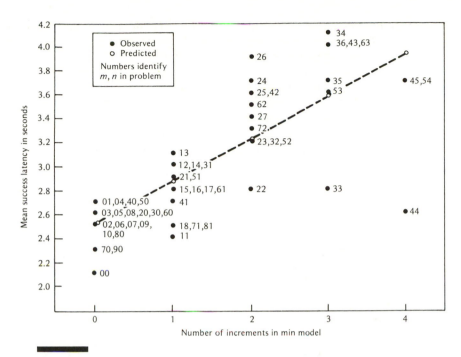

Figure 6.3
Response time depends on the number of increments required in the min model.
Number pairs represent the two numbers to be added; e.g., 13 means 1 + 3. (From Groen
and Parkman, 1972.)

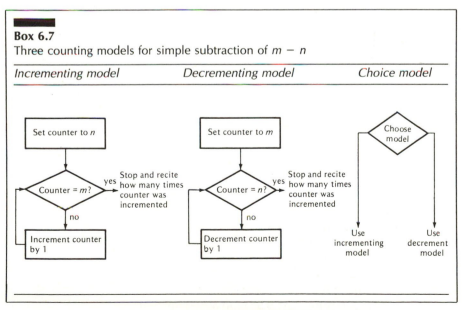

Box 6.7
Three counting models for simple subtraction of $m - n$

Incrementing model   *Decrementing model*   *Choice model*

Set counter to n

Counter = m? yes→ Stop and recite how many times counter was incremented

no

Increment counter by 1

Set counter to m

Counter = n? yes→ Stop and recite how many times counter was incremented

no

Decrement counter by 1

Choose model

Use incrementing model

Use decrement model

Incrementing model. Set a counter to the *n* and count up until you reach *m*. For example, 5 − 3 would require that you start with 3 and, as you recite "4, 5," you extend one and then two fingers.

Decrementing model. Set a counter to *m* and count down *n* times. For example, 5 − 3 would require that you start with 5 and, as you recite "4, 3, 2," you extend one, two, and then three fingers.

Choice model. Use either the incrementing or decrementing model, depending on which requires the lesser amount of counting. For example, 5 − 3 requires three decrements using the decrementing model, but only two increments using the incrementing model; in contrast, 5 − 1 requires one counting step using the decrement model, and four steps using the incrementing model.

In order to discover which model best predicted children's performance, Woods et al. (1975) asked second and fourth graders to solve all single-column subtraction problems. Each of the three models shown in Box 6.7 makes different predictions about response time for different problems, as follows.

Incrementing model. Response time is a function of *m* − *n*. For example, 5 − 3 requires two steps.

Decrementing model. Response time is a function of *n*. For example, 5 − 3 requires three steps.

Choice model. Response time is a function of the lesser of *n* or *m* − *n*. For example, 5 − 3 requires two steps (using the more efficient incrementing model), and 5 − 1 requires one step (using the more efficient decrementing model).

Woods et al. (1972) found that most second graders and all fourth graders behaved as predicted by the choice model. Figure 6.4 shows the response times of the fourth graders for problems requiring zero to four steps based on the choice model. As can be seen, response time seems to increase for problems as a function of the lesser of *n* or *m* − *n*. The other models did not fit the fourth graders' performance as well. However, for about 20 percent of the second graders, less-sophisticated models, such as the decrementing model, provided the best fit. Thus, there is some evidence that as children acquire more experience, they move from a less-sophisticated counting procedure to a more-sophisticated counting procedure for simple subtraction.

Once students have acquired some proficiency in simple addition or subtraction (i.e., as these procedures become automatic), simple computation can become a component in larger algorithms. For example, algorithms for two- or three-column addition (with carrying) or subtraction (with borrowing) incorporate simple computations as a single operation. Box 6.8 shows the algorithms for three-column subtraction, with decisions indicated as diamonds and operations indicated as rectangles.

Although the algorithm shown in Box 6.8 is the one that students are supposed to acquire, some students may acquire slightly flawed versions of it. For example, a student may know a procedure for three-digit subtraction that is identical to the one in Box 6.8, except that it contains one small "bug" (i.e., one step that is wrong). A student who uses an algorithm with one or more bugs may

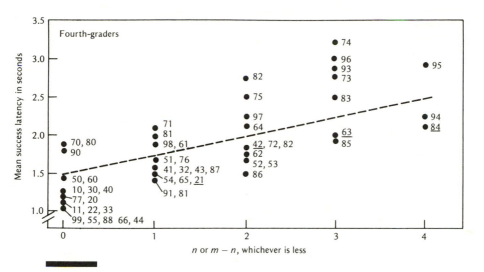

Figure 6.4
Response time depends on the number of increments or decrements required in the choice model. Number pairs represent subtraction problems; e.g., 83 means 8 − 3. (From Woods et al., 1975.)

be able to generate the correct answer on some problems but make errors at other times.

Here are the answers given by a student to several subtraction problems.

521	819	712	481	655
−418	−203	−531	−380	−160
117	616	221	101	515

As you can see, this student sometimes produces the right answer, and sometimes does not. One way to characterize this student's knowledge is to say that 40 percent of the time he is correct. However, another way to characterize the student's knowledge is to say that the student is using a subtraction algorithm that has a bug: at steps 2a, 2b, and 2c in Box 6.8, the student subtracts the smaller number from the larger number no matter which number is on top. Brown and Burton (1978) have argued that students' computational performance can be described by saying they are using a procedural algorithm, perhaps with one or more bugs, and applying this procedure consistently to problems.

In order to test this idea, Brown and Burton (1978) gave a set of 15 subtraction problems to 1325 primary school children. Brown and Burton developed a computer program called BUGGY to analyze each student's procedural algorithm for three-column subtraction. If the student's answers were all correct, BUGGY would categorize that student as using the correct algorithm. If there were many errors, BUGGY would attempt to find one bug that could account for most or all of the errors. If no single bug seemed to account for the errors, then all possible combinations were tried, until BUGGY found combinations that best accounted for the errors. Box 6.9 shows some of the most

Box 6.8

A procedure for three-column subtraction (from Mayer, 1981b)

Problem form

TTT   where T's are digits and B's are digits and computation begins on rightmost
−BBB   column.

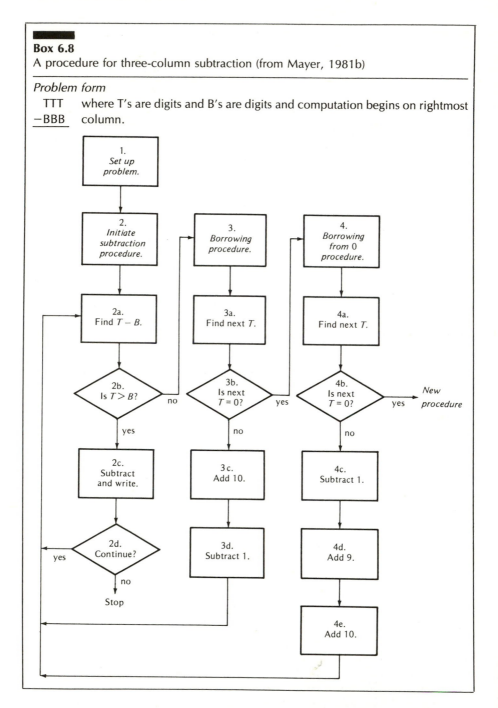

common bugs: 57 students out of 1325 seemed to have the "borrow from zero" bug; 54 seemed to have the "smaller from larger" bug; and so on.

Although the BUGGY program was based on hundreds of bugs or bug combinations, it was still not completely successful in diagnosing students'

■■■■■
Box 6.9
Some subtraction bugs[a]

Number of occurrences in 1325 students	Name	Example	Description
57	Borrow from zero	103 − 45 158	When borrowing from a column whose top digit is 0, the student writes 9, but does not continue borrowing from the column to the left of zero.
54	Smaller from larger	253 −118	The student subtracts the smaller digit in each column from the larger, regardless of which one is on top.
10	Diff 0 − N = N	140 − 21	Whenever the top digit in a column is 0, the student writes the bottom digit as the answer.
34	Diff 0 − N = N *and* move over zero	304 − 75	Whenever the top digit in a column is 0, the student writes the bottom digit as the answer. When the student needs to borrow from a column whose top digit is zero, he skips that column and borrows from the next one.

[a]Adapted from Brown and Burton, 1978.

---

subtraction algorithms. The BUGGY program was able to find algorithms (including bugs) that either completely or partially produced the answers given by 43 percent of the students. The other students seemed to be making random errors, or they were inconsistent in their use of bugs. Brown and Burton's work allows for a precise description of individual differences in some students' knowledge of subtraction algorithms.

Conclusion

In summary, this chapter has shown how mathematical ability for solving algebra word and story problems can be analyzed into four major steps: translation, integration, planning, and execution. In addition, this chapter has provided examples of the ways in which people may differ with respect to what they know about each step.

1. In the translation step, people may differ in their ability to comprehend linguistic expressions such as relational propositions.
2. In the integration phase, people may differ in the detail of their knowledge of different types of word and story problems.
3. In the planning phase, people may differ in general problem-solving strategies.
4. In the execution phase, people may differ in the sophistication, correctness, and automaticity of their algorithms for basic operations, such as addition and subtraction.

This chapter has not explored some other possible sources of individual differences in mathematical problem-solving performance, such as differences in cognitive systems, in capacity of memory, or in the speed with which mental operations can be carried out. However, Chi (1980) has provided some evidence that differences in knowledge are closely related to differences in memory capacity or speed.

More information about mathematical problem solving may be found in Carpenter et al. (1982), Mayer (1983), and Resnick and Ford (1981).

References

Bobrow, D. G. 1968. Natural language input for a computer problem solving system. *In* M. Minsky, ed., *Semantic Information Processing* (Cambridge, Mass.: M.I.T. Press).

Brown, J. S. and R. R. Burton. 1978. Diagnostic models for procedural bugs in basic mathematical skills. *Cognitive Science,* 2, 155–192.

California Assessment Program. 1980. *Student Achievement in California Schools: 1979–80 Annual Report.* Sacramento, Calif.: California State Department of Education.

Carpenter, T. P., M. K. Corbitt, H. S. Kepner, M. M. Lindquist, and R. E. Reyes. 1980. National assessment: a perspective of mathematics achievement in the United States. *In* R. Karplus, ed., *Proceedings of the Fourth International Conference for the Psychology of Mathematics Education* (Berkeley, Calif.: International Group for the Psychology of Mathematics Education).

Carpenter, T. P., J. M. Mosner, and T. A. Romberg, eds. 1982. *Addition and Subtraction: A Cognitive Perspective.* Hillsdale, N.J.: Erlbaum.

Chi, M. T. H. 1978. Knowledge structures and memory development. *In* R. S. Siegler, ed., *Children's Thinking: What Develops?* (Hillsdale, N.J.: Erlbaum).

Fuson, K. C. 1982. An analysis of the counting-on solution procedure in addition. *In* Carpenter et al. (1982).

Greeno, J. G. 1980. Some examples of cognitive task analysis with instructional implications. *In* R. E. Snow, P. Federico, and W. E. Montague, eds., *Aptitude, Learning, and Instruction, Vol. 2* (Hillsdale, N.J.: Erlbaum).

Groen, G. J. and J. M. Parkman, 1972. A chronometric analysis of simple addition. *Psychological Review,* 97, 329–343.

Hayes, J. R. 1981. *The Complete Problem Solver.* Philadelphia: Franklin Institute Press.

Hayes, J. R., D. A. Waterman, and C. S. Robinson. 1977. Identifying relevant aspects of a problem text. *Cognitive Science,* 1, 297–313.

Hinsley, D., J. R. Hayes, and H. A. Simon. 1977. From words to equations. *In* P. Carpenter and M. Just, eds., *Cognitive Processes in Comprehension* (Hillsdale, N.J.: Erlbaum).

Loftus, E. F., and P. Suppes. 1972. Structural variables that determine problem-solving difficulty in computer assisted instruction. *Journal of Educational Psychology,* 63, 531–542.

Mayer, R. E. 1978. Qualitatively different encoding strategies for linear reasoning: Evidence for single association and distance theories. *Journal of Experimental Psychology: Human Learning and Memory,* 4, 5–18.

———. 1981a. Frequency norms and structural analysis of algebra story problems into families, categories, and templates. *Instructional Science,* 10, 135–175.

———. *The Promise of Cognitive Psychology.* 1981b. San Francisco, Calif.: W. H. Freeman and Co.

———. 1982a. Memory for algebra story problems. *Journal of Educational Psychology,* 74, 199–216.

———. 1982b. Different problem solving strategies for algebra word and equation problems. *Journal of Experimental Psychology: Learning, Memory and Cognition,* 8, 448–462.

———. 1983. *Thinking, Problem Solving, and Cognition.* San Francisco: W. H. Freeman and Co.

Paige, J. M., and H. A. Simon. 1966. Cognitive processes in solving algebra word problems. *In* B. Kleinmuntz, ed., *Problem Solving: Research, Method, and Theory* (New York: Wiley).

Resnick, L. B., and W. Ford. 1981. *The Psychology of Mathematics for Instruction.* Hillsdale, N.J.: Erlbaum.

Riley, M., J. G. Greeno, and J. Heller. 1982. The development of children's problem solving ability in arithmetic. *In* H. Ginsburg, ed., *The Development of Mathematical Thinking* (New York: Academic Press).

Robinson, C. S., and J. R. Hayes. 1978. Making inferences about relevance in understanding problems. *In* R. Revlin and R. E. Mayer, eds., *Human Reasoning* (Washington: Winston).

Schoenfeld, A. H. 1979. Explicitly heuristic training as a variable in problem solving performance. *Journal for Research in Mathematics Education,* 10, 173–187.

Simon, H. A. 1980. Problem solving and education. *In* D. T. Tuma and F. Reif, eds., *Problem Solving and Education* (Hillsdale, N.J.: Erlbaum).

Soloway, E., J. Lochhead, and J. Clement. 1982. Does computer programming enhance problem solving ability? Some positive evidence on algebra word problems. *In* R. J. Seidel, R. E. Anderson, and B. Hunter, eds., *Computer Literacy* (New York: Academic Press).

Sternberg, R. J. 1977. *Intelligence, Information Processing, and Analogical Reasoning.* Hillsdale, N.J.: Erlbaum.

Trabasso, T. 1977. The role of memory as a system in making transitive inference. *In* R. V. Kail and J. W. Hagen, eds., *Perspectives on the Development of Memory and Cognition* (Hillsdale, N.J.: Erlbaum).

Weaver, J. F. 1982. Interpretations of number operations and symbolic representations of addition and subtraction. *In* T. P. Carpenter et al. (1982).

Wickelgren, W. 1974. *How to Solve Problems.* San Francisco: W. H. Freeman and Co.

Woods, S. S., L. B. Resnick, and G. J. Groen. 1975. An experimental test of five process models for subtraction. *Journal of Educational Psychology, 67,* 17–21.

7

MENTAL IMAGERY ABILITY

Stephen M. Kosslyn
Harvard University, Cambridge

You have once again made the mistake of traveling with somebody who brings lots of luggage, and are struggling to figure out how to fit it all into the car's trunk. You stare at one bag, mentally picture it placed just so in the trunk, but then realize it won't leave enough room for another suitcase. So you mentally rotate the image of the first suitcase around, and "see" that enough room is produced. The image (the "mental picture") saved you time and wasted effort; watching what would happen in the image was much easier than actually hefting the bags into the trunk and shifting them around.

Albert Einstein is sixteen years old and looking off into the distance, his eyes almost glazed over. In his mind he is seeing himself chasing a beam of light, which is plunging ahead at 186,000 miles per second. Einstein realizes that if contemporary theories were correct, the faster he went the slower the light would be traveling relative to him, until he matched its velocity and the light would seem to be "at rest." The young Einstein then realizes that, contrary to the results of this mental imagery "thought experiment," the laws of optics do not seem to depend on an observer's viewpoint. This imagery experiment provided Einstein with the first glimmer of insight that later led to his special theory of relativity.

In both examples mental images were used to advantage, serving as a kind of "mental blackboard" on which ideas can be developed and their implications explored. But what *is* a mental image? It cannot literally be a picture in the head; think of how uncomfortable this would be! And besides, who would look at such pictures in the head? And how are images, whatever they are, used in thinking?

These questions have preoccupied philosophers and psychologists since both disciplines began. But in the last fifteen years or so, more progress has been made in answering these questions than was made in all the preceding centuries combined. In this chapter we will review the progress made in studying mental imagery. In so doing, we will consider the questions of what a mental image is and of how we might go about studying such quintessentially private entities.

Imagery in Historical Perspective

Interest in mental imagery has waxed and waned dramatically over the years. Imagery has been a central topic in psychology, been banished from scientific discussion, and then come back again. To understand the erratic status of imagery, we must first understand why it appealed to the early philosophers, from Aristotle on. (Aristotle, often considered one of the greatest minds who ever lived, claimed that "thought is impossible without images.")

The early philosophers talked about psychology in terms of the mind, which was thought to take in information, cogitate, and direct behavior. The mind can contemplate things that are absent; it does so by using *representations* of objects and events. When something is no longer in front of you, to think about it you must somehow re-present it to yourself. The problem is, what can serve as this representation in the mind? Words won't do, because they are *arbitrarily* related to the things they stand for. That is, when you learned the word "cat," associating it with that small, four-legged feline that purrs, you could have just as easily been given the word "goober" instead; there is nothing special about the sounds we use to denote the feline. Given that the word is arbitrarily assigned to the animal, you are faced with another problem: how do you remember the animal itself, so you can remember the association between it and the word? If you use other words, such as "four-legged feline that purrs, drinks milk, and has sharp claws," this only pushes the problem back a step: how do you remember what those other words stand for?

Images, unlike words, are not arbitrarily related to the things they represent. Having an image is like seeing the object, but without the object actually being present. You recognize the object in the image in the same way that you recognize the object when you actually see it. Images thus seemed to offer a solution to the problem of how the mind represents objects and events; hence many philosophers thought of thought as being sequences of images. This idea soon began to lose its appeal, however, because (among other problems) people can think about *classes* of objects, not just particular ones. You can think about triangles in general, not just right triangles, isosceles triangles, and so on. But images can only represent particular instances, such as particular triangles; they cannot represent a class of objects or abstract concepts such as "justice" or "meaning." Even if images are used to represent information, they therefore cannot be the only kind of representation we use.

Nevertheless, images proved popular with the early psychologists, at least in part because they were accessible to introspection. Wilhelm Wundt founded the first psychology laboratory in Leipzig, Germany, in 1879, and introspection, "perceiving within," was his main methodology. Wundt's approach to psychology was to construct something like a "periodic table" of consciousness in which the elements were images. Rules of combination would dictate all the possible kinds of experiences a person could have. This focus led to a furious debate around the turn of the twentieth century with the discovery of "imageless thought."

To repeat one of the early experiments revealing imageless thought, try the following: lift up a pencil, put it down, and then lift up a book. Which is heavier? How do you know? In the original experiment the subjects claimed that they had images of the weights, but no image of the decision process itself. That is, there was no orderly syllogistic sequence of steps that led to the decision; it just seemed to pop into mind all at once. Some Wundtians, in particular the American E. B. Titchener, consulted their introspections and begged to differ. Titchener went so far as to claim that he had images even for very abstract ideas, like "meaning" (which was a little blue-gray shovel with a yellow handle).

The real problem raised by the so-called imageless thought controversy was not the fact of the disagreement, but the fact that there was no way to resolve it. One group reported one kind of introspection, and another reported another kind of introspection; how could it be demonstrated that one group was right and the other wrong?

John B. Watson, who taught for a while at Johns Hopkins University (before going on to a career in advertising on Madison Avenue), stepped into the impasse. His solution was radical: he rejected the entire notion that mental events, of *any* sort, are the proper subject matter of psychology. Watson nudged psychology in a new direction, and soon Behaviorism held sway. Psychologists focused on studying behavior as such, not the putative mental events that underlie the behavior. Watson considered talk about imagery to be just that: talk. He asserted that if we want to study "thought," we should measure subtle activity in various throat muscles, because thought (Watson thought) was simply talking to yourself. During the reign of the Behaviorists, from about 1913 to the late 1950s, the study of all mental events was eschewed, and imagery was virtually ignored.

The pendulum began its swing back in the late 1950s, and today imagery is the object of much research. Why has it made this comeback? I believe there are three reasons.

First, the weakness of Behaviorism became apparent. In particular, it was not at all clear how behaviorists could explain perception or language use and acquisition. As they struggled to explain these basic human abilities, they began to use the terms "stimulus" and "response" to refer to hidden events in the brain, not the observable events and muscle twitches Watson talked about. As soon as they began to make inferences about such implicit stimuli and responses, it was only a small step for others to make inferences about mental representations.

Second, the methodological impasse evident in the imageless-thought controversy was broken. New methodologies were invented that have enabled researchers to study mental events objectively. These methodologies involve the *externalization of mental events;* instead of studying the mind itself, we measure the observable consequences of internal processing. If a given introspection is valid, then there ought to be externally observable consequences of the observed internal events. The experimenter does not linger too much on the introspection itself, but quickly moves on to the observable ramifications and tries to document these. Virtually all the experiments to be described in the following sections rest on methodologies that exploit this basic idea.

The third reason for the resurgence of interest in imagery centers on developments in linguistics and artificial intelligence (that discipline in which computers are programmed to behave "intelligently"). Noam Chomsky's work in linguistics demonstrated the necessity of positing unobservable representations in order to understand how people can use language. And the mere fact that computers could be programmed to solve problems suggested that the mind may operate something like a computer program. This analogy was important because we understand how computers work, and thinking of the mind in the same way removed the aura of mysticism that had previously surrounded talk of mental events.

The computer analogy paved the way for wholesale investigations of how information is represented in the mind. It also made imagery once again a controversial topic: computers more naturally store descriptions than pictures, and many researchers thereby inferred that the same would be true of the human mind. Unlike the earlier controversy over imagery, however, this one was productive, largely because methodological tools were available for testing ideas instead of just arguing about them. In the remainder of this chapter we will review evidence that demonstrates that the mind can store information using mental images, and that reveals some of the properties of images and some of the ways they are used in thinking.

Stalking the Mental Image

What is a mental image? There have been two general approaches to trying to answer this question. One of them centers on the relationship between imagery and perception; the other centers on the structure of images in their own right.

Inner Visions

Almost from the very beginning, imagery has been identified with perception. Having a visual image, for example, was likened to seeing an object in the absence of the appropriate visual input. The philosopher David Hume claimed that the only differences between an *impression* formed during perception (that is, a "percept") and a mental image in the same sensory modality, which he called an *idea,* was "in the degree of force and liveliness with which they strike upon the mind, and make their way into our thought or consciousness." Given the longstanding popularity of this idea, it is not surprising that much research has been conducted to demonstrate that imagery and perception are similar events in the brain. One approach has focused on the idea that if the same brain events are used in imagery and perception, then visual imagery should interfere more with visual perception than with auditory perception, but auditory imagery should interfere more with auditory perception. Another approach has been to try to demonstrate that an imaged stimulus can "stand in" for an observed one, producing a specific perceptual-like effect. Let us consider some representative examples of each type of research.

The classic interference study was reported by Perky in 1910. It is useful not so much for what it tells us about imagery but for what it tells us about the recent progress in studying imagery. Perky asked subjects to image a common object, such as a banana, as if it were on a pane of glass mounted on the wall. Little did they know, but the glass was actually a one-way window into an adjoining room containing a projector, and the projector was actually displaying a picture of the imaged object. The intensity of the projector was gradually turned up to the point where the picture was easily seen by anyone else in the room. But the subjects never reported seeing the picture; they reportedly thought they were "seeing" their mental image. But does this result really show that visual imagery impairs visual perception? The problem here is that forming the image may simply have distracted them; talking aloud instead may have had the same results. To show that the percept and image are similar, we would have to show *selective* effects of forming one kind of image (e.g., visual, auditory) on one kind of perception (visual, auditory); if auditory images interfere with seeing as much as visual images do, we could not argue that images are similar to percepts.

Because of the influence of Behaviorism, no work was done on this topic for more than 50 years. However, in 1970, Segal and Fusella redid the Perky experiment with improved methodology. They asked people to form either a visual or an auditory mental image (such as the sight of a flower or the sound of a telephone ringing). At the same time, a very faint dot might be quickly shown to them or a very faint sound might be presented over some headphones. If images really are like the brain representations formed during perception, except that they are formed from memory instead of via the senses, then images should be confused with perceptions in the same modality (visual, auditory) at least some of the time. And because visual perception involves different kinds of representations than auditory perception does, we should not be as likely to confuse visual images with sounds, or auditory images with things seen. The results of the experiment were exactly as expected: visual images did selectively interfere with visual perception, whereas auditory images selectively interfered with hearing.

The Segal and Fusella findings showed that images in some way resemble the representations formed during perception in the same modality, perhaps because the same parts of the brain are used for both. Besiach and Luzzatti (1978) provided some evidence that this is true, by studying people afflicted with brain damage. Brain damage often results from a stroke, which occurs when a blood vessel breaks, cutting off oxygen to some parts of the brain, resulting in the death of some brain cells. When cells in the parietal region of the right hemisphere are affected, patients sometimes develop "visual neglect" on the left side. That is, they are not blind, but they ignore everything on the left side. For example, these patients sometimes forget to shave the left side of their face, will leave off the left side when drawing, and will read only the right side of words. One patient is reported to have thought she was going crazy because she kept hearing voices; the speakers were on her left, and she did not realize they were there. Bisiach and Luzzati found that when brain damage caused this syndrome in vision, it also caused it in mental imagery. In one of their studies, a patient was asked to imagine standing on one end of a plaza that he had known well prior to the stroke. When asked to describe everything he "saw" in the image, he mentioned only things to the right. He was then asked to imagine standing on the opposite side of the plaza, looking toward the spot he had just occupied. When asked to describe everything in the image, he now mentioned only things on the right, which were the things previously ignored because they had been on the left from the other perspective! Clearly, the brain damage affected in a special way the mechanisms underlying both seeing and imaging.

The Besiach and Luzzati study is an example of the other major approach to studying the relationship of imagery and perception: finding analogous effects when images are used in place of sensory input. As another example, consider Natadze's (1960) mental analogue of the "weight-contrast" illusion. To induce this illusion, a person is asked first to heft a very heavy object in one hand and a very light one in the other, and then to lift two equally heavy objects. The subject is then asked which one feels heavier. If the left hand had held the heavy object initially, the object held in it now feels lighter than the object held in the other hand. In Natadze's experiment, subjects were first asked to *imagine* holding two balls of different weights, and then were given two balls which weighed the same amount. The subjects were then asked which one felt heavier. These subjects reported the usual illusion, even though they used images to stand in for the actual heavy and light weights at the beginning.

The logic underlying this approach to studying imagery has recently been moved one step further by Ronald Finke and his colleagues. Their approach is to show that images can produce perceptual effects only when the perceptual effects are due to "central " brain processes. That is, some perceptual effects are due to the operation of the eyeball and nerves leading directly from it; if images are representations in the central parts of the brain, then we would not expect them to be able to induce these effects. However, we would expect images to induce perceptual effects due to central brain processing.

A good example of this kind of research was reported by Finke and Schmidt (1977). They showed that imaged stimuli could substitute for actual stimuli in producing a very unusual phenomenon called the McCollough effect. The McCollough effect is produced by the following sequence of events. Subjects are first shown alternating stripes aligned either vertically or horizontally. Each pattern is presented for about ten seconds, and the patterns are alternated back and forth for about five minutes. The trick is that one pattern contains black and red stripes, whereas the other contains black and green stripes. After the patterns have been presented, two new patterns are presented, one containing horizontal black and white bars, the other containing vertical black and white bars. The McCollough effect is the finding that people will now see the white stripes in the new pattern as tinted in the color opposite to that in the original patterns: the vertical white bars will seem green if the original vertical pattern had red stripes, and horizontal white stripes will seem red if the original horizontal pattern had green stripes. This perceptual effect can last up to two weeks after subjects study the original colored patterns, and clearly is not like the afterimages formed by cells in the eye or the nerves leading directly from it (such as those produced when you look into a flashbulb). Finke and Schmidt found that the McCollough effect could be produced when subjects were initially shown not alternating bars, but solid fields of red and green, and were asked to *project* images of vertical black bars on one and horizontal black bars on the other!

The upshot of this work is that visual images are like the representations produced in the central parts of the brain when we look at something. But even having established this relationship, we still do not know much about either sort of representation. A second major class of research has focussed on understanding the properties of images as such.

Anatomy of an Image

The images people experience appear to share many of the properties of pictures. But because images are not actual pictures, there is no necessary reason why they should have *any* properties of pictures. Whatever is going on in the brain when we have an image, it produces a representation that has certain functional properties. Visual mental images may *act as if* they were rigid spatial objects that could be looked at and so on, but this is not guaranteed or obviously true.

One way to study the properties of mental images is to observe their characteristics under transformation. This method has been extensively explored by Roger Shepard (1975) and his colleagues. In a now-classic experiment, Shepard and Metzler presented subjects with stimuli like those illustrated in Figure 7.1. The subjects were asked to decide, as quickly as they could, whether the figures were the same shape, differing only in orientation. The pairs were constructed in such a way that different amounts of mental rotation would be necessary to align the two objects to "see" if the shapes matched. Figure 7.2 illustrates the time that the subjects required to decide that two figures were the same, depending on the disparity in their orientations in the picture. More time was required when a member of the pair had to be rotated more in order to match up with the other. Perhaps the most fascinating aspect of Shepard and

Metzler's findings is that times not only increased when greater tilts were presented, but also increased even when the tilts were in depth. It is as if we see little models of objects in the world, and can manipulate these models much like the actual objects themselves (see Shepard and Cooper, 1982).

One implication of Shepard and Metzler's findings is that images behave as if they were physically rigid. If this were not true, why should subjects have

Figure 7.1
Examples of Shepard and Metzler's stimuli; are both objects in a pair the same except for their orientation?

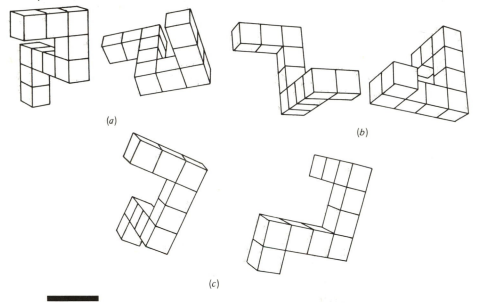

(a)

(b)

(c)

Figure 7.2
The results of the Shepard and Metzler experiment; decision time increases when one of the objects must be "mentally rotated" further to match up with the other.

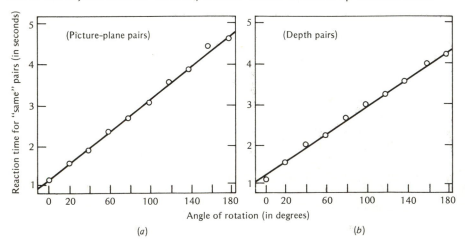

(a)

(b)

apparently rotated the figures by passing through intermediate positions along a trajectory? Shepard and Feng (1972) explored another mental transformation task that buttressed this conclusion. In this experiment, subjects were presented with stimuli like those illustrated in Figure 7.3. The task was to decide whether the two arrows would meet if the figure were folded into a box, with the shaded square being at the bottom of the box. The amount of time to reach this decision depended on the number of squares a subject would have to "mentally fold" before the arrows came together. Interestingly, the same additional amount of time was required for each mental *fold* that was necessary, not for each additional square that was folded (sometimes two or more squares were folded at once.) Apparently images can act like three-dimensional models. This does not mean that images occur in a three-dimensional space, a cavity in your brain, but rather that the brain operates in a way that can mimic the properties of a three-dimensional space. Another example of such mimicry occurs in a computer, which can be programmed to present a three-dimensional array, even though you could look forever and never find an actual array inside the computer (Kosslyn, 1983).

Other researchers have tried to discover the properties of images by considering what kinds of pictorial characteristics are mimicked by them. If images function at all like pictures or models, they must depict information. That is, parts of images must correspond to parts of the represented object, and distances

Figure 7.3
Examples of Shepard and Feng's stimuli; if the shaded square is the bottom, can you fold the other squares to form a cube where the arrows meet?

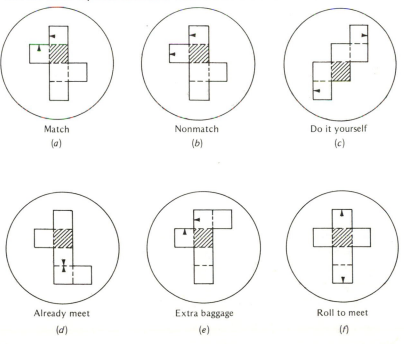

Match	Nonmatch	Do it yourself
(a)	(b)	(c)
Already meet	Extra baggage	Roll to meet
(d)	(e)	(f)

between the parts of the objects (as they appear from a particular point of view) must be preserved by the distances between the parts in the image. Numerous experiments have been conducted to demonstrate that images really do preserve information about interval distance between parts (Kosslyn, 1980; 1983). In some of these experiments people were asked to scan over images, and the time needed to scan different distances was used as a kind of "tape measure." The idea was that if images do indeed depict objects, then parts of an object that are further apart should require more time to scan between (provided that the rate of scanning was kept constant). In one experiment of this sort, people first learned to draw a map of the mythical island shown in Figure 7.4. This map contained seven key objects (e.g., the hut, tree, rock) located in such a way that the 21 distances between the pairs all had distinct values (each one being at least .5 cm longer than the next shortest). After subjects learned to draw the map, it was removed. The subjects were then asked to form an image of it, and then to focus mentally on a given location (each location was used as a focus point equally often). Next an object was named, and the subject was to scan to that object if it was on the map; when reaching the object, he or she was to push one button. Each subject repeatedly scanned between every pair of objects. If the subject "looked" but could not find the object, he or she was to push another button. The time to respond was measured. The results are presented at the bottom of Figure 7.4 for the probes where subjects presumably scanned between two objects on the map. The results clearly reflect the fact that different distances were being scanned, with a constant amount of time being added for each additional unit of distance traveled.

The scanning experiment, unlike the earlier ones, depended on subjects' following instructions. Perhaps they followed the instructions too well, figuring out what was expected, perhaps by responding to subtle cues given by the experimenter, and "faking" the results. Some other experiments were therefore designed to control for this possibility. In one, two new experimenters were not told the correct predictions, but were told that the shorter distance should be harder to scan across because the objects are cluttered together. The same results were obtained with both new experimenters as in the original experiment, showing that the experimenters did not lead the subject to respond simply to produce the expected results. In another experiment, the instructions to scan were eliminated. Here, subjects imaged animals and focused on one end. Next, they heard a property named, and simply decided as quickly as they could whether that animal had that property (half the time it did, and half the time it did not). These subjects were explicitly told that they did not have to use their images to answer; the word "scan" was never mentioned. Half the properties were located on the end that the subject was focusing on, and half were located on the other end of the imaged animal. What the subject did not know was that half the properties had previously been rated by other subjects as *requiring* imagery to evaluate (such as "dark head" for bee), and half had been rated by other subjects as not requiring imagery (such as "two eyes" for dog). The two kinds of properties were randomly intermixed in the presentation order. The results were clearcut: the time to evaluate properties increased if they were on the end of the image not

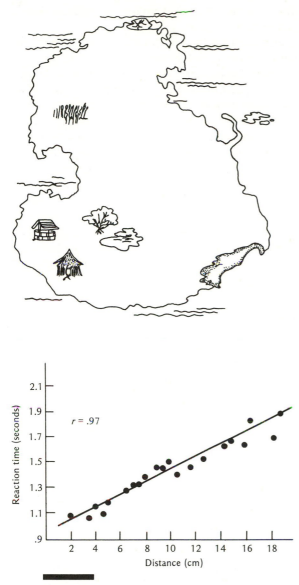

Figure 7.4
    The imaginary island that subjects imaged and scanned (top), and the time to scan
increasingly longer distances across the image (bottom).

being focused on, but *only* for those properties previously rated as requiring
imagery. The location of the properties did not matter if the properties did not
require imagery. These findings are what you would expect if the increase in
time results from having to scan the image to "see" one kind of property but not
the other. Clearly, time increases when subjects scan greater distances, and
these increases do not reflect the subjects' overly enthusiastic efforts to cooper-

ate with the experimenter. Thus, we can infer that images do indeed depict information, portraying parts arranged in a spatial array.

The scanning technique was used by Steven Pinker to study the three-dimensional properties of imagery in more detail. Pinker (1980) had his subjects first learn the positions of objects hanging in a tank. They then formed an image of the tank, focused on one object, and then scanned to another. Scan times increased with the three-dimensional distance between objects. However, Pinker also asked subjects to imagine they were viewing the tank through cross-hairs, like those found in a rifle site. Now, they were to shift the cross-hairs from one object to another, and time increased not with the three-dimensional distance, but with the distance in the two-dimensional "picture plane" (what you would see in a photograph). This result shows that although images do preserve three-dimensional information, we "see" them from a particular point of view, and we can focus just on the two-dimensional impression seen from that point of view. Other results reported by Pinker suggest that images do not occur in a 3-D "tank," but are more like pictures in bas relief. When you rotate or bend an image in depth, you fill in the back as you "see" it; the back was not in the image when it was hidden, unlike actual models.

The Medium and the Message

In order to depict something, you must depict it *on* a medium. If you draw a picture, it must be drawn on a canvas or page; if you display a TV picture, it must appear on a tube; and so on. Similarly, if images function to depict objects, we can ask about the medium in which the image occurs, the "mental screen." Obviously, there is no actual screen in the brain; no matter how hard you hit somebody in the head, you won't hear breaking glass. But just as an array in a computer can function as a space, with some parts of the array being relatively close and some far, so too can brain cells function as a space. The cells would be connected up in such a way that they act as if they form a screen, even if ones that are "next" to each other (perhaps being directly connected) are separated by real distance in the brain.

Whenever something is depicted on a medium, properties of the medium affect the possible size and detail that can be presented. On a TV screen, for example, the size of the picture tube determines the maximum size of a picture, and the "grain" (the dots used to display the picture; look at a TV very close up if you have not done so before) determines how small the details can be and yet remain visible. The mental medium in which images occur determines how easily parts can be seen on objects in images, and how large an image can be before it seems to "overflow" the mental screen.

The experiments demonstrating effects of the "grain" of the mental medium all involve asking subjects to image an object and then to "look" for a property of the imaged object. In one experiment, subjects imaged a given animal at one of the four relative sizes (the sizes were learned beforehand), and then "looked" for a named property of the animal. Half the time the property was true of the animal, and hence should have been visible on the image, and half the time it was not true of the animal (e.g., for a goose, feet and horns). The subject was told that if the animal had the property, he or she should be able to find it on the image; once the property was "seen," the subject was to press one button. If the subject "looked" and could not find the property, he or she was to press the other button. The time to respond was measured, and we found that the subjects needed more time to find properties on smaller images, as if smaller images were blurrier because of the limited grain of the mental medium. In fact, subjects in this experiment often reported afterward that they had to "zoom in" in order to "see" parts of objects imaged at smaller, but not larger, sizes.

The foregoing results suggest that people "look" at objects in their images much as they look at actual objects, and that parts of smaller images are more difficult to resolve. If this is true, we reasoned, then smaller parts as such should be more difficult to see in an image. We therefore conducted another experiment in which people imaged animals at a single size, but we asked about properties that were different sizes on the image. In this experiment, we varied not only the size of the parts, such as claws and head for a cat, but also how strongly associated the parts were to the animal. It is a well-known finding that when imagery is not used, people can decide more quickly that more strongly associated parts belong to an object than they can decide that less-associated parts belong. For example, people can decide that the statement "A tiger has stripes" is true more quickly than they can decide that "A tiger has knees" is true. This finding is usually interpreted as reflecting the way in which people search down mental lists of verbal associations, with more strongly associated properties being stored higher on the list, and thus being looked up more quickly. The reason we made the smaller properties more highly associated than the larger ones, then, is that it allowed us to show that imagery operates differently than verbal memory. In this experiment, we asked subjects to use imagery to evaluate the properties on only half the trials; on the other half, they were told simply to answer as quickly as possible. The results are presented in Figure 7.5. As is evident, when imagery was used, larger but less-associated properties were "seen" more quickly than the smaller but more highly associated properties. When imagery was not used, however, now association strength determined the results, with the smaller but more highly associated properties being evaluated faster (Kosslyn, 1980; 1983).

The results, then, are just as expected if images occur on a kind of grainy "mental screen," on which smaller details are harder to "see" than larger ones are. And inspecting an image is clearly different from recalling verbal information, as you would expect if images are "viewed" in a specifically visual part of the brain.

Other research has focused on another property of the mental screen: its limited extent. Try the following: image an elephant far off, facing to the left. Imagine you are walking toward it, fixating your gaze on the center of its flank. Does it seem to loom larger as you imagine getting closer? Most subjects say it does. Now, is there a point where you can't get any closer and still "see" the entire animal? Again, most subjects say there is. Now try this task with a rabbit. Does the rabbit seem to be closer than the elephant was before it begins to

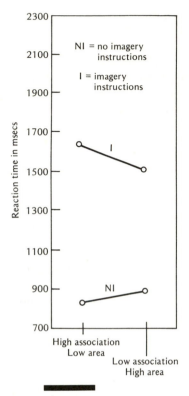

Figure 7.5
The time to decide whether an animal had a named property, when imagery was used or was not used.

overflow? When this task was done carefully, showing subjects drawings of objects and having them estimate the distance at which the object seems to overflow the image, Kosslyn (1978) found that the larger the object, the further away it appears when it just begins to overflow. Further, the apparent spread of the image at the point of overflow was usually the same for different objects. This is exactly what you would expect if the mental screen has a fixed extent, and if the image begins to overflow when it hits the "edges" of the screen.

In summary, these and similar experiments have shown that images depict information, occur in a mental medium that acts like a screen (with a limited extent and a grain), and can be manipulated much like the objects they represent. As you can imagine, some of these properties make imagery very useful in thinking; let us now consider a few of the roles imagery plays in different mental functions.

Using Images

We began this chapter with some examples of when imagery may be used in thinking, from the mundane act of loading suitcases into a trunk to Einstein's lofty thoughts about the universe. Psychologists have studied three ways in which images can be used: as a memory aid, as a way of practicing a physical activity without leaving your armchair, and as a tool in reasoning.

The oldest recorded use of mental imagery is as a memory aid. The origin of this practice is usually attributed to the ancient Greek bard Simonides. In those days no banquet was complete without a bard telling stories; on one such occasion, Simonides had the good fortune to be called outside the banquet hall right before the roof caved in. The guests were mangled beyond recognition, and wives and tax collectors were very anxious to know who was in attendance. Simonides found that he could easily remember the guests by imaging the table, and scanning from person to person around it. This realization led to development of the so-called "method of loci," where imagery is used to help recall a series of words. In this method, you first memorize a sequence of locations in a familiar setting. When you later want to memorize a list, you mentally walk through this setting and place an image of each item on the list at each successive location. So, for example, you might memorize the following locations in your home: the front door, the entrance hallway, the lamp in the living room, the sink in the bathroom, etc. When later trying to memorize the items on a shopping list, you might now imagine walking the route, leaving an image of a loaf of bread at the doorway, some lettuce at the entranceway, and so on. Finally, when you arrive at the market and want to remember the list, you now simply image the scene, and imagine walking through it, "seeing" each item that you previously placed at each location. Psychologists have shown that this technique vastly improves memory for lists of words, compared to simple rote repetition or the like (Denis, 1979).

Gordon Bower and his colleagues have investigated the reasons why imagery improves memory. Bower (1972) gave people pairs of words, such as "dog" and "bicycle," and asked different groups to memorize the pairs in different ways. One group was asked simply to say the words in a pair over and over; another was asked to form an image of each item, but to make the images separate and unrelated; and a third group was asked to image each item, but to make the images touching and interacting in some way (e.g., a dog riding a bicycle). This last group showed far better memory for the pairs of words than the other groups. But even so, the group asked simply to form separate images did better than the group told to repeat the words over and over. Paivio (1971) has shown that simply being able to form an image of what the word refers to ensures better memory for the word; concrete words like "cow" are remembered better than abstract ones like "truth."

In short, imagery appears to improve memory in two ways. First, you can store not just the word itself, but an image of the thing being named. Recall that verbal memory and imagery are different, and this difference can be used to advantage to ensure that you will remember something. Second, images can be combined into scenes that themselves can be remembered, producing yet another route to improving memory.

The second use of imagery investigated by scientists involves imagery as a substitute for actual practice at performing some activity. Recall that images can act as substitutes for actual objects, being rotated or bent much as objects can be. Further, recall that images can stand in for perceptual stimulation, producing effects like those evoked when subjects actually view a stimulus. As it turns out, imagining yourself doing something can also substitute, to some extent, for the actual activity. For example, Richardson (1969) describes a study in which subjects were asked to mentally practice a simple gymnastic exercise on the horizontal bar. Subjects were asked to "see and feel themselves" moving through each set of movements for periods of five minutes on each of six days. None of these people had any actual experience doing the exercise on the bar. On the day after the mental practice the subjects were taken to a horizontal bar and asked to perform the exercise; the quality of their performance was scored. In this study, Richardson expected that if imagery was an effective means of practicing, then people with more vivid and controllable imagery would perform better than those with less acute imagery abilities. And, indeed, people with better imagery *did* perform better than those who scored low on the imagery-abilities tests that Richardson used (included as appendices to Richardson, 1969). Similar results have been obtained by asking people to imagine shooting balls through the hoop in basketball, which resulted in better actual shooting ability than was found in a control group that did not perform any mental practice. Although mental practice is usually better than no practice, it usually is not as good as actual practice; consider the implications if it were!

The third use of imagery investigated by scientists focuses on its role in reasoning. Some of this work has centered on the use of imagery in spatial reasoning. For example, Brooks (1968) studied one situation in which imagery was used spontaneously to reason about the shapes of letters. In one task, he asked people to decide whether each corner of a block letter was at the extreme top or extreme bottom. Subjects were asked to start classifying the corners from a specific starting place, as illustrated in Figure 7.6. In this example, the subject should have responded, "yes, yes, yes, no, no, no, no, no, no, no, yes." The figure was removed as soon as the subject began, forcing him or her to classify the corners from memory. Brooks showed that imagery was, in fact, being used; to do so, he took advantage of the fact that imagery interferes with perception in the same modality (as we discussed earlier). He asked subjects to indicate their "yes/no" responses in different ways. One involved giving the subject a sheet of paper containing a crooked column of "y's" and "n's"; the subject was to indicate "yes" by pointing to a "y," and "no" by pointing to an "n," working his or her way down the sheet. Because the response letters were arranged haphazardly on the page, subjects had to look carefully when making their responses. In contrast, on other trials subjects simply said the words "yes" and "no" aloud, which does not involve any visual perception. Given the findings described earlier on interference, we would expect that the looking-then-pointing method of responding would be more difficult if visual imagery were being used. And in fact this is what Brooks found. In another task Brooks gave subjects a sentence, like "A bird in the hand is worth two in the bush," and asked them to classify each word as being a noun or not. In this example, the correct response would be "no, yes, no, no, yes, no, no, no, no, yes." In this task, saying the responses aloud was more difficult than pointing to the appropriate letters on

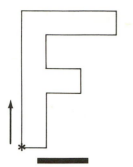

Figure 7.6
A letter used by Brooks to study the use of imagery in reasoning; subjects started at the star and classified each corner of the figure from memory.

a page. Here the subjects presumably held in memory an auditory image of the sentence, which was interfered with by saying the words aloud.

Imagery is used in other kinds of spatial reasoning, such as deciding whether the tip of a horse's tail or its rear knees is higher off the ground, or in deciding whether a hamster or a mouse is larger. When a subject is making judgments of the relative sizes of similar-sized objects, more time is taken if the subject begins with a small image, which must be "mentally enlarged" to a normal-size before being examined, than if the subject begins with a normal size image. In general, experiments have shown that imagery is used when people reason about spatial relations that are implicit in the appearance of objects, but that had not been explicitly considered before.

What are perhaps the most interesting uses of mental imagery in reasoning are not concerned with reasoning about spatial relations for their own sake. Janellen Huttenlocher (1968) has studied the role of mental imagery in how people solve simple problems of logical deduction. Her subjects are given sets of premises, such as "John is smarter than Bill, Bill is less smart than Herbert, and Susan is smarter than John." They then are asked to decide whether a statement, such as "John is smarter than Herbert," is true or false. Huttenlocher found that the way the premises were initially presented was critical in determining how many errors subjects would later make. Furthermore, the variables that were important were the very same ones that impaired performance when subjects were asked to order three blocks on a shelf; use of negatives, switching from "more" to "less," and similar complications had the same effects in the two tasks. This led Huttenlocher to take seriously the subjects' reports that they often solved the problems by constructing an image of a line and placing dots (one representing each person) along it. The smarter a person was supposed to be, the further to the right the dot was placed. Thus, as long as they remembered whom each dot stood for, it was easy to "read off" who was smarter than whom.

However, imagery is not the only way in which people can reason about three-term series problems. Clark (1969) and Sternberg (1980), among others, have shown that at least some people will occasionally use a linguistic strategy in this task. That is, they will describe the relations between the things being compared, and use these descriptions to draw inferences about relative orderings. This view received some support from an experiment conducted by Kosslyn and Phil James. They asked people to form images of lines with dots in Huttenlocher's task, but had them image the dots "in front of them" or "off to one side." When the dots were moved toward the side, and hence were harder to "see" in the image, more time was taken to evaluate a statement about the relative intelligences of two people, but only when subjects were relatively unfamiliar with the information. If subjects were given plenty of practice ahead of time, so that they had thoroughly memorized each person's level of intelligence, then the position of the image did not affect judgment times. Apparently imagery is a handy means of dealing with abstract problems, but its usefulness can be eliminated if the material is highly familiar and the appropriate verbal information is well learned.

People Are Different

It has long been believed that people differ in the quality and kind of imagery they can use. In fact, the first scientific studies of imagery focused on this claim. For example, Galton (1883) asked people to describe various characteristics of their breakfast tables from memory. He discovered that a relatively high percentage of his respondents claimed not to use imagery at all in answering this question, and denied ever using "mental images" in thinking. Further, it turned out that this group, about 12 percent of the sample, was composed mostly of doctors, lawyers, and other professionals, leading Galton to speculate that imagery was a relatively primitive form of thinking. However, this sort of research is based on subjects' introspective reports, and it should not be surprising that the data are somewhat suspect. Of particular interest is McKellar's (1965) finding that 97 percent of a sample of 500 members of Mensa claimed to experience visual mental imagery. This result is surprising in view of Galton's earlier result, because Mensa is an organization requiring a high IQ score for admission, and is presumably composed of the same kind of people who earlier had composed the group claiming not to have imagery! This disparity in findings could result from many different factors: perhaps the advent of television has caused people to think "more visually"; perhaps the fact that Albert Einstein claimed to think in images has made it "fashionable" to claim to do so also.

Individual differences in imagery are usually studied by using two kinds of measures. Self-report measures require the subject to make some kind of rating about his or her imagery. The two kinds of ratings most often studied require the subject to rate the *vividness* of images or the degree of his or her *control* over various image transformations. After ratings are collected, they usually are then correlated with performance on some other task, with the aim of finding out whether "high" imagers tend to be better or worse at the task than "low" imagers (Marks, 1977; Paivio, 1971; White et al. 1977). And in fact, people reporting vivid images differ from those reporting dim images. For example, they tend to remember pictures better, to read concrete text more slowly (presumably because they "mentally illustrate" while they read; see Denis, 1982), to show fewer eye movements when recalling pictures, and to report experiencing "larger" images. However, the results of this sort of research have in the main been disappointing. The findings are usually of small magnitude, and often fail to be repeated when another researcher carries out the experiment. One of the problems, of course, is the subjective nature of the task; it relies on all subjects understanding the instructions the same way, and on their using the same internal criteria for rating their images. Because all this is private, we have no way of calibrating the subjects to use the same scale when giving ratings.

The other kind of measure used to study individual differences is performance on some objective test. These tests require subjects to decide whether two forms are the same but in different orientations, whether a form can be constructed from a set of parts, whether a piece of paper would look a certain way if it were folded, hole-punched, and unfolded, and so on. Unfortunately, for the most part these tests have not been shown to measure imagery as such. That is, they could be measuring some more generalized "spatial ability," which involves using descriptions and deductions about the descriptions. For the most part, however, the scores on these tests seem to be relatively good predictors of how well a person will do in a real spatial task (such as using a map).

Finally, a very recent finding from our laboratory has shown that a common assumption about individual differences in imagery is wrong. It often is assumed, both in the scientific literature and in common conversation, that a person is either "good" or "bad" at imagery. In fact, it turns out that imagery is not a single ability. Rather, imagery is a collection of distinct abilities, such as the ability to rotate images, the ability to "inspect" them, the ability to hold many parts of an image at once, and so on. Further, people can be relatively "good" at one or more of these abilities, and poor at others (see Kosslyn et al., in press).

Conclusions

In this chapter we have briefly reviewed the nature and function of mental imagery. Imagery provides a special way of storing information that is unlike verbal means. Images depict information, and objects in images can be mentally manipulated much like the corresponding actual objects. Images share some of the same brain mechanisms used in perceiving in the same modality, and hence can interfere with like-modality perception. Images can depict three dimensions, but are seen from a particular point of view. Images occur on a "mental screen" that has a grain, obscuring details if they are too small, and has a limited extent, imposing a maximum size for images; and images can be used in a number of ways, from improving one's memory to reasoning.

Research on mental imagery is now progressing so rapidly that we are learning enough to program computers to mimic human mental imagery. One effort in that direction was reported by Kosslyn and Shwartz (1977, 1978). Figure 7.7 is a computer image of a car. This picture was printed out after the program had been asked to image a car and then was asked whether the car had a rear tire. The program scanned to the rear, found the tire, and responded. More time was required to do this than when the program was already focused on the rear, and scanning was not required, just as was found to be true of humans in the experiments described earlier. In Figure 7.7, you can see how the image has "overflowed" at the right-hand side of the mental screen; note also that the

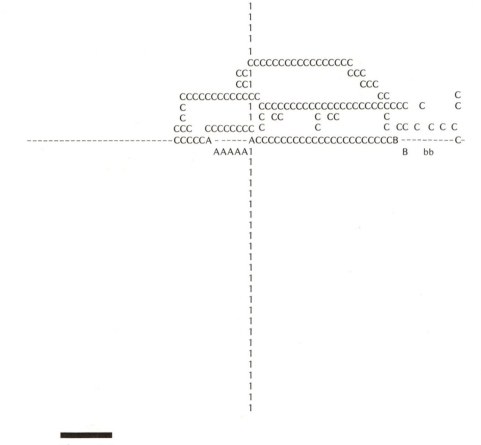

Figure 7.7
An example of a computer's "mental image," after the computer had been asked to find the rear tire and was focused upon it. Programming computers to mimic the human mind is one way to test theories of mental activity.

overflow is gradual, not sudden and sharp, which is also true of humans. The theory of imagery that guided construction of the computer program allows us to explain virtually all the effects of imagery on response time that have been described in this chapter, and most of the other results as well. (The theory has the most trouble with the imagery-induced illusions, which are not well-understood even in perception.) However, the point of formulating any theory is not only to explain the available results, but also to make new predictions, to help researchers collect new and interesting results. The computer model makes a number of such predictions. For example, it leads us to expect that smaller mental images can be rotated faster than larger images. Why? Because the image is represented as a set of points in a coordinate space. A rotation requires moving all the points in specified ways. Larger images cover a larger area in the space (a matrix in the computer), and hence more area must be processed when the points are moved around, which takes more time than when a smaller area is processed (Kosslyn, 1983).. This prediction has been supported by experiments with humans, who do indeed take less time to rotate smaller images.

In short, the Renaissance in interest in mental imagery has produced a host of new facts about imagery and new ways of theorizing about it. We truly have learned more about imagery in the past fifteen years than in all the preceding centuries combined, and the end of progress is not in sight.

References

Bisiach, E., and C. Luzzatti, 1978. Unilateral neglect of representational space. *Cortex,* 14, 129–133.

Bower, G. H. 1972. Mental imagery and associative learning. *In* L. Gregg, ed., *Cognition in Learning and Memory* (New York: Wiley).

Brooks, L. 1968. Spatial and verbal components of the act of recall. *Canadian Journal of Psychology,* 22, 349–368.

Clark, H. H. 1969. Linguistic processes in deductive reasoning. *Psychological Review,* 76, 387–404.

Denis, M. 1979. *Les Images Mentales.* Paris: Presses Univ. de France.

Denis, M. 1982. Imaging while reading text: a study of individual differences. *Memory and Cognition,* 10, 540–545.

Finke, R. A., and M. J. Schmidt. 1977. Orientation-specific color aftereffects following imagination. *Journal of Experimental Psychology: Human Perception and Performance,* 3, 599–606.

Galton, F. 1883. *Inquiries into Human Faculty and Its Development.* London: Macmillan.

Huttenlocher, J. 1968. Constructing spatial images: a strategy in reasoning. *Psychological Review,* 75, 550–560.

Kosslyn, S. M. 1978. Measuring the visual angle of the mind's eye. *Cognitive Psychology,* 10, 356–389.

———. 1980. *Image and Mind.* Cambridge, Mass.: Harvard Univ. Press.

———. 1983. *Ghosts in the Mind's Machine.* New York: Norton.

Kosslyn, S. M., J. L. Brunn, K. R. Cave, and R. W. Wallach. In press. Individual differences in mental imagery: A computational analysis. *Cognition.*

Kosslyn, S. M., and S. P. Shwartz. 1977. A simulation of visual imagery. *Cognitive Science,* 1, 265–295.

————. 1978. Visual images as spatial representations in active memory. *In* E. M. Riseman and A. R. Hanson, eds., *Computer Vision Systems* (New York: Academic Press).

Marks, D. F. 1977. Imagery and consciousness: A theoretical review from an individual differences perspective. *Journal of Mental Imagery,* 1, 275–290.

McKellar, P. 1965. The investigation of mental images. *In* S. A. Barnett and A. McLaren, eds., *Penguin Science Survey* (Harmondsworth, England: Penguin).

Natadze, R. 1960. Emergence of set on the basis of imaginal situations. *British Journal of Psychology,* 51, 237–245.

Paivio, A. 1971. *Imagery and Verbal Processes.* New York: Holt, Rinehart & Winston.

Perky, C. W. 1910. An experimental study of imagination. *American Journal of Psychology,* 21, 422–452.

Pinker, S. 1980. Mental imagery and the third dimension. *Journal of Experimental Psychology: General,* 109, 354–371.

Richardson, A. 1969. *Mental Imagery.* New York: Springer.

Segal, S. J., and V. Fusella. 1970. Influence of imagined pictures and sounds on detection of visual and auditory signals. *Journal of Experimental Psychology,* 83, 458–464.

Shepard, R. N. 1975. Form, formation, and transformation of internal representations. *In* R. L. Solso, ed., *Information Processing and Cognition: The Loyola Symposium* (Hillsdale, N.J.: Erlbaum).

Shepard, R. N., and Cooper, L. A. *Mental Images and their Transformations.* 1982. (Cambridge, Mass.: MIT Press.)

Shepard, R. N., and Feng, C. 1972. A chronometric study of mental paper folding. *Cognitive Psychology,* 3, 228–243.

Sternberg, R. J. 1980. Representation and process in linear syllogistic reasoning. *Journal of Experimental Psychology: General,* 109, 119–159.

White, K., P. W. Sheehan, and R. Ashton. 1977. Imagery assessment: a survey of self-report measures. *Journal of Mental Imagery,* 1, 145–170.

8

DEDUCTIVE
REASONING ABILITY

Philip N. Johnson-Laird
MRC Applied Psychology Unit of the Medical Research Council.
Cambridge, England

Suppose that someone is telling you about a newly married
couple, and says,
The husband speaks only Polish.
The wife speaks only English.

What conclusion would you draw? You might conclude that the couple
could not speak to each other and must communicate by signs and gestures, or
that they rely on an intermediary to translate between them. (You might even
suspect it was a marriage of convenience, perhaps to allow the man to leave
Poland.) What you have done is to combine the information that you have been
given with your general knowledge in order to deduce a conclusion. But is your
conclusion logically valid? Given that the premises are true, is your conclusion
that the couple cannot speak to each other also bound to be true? A moment's
thought should convince you that there is another possibility: although each

person *speaks* only a single language, at least one of them may *understand* the other's native tongue and therefore verbal communication would be possible between them.

This example illustrates most of the features of deduction that are likely to concern a psychologist. It suggests the following working definition that helps to delimit the field of inquiry: a *deduction* is a systematic process of thought that leads from one set of propositions to another, and that is supposed to be based on principles of logic. The purpose of logical principles is to guarantee validity, and a deduction is valid if and only if the truth of its premises suffices to ensure the truth of its conclusion. If the conclusion does not follow validly from the premises, then, strictly speaking, the deduction is fallacious, although it may be highly plausible and may lead to a conclusion that is, in fact, true. Often in daily life, reasoners will settle for a plausible conclusion, but they will also occasionally attempt to draw a logically valid one.

Psychologists have studied deductive ability for a long time, and there are two distinct tacks that they have taken toward it. The first is concerned with the practical business of assessing an individual's ability in relation to a norm, and the second with unravelling the different mental processes that underlie a deduction. The first approach predominated until recently because, surprisingly, psychologists can measure deductive skill even if they do not know what it consists of. The second approach has blossomed in the last decade or so, because of the progress that has been made in computers and computer programming. I will begin this discussion by considering the traditional studies of deductive ability, and then go on to examine investigations of the mechanisms of thought. I will also consider possible effects of culture on reasoning, the development of logical thinking in children, differences from one individual to another in deductive ability, and various sorts of pathological thinking.

The Assessment of Deductive Ability

During World War II, psychologists working for the British Air Ministry were asked to devise a test that would assess the ability of potential rear-gunners in bomber planes. What was needed was some way of predicting their likely competence without putting them and their crews at risk. A plausible test would be to seat them in the rear turret of a plane on the ground and have them shoot at various targets moving in three dimensions. A sample of gunners that had been tested could then be sent into the air, and, after some suitable period of time in combat, each gunner's performance could be examined to decide whether it was predicted by his score on the test. If it was, then the test could be used to select those people who were likely to be good at shooting down enemy aircraft.

In practice, however, tests of this sort, despite appearing to have considerable validity, often turn out to be rather poor predictors. Such was the case with the test for rear-gunners: the Air Ministry's psychologists discovered that a better test was simply to see how well an individual could shoot at targets moving only in the horizontal dimension. Hence, the general strategy for constructing such tests is to try out a whole range of potential measures, to examine how well each of them predicts actual performance, and to select the test (or set of tests) that makes the best predictions.

Exactly this technique was used to construct early tests of intelligence, and it was soon discovered that tests which require deductive ability are a good predictor of conventional academic excellence; clever people are skillful in making deductions. Since then, although a whole variety of different sorts of intelligence tests have been developed, tests of deductive ability continue to be used in measuring intelligence. Remarkably, psychologists never know what these tests are actually measuring. All they know is that different people perform at different levels, and that their performance predicts (with some margin of error) their competence in other, more conventional intellectual tasks.

By far the most controversial issue about reasoning ability arises from its alleged relation to race and culture. Undoubtedly, peoples from so-called "primitive" cultures do not score very highly on tests of reasoning. It would be silly to give a verbal test that had been standardized on urban Americans to a group of African tribesmen. Even if it were possible to translate the test into the appropriate language, most of the items would probably refer to ideas and entities totally unfamiliar to them. There have accordingly been attempts to devise tests that are independent of a person's cultural background. Although some tests are certainly less dependent than others on such a background, there is at least one reason for supposing that it is impossible to make sensible comparisons between the gross deductive abilities of individuals from different cultures. Cultures differ in the extent to which reason is employed for its own sake and divorced from the demands of daily life. Perhaps the best way to illustrate this point is to consider the findings of cross-cultural psychologists.

Sylvia Scribner (1977) and her colleagues have shown that people in nonliterate cultures are often not prepared to play the "game" of making deductions in a laboratory setting. The following dialogue illustrates the performance of such a nonparticipant. The subject was given the following deductive problem.

> *All Kpelle men are rice farmers.*
> *Mr. Smith is not a rice farmer.*
> *Is he a Kpelle man?*

The subject was himself a member of the Kpelle (a group who live in the African state of Liberia), but, as the following dialogue shows, he was not prepared to play the experimenter's game.

> *Subject (S): I don't know the man in person. I have not laid eyes on the man himself.*
> *Experimenter (E): Just think about the statement.*
> *S: If I knew him in person, I can answer that question, but since I do not know him in person, I cannot answer that question.*
> *E: Try and answer from your Kpelle sense.*
> *S: If you know a person, if a question comes up about him you are able to answer. But if you do not know the person, if a question comes up about him it's hard for you to answer.*

Although the Kpelle subject is not prepared to make the deduction, it would be a mistake to assume that he is incapable of rational thought. Indeed, it is quite clear from the dialogue that he is able to make a deduction, moreover, one of the same general form that interests the experimenter. The argument underlying the subject's remarks can be paraphrased as follows.

All the deductions that I can make are about individuals that I know.
I do not know Mr. Smith.
Therefore I cannot make a deduction about Mr. Smith.

It seems that the Kpelle subject can make deductions if they are really demanded by the context, but cannot or will not make them otherwise. Hence, he makes a deduction (one demanded by the situation) to explain why he cannot make the deduction asked for in the experiment.

The Russian psychologist A. R. Luria (1977) reported similar findings in a study with nonliterate Uzbekistanian women. It is likely, as Scribner argues (1977), that literacy, rather than other cultural differences, is the critical variable. In all the experiments that my colleagues and I have carried out on European students, we have encountered only one subject who was not prepared to play the game of deductive reasoning, again on the grounds of not being acquainted with the people referred to in the premises.

No doubt there are cultural differences in intelligence. Few of us would be able to make fire from a wooden drill, to track an animal in an arid desert, or to navigate a boat on the basis of the rising and setting of the stars. Conversely, it is hardly surprising that most people outside the middle classes of the Western world have difficulty in coping with the experience of a psychological test. Certainly, the most profound effect on deductive reason appears to be exerted not by cultural background, but by education and, in particular, by learning to read. It is easy to speculate on why reading should enhance the propensity to make deductive inferences, but the precise nature of the relation between reading and reasoning is not yet known. A reluctance to make inferences is not the same as an inability, however, and there remains no evidence that culture directly affects the fundamental operations of thought.

Deductive Reasoning and Mental Representation

The measurement of reasoning ability has revealed very little about the mental processes that occur in deduction, and we must turn to experimental investigations to learn more. The general procedure in such studies is to give subjects deductive problems to solve, to observe the characteristics of their performance, and to try to develop an account of the underlying mental processes. Here is an example of a so-called "three-term series" problem, which the reader can solve deductively.

Joyce is taller than Evelyn.
Evelyn is taller than Vivian.
Who is tallest?

Although the answer is obvious, the processes by which you arrive at it are surprisingly complex. As with any intellectual problem (Polya, 1957), they require several stages.

First, you must understand the problem. You have to grasp the initial conditions, and the goal, which is to determine which of the three individuals (Joyce, Evelyn, or Vivian) is the tallest. You must also appreciate any general constraints or conditions that apply to the problem. A logician, for example, would argue that you must grasp that the relation of "taller than" is transitive, though perhaps such a statement is slightly misleading.

Second, you have to devise a plan. Most people immediately realize that they should try to put together the information in the two premises. This procedure is so obvious that they hardly have to think about it; nevertheless, the decision to use this procedure does require a process of thought. A computer program for solving a variety of problems would have to contain a procedure to select a method that is appropriate for any given problem. Young children, who have great difficulty in putting things into serial order (Inhelder and Piaget, 1964; Young, 1978), may not grasp the need to do so in solving a three-term series problem. Certainly, the ability to arrange objects in a serial order generally develops before the ability to make transitive inferences (Murray and Youniss, 1968).

Third, you must execute the plan without error. The solution of the current problem is simple, but a mistake can occur if, for example, you forget one of the premises. Children's inability to solve three-term series problems is often nothing more than a trivial failure in memory rather than a serious logical deficiency (Bryant and Trabasso, 1971).

Fourth, you should check your answer and perhaps consider whether there is another way to proceed. Here there is probably no simpler solution, but other relational inferences can be very much more complicated, as in the following example.

> John stood in the last local elections in Camden.
> Camden is a borough of London.
> London had its annual borough election on Tuesday.
> Therefore John stood in the election on Tuesday.

However, you should be cautious. Once you have deduced the correct answer to a problem, it is all too easy to apply the method by rote. What do you do if you have a four-legged table that wobbles? Wedge something under one of the legs. And what do you do if you have a three-legged table that wobbles? Many people volunteer the same answer. They are mistaken; a three-legged table cannot wobble.

Deductive inferences in daily life seldom call for a complicated strategy, but many problems in which deduction plays a part can be solved only by following a complex method. Workers in the field of Artificial Intelligence have developed computer programs that model overall problem-solving strategies. For example, Newell and Simon (1972) have developed a computer program, the General Problem Solver, that models the process of reducing problems to subproblems; the program can be used for any domain in which the basic elements and operations can be spelled out explicitly, including problems that depend on deduction. Most of the experimental work on deductive reasoning, however, has concerned the elementary steps by which information in premises is combined to yield new information.

With three-term series problems, the main puzzle is the precise nature of the mental representation of the premises and of the mental processes by which the conclusion is derived. Hunter (1957), in a classic paper on the topic, suggested that the reasoner's basic goal, given such premises as

> B > C   (B is larger than C)
> A > B   (A is larger than B)

is to construct a linear order of the form

> A > B > C

It is therefore necessary to make a mental reordering of the premises:

> A > B
> B > C

It is then relatively straightforward to combine them into

> A > B > C

and to use this representation to answer any question about which entity is the largest or smallest, or to delete the middle term to yield the conclusion

> A > C   (A is larger than C).

Later workers advanced the similar idea that subjects construct a mental array of the three items, and that there are various constraints on this process that render it harder for certain premises. De Soto, London, and Handel (1965) argued that in constructing a vertical array, it is harder to work from the bottom upward than from the top downward; and Huttenlocher (1968) claimed that it is easier to encode a premise if the first item is an *end anchor* (i.e., an item that occurs at one end of the array) than if it is the middle term.

These approaches are often supposed to conflict with a psycholinguistic theory advanced by Clark (1969). Clark argued that a term such as "better" is easier to understand than its antonym "worse," because the former is essentially neutral and affirmative in tone, whereas the latter is clearly contrastive and negative in tone. An example of the contrast that underlies Clark's thinking here is the difference between asking

> *How good is it?*

which does not convey any strong presupposition about its worth, and asking

> *How bad is it?*

which does suggest that the speaker presupposes that it is bad. Clark likewise argued that explicit negation, as in a premise of the form

B *is not as good as* A

would cause difficulty. He also supposed that if there is a mismatch between the comparative in the premises

B *is better than* C
A *is better than* B

and the comparative in the question

Is C *worse than* A?

then the problem will be harder. Clark's experimental results corroborated these claims.

There is nothing essentially irreconcilable about a theory based on constructing an internal array and a theory that emphasizes the importance of linguistic variables. I proposed a reconciliation of the two approaches (Johnson-Laird, 1972), and many experimental results suggest both that different subjects may employ different procedures (Shaver et al., 1974; Ormrod, 1979; Egan and Grimes-Farrow, 1982), and that individuals can be induced to change their representations of linear orders (Wood, 1969; Mynatt and Smith, 1977; Mayer, 1979; Sternberg and Weil, 1980).

Three-term series problems are examples of deductions that depend on the "logic" of relations. A crucial aspect of such deductions, regardless of their mental representation, is how reasoners grasp their logical validity. One view is that children learn that certain relations, such as "greater than," are transitive, whereas other relations, such as "father of," are not. This doctrine posits logical knowledge in the mind. Until recently, there seemed to be no other possibility, and the doctrine of mental logic was largely taken for granted by workers in the field. It is worth examining the doctrine closely, however, since there is now a viable, and perhaps more plausible, alternative to it.

Mental Logic and Children's Development of Logical Ability

The fundamental principle of all deductive inference is that a conclusion is warranted if there is no counterexample to it. In other words, a deduction is valid provided that there is no way of interpreting the premises that is consistent with the conclusion's being false. Logicians have made it their business to try to capture the principles of valid deduction within formal logical calculi. Psychologists, however, are concerned with the mental processes by which people attempt to make valid deductions. They are confronted with this puzzle: how is it possible to make valid deductions without the use of logic? The question is paradoxical, because the invention of logic would seem to require the ability to reason validly, but this ability in turn might seem to depend on an existing logic.

One possible resolution of the riddle was provided by the Swiss scholar, the late Jean Piaget.

Piaget's concern was to understand the growth of knowledge from childhood to adulthood, and to explain how human beings come to know the world, how they develop the power of rational thought, and how they create abstract disciplines, such as mathematics and formal logic. The central assumption of his theory is that the evolution of knowledge is governed by the same principles that govern the evolution of species. The mind is an organism that grows and adapts like any other; it assimilates reality or else transforms itself to accommodate it, much as an amoeba copes with its environment. Indeed, the evolutionary process, which starts with the simple behavior of single-celled organisms, leads to the actions by which human infants come to act on the world, and in turn to the mental representation of these actions, which (according to Piaget) is the basis of all rational thought.

Piaget divided the development of intelligence, which culminates in deductive competence, into several separate stages, though perhaps his followers make more of the chronology of these stages than Piaget did himself. During the first eighteen months or so of life, infants are primarily mastering simple sensory and motor skills. Around the time when children seem to evince a grasp of such concepts as cause and effect (and intention), they begin to develop language, and enter the second stage of intellectual growth, the *preoperational* stage. For Piaget, the main importance of language was that it provides a symbolic system for representing the world. But even when children have become very competent in their native tongue, they are still likely to make surprising errors in thought.

A typical Piagetian investigation illustrates a failure in reasoning about sets. The experimenter places about twenty beads in a box, and the child acknowledges that they are "all made of wood." Most of the beads are brown, and the remainder are white. In order to find out whether the child understands that the set of beads is composed of the set of brown beads and the set of white beads, the experimenter asks the question, "Which are there more of, wooden beads or brown beads?" Children in the preoperational stage almost always respond that there are more brown beads "because there are only two or three white ones." They fail to grasp that the question is comparing the size of a set with the size of one of its own subsets.

The difficulty that these children experience arises, according to Piaget, because they have great trouble in mentally representing operations that are reversible. Only when children appreciate that constructing the complement of a set is a reversible operation will they understand that one set can be included within another. A successful grasp of this principle leads directly to the third stage in intellectual development, the stage of so-called *concrete operations.*

The final mastery of deductive reasoning depends on one further stage in the Piagetian saga, a grasp of *formal operations* (Inhelder and Piaget, 1958). Consider the following problem, which children cannot normally solve until about the age of twelve. There are four colorless, odorless liquids (1 to 4), each in a similar flask, and a smaller flask that contains another test liquid. The experimenter presents two glasses to the subject: one in fact contains two of the liquids (1 and 3) mixed together, and the other contains just one of them (2). In front of the subject, he pours several drops of the test liquid from the smaller flask into both glasses. The mixture of 1 and 3 turns yellow, the other liquid does not. The child's task is to work out how to produce yellow. Younger children will try mixing the test liquid with each of the four liquids separately; only the older children will appraise the effects of adding the test liquid to systematic combinations of the four liquids. Piaget's view was that the ability to solve this sort of problem depends on the capacity to carry out operations, not on concrete objects, but on abstract propositions. These formal operations are made possible only by the development of a complete mental logic, which corresponds to the logicians' propositional calculus.

The work of Piaget and his colleagues in Geneva is both influential and controversial. It has had a great and probably beneficial impact on what happens in the primary schools of the Western world. It has also been criticized on several distinct grounds. The theory is vague, and contains many loopholes that allow inconvenient facts to be explained away. There are feasible alternative explanations for the main phenomena. Children of a much younger age than the theory would allow can reason correctly if care is taken to ensure that they remember the information given to them (Bryant and Trabasso, 1971), that they are not misled by confusing questions (Donaldson, 1978), and that they are given problems about familiar objects in familiar relationships (such as parents and children within a family, rather than brown and white beads within a set of wooden ones—see Markman and Seibert, 1976). Nevertheless, Piaget's theory gives a comprehensive account of how mental logic could in principle develop. For many years, psychologists have indeed taken logic for granted, and assumed that their business is to discover which particular logic and formal rules of inference are to be found in the mind. The difficulties for the doctrine of mental logic itself have only gradually emerged.

One obvious problem is that people commit fallacies. They do not invariably draw valid conclusions. Indeed, there are some inferential tasks that children ought to have mastered by the stage of formal operations, and that most adults nevertheless get wrong. Here is an example of one such task that defeats many people. It was invented by Peter Wason, and he and I carried out many investigations of it (Wason and Johnson-Laird, 1972).

> You are given a pack of special cards, and you check that each card has a letter on one side and a number on the other side. The experimenter takes four cards at random from the pack, and the rest of the experiment concerns only these four cards. They are laid out in front of you on the table, e.g., E, K, 4, and 7. The experimenter then states a general rule: If a card has a vowel on one side, then it has an even number on the other side. Your task is to decide which cards you need to turn over in order to find out whether the rule is true or false. You could elect to turn over all four cards, but this selection would not be economical: you have to choose just those cards that it is necessary to turn over. Likewise, you should not worry about

the order in which you turn over the cards: imagine that you are going to turn them over at one and the same time.

The problem is difficult, as you can find out by trying it. If you are not forewarned of its difficulty, however, you may consider it to be trivial. Even if you do see that it is deceptive, you may still fail to make the correct selection. Typically, subjects choose the card with the vowel on it (*E*) and the card with the even number on it (4), though some people prefer to select just the former card. Obviously, it is correct to choose the card with the vowel on it, because if there is an odd number on its other side, then the general rule is false. However, there is no point to choosing the card with the even number on it. If it has a vowel on its other side, then it is consistent with the rule; and if it has a consonant on its other side, then it is not inconsistent with the rule. The rule as stated does not imply that if a card has an even number on one side, then it has a vowel on its other side. Choosing the card with the even number on it is therefore merely a waste of time.

The subjects' real error in this task is one of omission. Almost always they fail to select the card with the odd number (7) on it. Indeed, they will often say, when questioned after the experiment, that the card is irrelevant to the truth of the rule. Yet, remember that if the card with the vowel on it has an odd number on its other side, then the rule is false; that was the motivation for choosing the card with the vowel. Therefore, if the card with the odd number on it is turned over to reveal a vowel, then the rule is also proved false. The importance of this common failure to make the correct selection is twofold.

First, it casts doubt on the idea that there is a mental logic. Piaget went so far as to claim that whenever adults seek to test a rule of the form, "If *X* is the case, then *Y* is the case," they use logic to form the contradiction of the rule ("*X* is the case and *Y* is not the case"), and then actively search for instances of this contradiction (Beth and Piaget, 1966). Plainly, the university students whom we tested in our experiments were not following this principle; yet, according to Piaget, they should have mastered it by the age of twelve.

Second, the phenomenon points toward what may be a more plausible account of human deductive reasoning. Wason and I devoted several years to the study of what causes the reluctance to falsify assertions. We tried numerous ways to overcome it (Johnson-Laird and Wason, 1977). Some of our experiments took a form that resembled brief psychotherapy directed toward engaging logical insight. By far the most dramatic way of inculcating insight, however, is merely to change the nature of the materials. It took us some time to discover this fact.

One way of doing the experiment, which Paolo and Maria Legrenzi and I developed, is to use a set of envelopes, including one that is face down and sealed, one that is face down and unsealed, one that is face up with a 50-*lire* stamp on it, and one that is face up with a 40-*lire* stamp on it. The subjects are then asked which envelopes they would like to turn over in order to discover whether or not they violate the following postal regulation: "If a letter is sealed, then it has a 50-*lire* stamp on it." With these materials, our subjects, who were

British, had no difficulty in realizing that they should turn over both the sealed envelope and the envelope with the 40-*lire* stamp on it. This insight did not transfer to an abstract version of the task, where the subjects once again failed to select the potentially falsifying instance (Johnson-Laird et al., 1972).

There has been controversy about why insight occurs with realistic materials and practical everyday rules. The phenomenon has been corroborated in some experiments (Gilhooly and Falconer, 1974; Mandler, 1980; Pollard, 1981; Pollard and Evans, 1981; Cox and Griggs, 1982), but not in others using slightly different materials (Manktelow and Evans, 1979; Brown et al., 1980). Undoubtedly, the content of a reasoning problem matters, presumably because it can engage memories that are relevant to the problem. Such effects of content, however, cannot be readily reconciled with a mental logic.

Reasoning and Mental Models

A system of logic contains rules of inference that apply to all assertions of a particular form, such as, "If *X* is the case, then *Y* is the case," regardless of their content. Since our results suggest that reasoners are very much affected by the content of premises, it looks as though the mind does not ordinarily follow any formal rules of inference contained within a mental logic. Many psychologists and philosophers find this claim very puzzling. How, they wonder, are people able to make valid deductions if they do not rely on a logic? One possible solution to the puzzle arises from the study of a different sort of deduction, such as the following.

All prudent men shun hyenas.
All bankers are prudent men.
Therefore all bankers shun hyenas.

This is an example, dreamed up by Lewis Carroll, of what logicians, following Aristotle, call a *syllogism*. Psychologists have been studying the errors that people make in syllogistic inferences for at least seventy years (Störring, 1908), and have proposed several theories about the causes of these errors. An early and influential hypothesis is that reasoners are seduced by the *atmosphere* of the premises (Woodworth and Sells, 1935). For example, consider the following premises.

All the pilots are artists.
All the skiers are artists.

Some subjects will judge that the following conclusion,

All the pilots are skiers

is valid. This mistake is supposed to result from the atmosphere created by the two premises containing "all." An alternative explanation, however, is that subjects assume illicitly that the premise

All the skiers are artists

is equivalent to its converse,

All the artists are skiers.

Once this step is made, the conclusion above is valid (Chapman and Chapman, 1959), but the fallacy of assuming that a premise containing "All" is equivalent to its converse is obvious from observing that "All dogs are animals" differs in meaning from "All animals are dogs."

The trouble with such proposals is that they tell us nothing about the mental processes underlying *valid* deductions. Indeed, only within the last decade have psychologists put forward explicit information-processing theories of syllogistic inference. Erickson (1974) has argued that subjects represent premises in a form corresponding to so-called *Euler circles,* in which circles are used to represent sets. A premise such as

All the pilots are artists

requires two separate arrangements of circles (see Figure 8.1).

In Figure 8.1, the left-hand arrangement represents the case where the set of pilots is properly included within the set of artists; the right-hand arrangement represents the case where the two sets are coextensive. Unfortunately, Euler circles suffer from two severe problems as a basis for psychological theory. First, the representations of the two premises can be combined in an embarrassingly large number of ways. Second, there are many nonsyllogistic inferences, such as,

Some of the pilots don't like some of the artists;
therefore not all the artists are liked by all the pilots.

These cannot even be expressed within Euler circles.

Erickson dealt with the combinatorial problem by assuming that reasoners do not always consider the full set of distinct ways in which an individual premise can be represented, and that they often fail to construct the complete set of combined representations of the two premises. However, in order to account for some of their *correct* responses, he had to assume that reasoners were prey to atmosphere effects. Sternberg and his colleagues have recently proposed a theory of syllogistic reasoning based on strings of symbols corresponding to Euler circles, and they likewise limit the number of combinations that reasoners

Figure 8.1

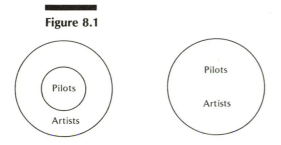

are supposed to construct (Guyote and Sternberg, 1981). Both theories accordingly imply that human beings are intrinsically irrational in dealing with many syllogisms; neither theory can be readily extended to explain simple nonsyllogistic inferences like the one just given.

A different approach could be based on the assumption that the mind contains the quantificational calculus: the general logic for expressions containing "all," "some," and other such quantifiers. In seeking to avoid this assumption of a mental logic, I have argued that making an inference is rather like constructing a *mental model* of the state of affairs described in the premises, and then searching for variants of this model in order to discover whether there are any conclusions that must be true (Johnson-Laird, 1983). Consider again the following premises:

> *All the pilots are artists.*
> *All the skiers are artists.*

One way in which you could try to make a deduction from these two premises would be by gathering together some actors in a room, and then assigning them the roles of pilot, artist, and skier, in accordance with the premises. Hence, you might interpret the first premise by establishing a scene in which there are six actors as shown in Figure 8.2.

Three of the actors play the part of pilots and, in accordance with the premise, they are all artists (as indicated by the identity signs). Three other actors play the part of artists who are not pilots, since the premise allows the existence of such individuals. However, you cannot be sure that they exist, because the two sets could be coextensive; so their doubtful status is indicated by parentheses. The actual number of actors (here, six) that you have employed is arbitrary, and makes no difference to the nature of the deduction. When you are given the second premise, "All the skiers are artists," you have to incorporate its information into the scene. A useful rule of thumb, which will ensure that you are always able to produce a tentative conclusion, is to be as economical as possible and to give the greatest number of different roles to the smallest number of actors. If you follow this rule, then you will assign the role of skier to precisely the same actors who are playing the part of pilots. You thus establish the scene in Figure 8.3.

Figure 8.2

---

pilot = artist
pilot = artist
pilot = artist
           (artist)
           (artist)
           (artist)

Figure 8.3

pilot	=	artist	=	skier
pilot	=	artist	=	skier
pilot	=	artist	=	skier
		(artist)		
		(artist)		
		(artist)		

You might be tempted, in perusing this scene, to draw the conclusion that

All the pilots are skiers.

Some subjects in the experiments that my colleagues and I have carried out do draw this fallacious conclusion. It is, of course, precisely the same error that the concepts of atmosphere effect and illicit conversion were independently invoked to explain; but neither of these hypotheses is required by the present theory (see Revlis, 1975, who has developed both of them into complete information-processing models). Moreover, if you are a prudent person, then you will attempt to submit your model to a "logical" test. You will try to apply what I referred to earlier as the fundamental principle of all deductive inference: an inference is valid if and only if there is no way of interpreting the premises that would render its conclusion false. You should readily appreciate that the roles could be reallocated to produce the scene in Figure 8.4.
This tableau may tempt you instead to draw the conclusion that

Some of the pilots are skiers.

Once again, although some of our subjects drew this conclusion (and it is one that cannot be predicted by the atmosphere hypothesis), it is fallacious. You can in fact rearrange the scene to correspond to Figure 8.5, which is still consistent with the meaning of the premises. It should now be clear that there is *no* valid conclusion that states a definite relationship between skiers and pilots.

Reasoning may consist in the manipulation of mental models that correspond to internal analogues of scenes of actors. Most people, however, are wholly unaware of how they reason, which suggests that mental models can be

Figure 8.4

pilot	=	artist	=	skier
pilot	=	artist	=	skier
pilot	=	artist		
		artist	=	skier
		(artist)		
		(artist)		

━━━━━━

Figure 8.5

pilot	=	artist		
pilot	=	artist		
pilot	=	artist		
		artist	=	skier
		artist	=	skier
		artist	=	skier

manipulated outside of conscious awareness. Nevertheless, the errors that subjects make in syllogistic inference are entirely consistent with this theory of models. People fail to consider all the possible models of the premises, as I illustrated in the preceding example. In fact, according to the theory, syllogistic premises that lead to valid conclusions fall into three categories: those that permit only one mental model to be constructed, those that permit two different models, and those that permit three different models. My colleagues and I have found, in a variety of experiments, a highly reliable trend in difficulty: one-model problems are easier than two-model problems, which in turn are easier than three-model problems (Johnson-Laird and Steedman, 1978; Johnson-Laird and Bara, in press). If all the different models are properly constructed, and if what they have in common is correctly evaluated, then (in accordance with the fundamental principle of deductive inference) no invalid conclusion will ever be drawn. Such a system does not embody a mental logic comprising formal rules of inference; nor does it resort to a systematic procedure for searching for counterexamples. However, unlike the use of Euler circles, the system can be readily extended to deal with nonsyllogistic deductions. The origins of logic as an intellectual discipline may well lie in conscious reflection on the problem of systematizing what is ordinarily done in a barely conscious and relatively haphazard way.

The theory of mental models also explains why the content of a problem may affect the ability to falsify a rule; subjects are not testing the rule according to a formal logic, but instead are constructing a mental model of the state of affairs described by the rule. This model will take into account their general knowledge of the situation. When this knowledge is rich, then it is relatively easy for them to entertain alternative rules to the one presented by the experimenter, and perhaps only then is a subject readily able to search for counterexamples to the rule.

Pathological Thinking and Logical Errors

Many psychologists who hold to the doctrine of mental logic argue that people never make logical mistakes; instead, they merely misunderstand or forget the premises, bring to mind irrelevant facts, or fail to use their knowledge of logic (Henle, 1978). Such claims are tendentious; they are motivated by an overwhelming faith in the rationality of conscious thought. There is, as we have seen, no need to give up the idea that human beings are fundamentally rational; this thesis can be maintained without arguing that there is *mental logic*. It is plausible to suppose that people do sometimes think irrationally, since, for example, they sometimes fail to make proper searches for counterexamples (Johnson-Laird, 1982). There are practical difficulties in fully investigating this conjecture in the laboratory. Nevertheless, several independent sources of evidence suggest that the process of thought can go wrong in this way.

First, it is a common observation that when people are upset, in a panic, or under the sway of a strong emotion or prejudice, they may cease to think rationally. Everyone has had the experience of making a silly mistake under stress. The annals of military history are full of notorious blunders committed in the heat of battle or in anticipatory fear of it. The British psychologist Norman Dixon has shown in a study of military incompetence that such mistakes can be made by otherwise clever and sensitive individuals (Dixon, 1976). The fall of the island of Singapore in World War II provides an excellent example. General Percival, who was an intelligent and sympathetic commander of the city, completely failed to set up adequate defenses against a possible attack by the Japanese from the mainland. He even failed to take such steps when explicitly ordered to do so by Churchill, and argued that they would be bad for the morale of civilians. The causes of such blunders are complicated and not well understood. It seems, however, that a sort of intellectual *tunnel vision* can result from anxiety, stress, or other highly emotional states of mind. People neglect to consider, or to search for, obvious counterexamples to conclusions that they hold dear.

Second, damage to the brain as a result of an accident or stroke can impair deductive thought. Damage to the right hemisphere may affect the ability to organize spatial relations. Damage to the left hemisphere may affect linguistic ability, and may lead to obvious errors in thought. For example, one patient denied that he had had an operation, but complained about the "hammering and sawing" that had been done to his head (Weinstein and Kahn, 1959). Brain damage may also lead to an inability to think about abstract matters (to find the characteristic common to a set of objects, for example). Such a patient can cope with the routine of daily life, but becomes incapable of solving simple reasoning problems (Goldstein, 1959).

Third, mental illness often interferes with an individual's thought processes. Certain psychiatrists have claimed that schizophrenics are governed by a mental logic that contains pathological rules of inference (von Domarus, 1944; Arieti, 1965; Matte-Blanco, 1965). In particular, patients are said to deduce that entities with similar properties are identical. They are accordingly supposed to make inferences of the following sort.

> *I am a virgin;*
> *the Virgin Mary was a virgin;*
> *therefore I am the Virgin Mary.*

Here is an example from a transcript of a patient talking to a therapist, and seeming to slip into this sort of fallacy:

"Do you know the difference between closeness, likeness, sameness, and oneness? Close is close, as with you; when you are like somebody, you are only like the other; sameness—you are the same as the other, but he is still he and you are you; but oneness is not two—it is one, that's horrible— horrible! (The patient jumps up in a sudden panic.) Don't get too close, get away from the couch, I don't want to be one with you." (Jacobson, 1954)

Similarly, psychotic patients often appear to be quite impervious to conterexamples to their delusions (McReynolds, 1960). Strangely, however, they can maintain them in a stubbornly dogmatic and often logical manner:

Therapist: *We are friends, aren't we?*

Patient: *Oh no, we are not; we hardly know each other and, besides you want me to change, so how can you say that you are a friend of the person I am now? (Fromm-Reichmann, 1959)*

People with extreme prejudices, or systematic delusions, often actively avoid counterexamples to them, and go out of their way to seek confirming evidence to support their folly.

Undoubtedly, there are pathological errors of thought, but there are no grounds for supposing that they derive from an aberrant mental logic. As we have seen, the study of normal people in a laboratory setting reveals that they often commit fallacies of a "pathological" sort. They will accept as valid arguments such as the following.

All the pilots are artists.
All the skiers are artists.
Therefore all the pilots are skiers.

And this form of argument is, of course, comparable to the example about the Virgin Mary. Obviously, people are perfectly capable of rational thought in daily life; yet, confronted with a relatively strange task in the laboratory, they no longer follow the fundamental principle of deductive reasoning. Since these errors can be explained in terms of the theory of mental models, the same theory (rather than an aberrant mental logic) may account for the pathological thinking of brain-damaged and psychotic patients. The crucial distinction between sanity and insanity concerns the prevalence of error, and the nature of the subject matter that elicits it. Psychiatric patients are likely to be disturbed in their reasoning about the most basic aspects of life.

Individual Differences in Reasoning Ability

People differ in their ability to make valid deductions. It is for this reason, as I remarked at the outset, that tests of intelligence so often include reasoning problems. One simple index of the range in ability is that the best subject that my colleagues and I have ever tested drew 85 percent valid conclusions from syllogistic premises, whereas the worst subject that we have tested drew only 15 percent. Why do subjects differ so markedly? It is no use replying that they differ in their intelligence, because the ability to make deductions is surely just one component of intelligence rather than vice versa. A more sensible approach, pioneered by, among others, the editor of this volume, is to examine the component skills underlying reasoning and to discover which differences in them correlate with reasoning performance.

Mental tests do provide us with one clue, however. Factor analysis of test scores in intelligence tests reveals a number of factors, including what are generally labeled *verbal ability* and *spatial ability*. You might suppose that both these factors are important in syllogistic reasoning. In fact, spatial ability turns out to be a much better predictor of accuracy in reasoning than does verbal ability (Frandsen and Holder, 1969; Guyote and Sternberg, 1981). This result may seem puzzling, especially to theorists who propose that deductive reasoning involves verbal manipulations or operations on strings of wordlike symbols. But there is a ready explanation of the phenomenon.

According to the theory of mental models, syllogistic inference depends on the following three component skills.

1. The ability to understand premises and to imagine a state of affairs that corresponds to them, i.e., the ability to construct integrated mental models based on verbal descriptions.
2. The ability to search for alternative models of premises, and to discover what, if anything, such models have in common.
3. The ability to express in words the state of affairs represented in a model or set of models.

The first and third of these abilities are essentially just a normal capacity to use one's native tongue. Of course, people do differ in their verbal competence, particularly in understanding, verifying, and producing discourse (Hunt, 1978; MacLeod et al., 1978; Goldman-Eisler, 1968). But this type of difference is not likely to affect accuracy in syllogistic inference, though it may affect speed. Subjects should therefore not differ very much in their performance with one-model syllogisms, because valid conclusions can be drawn from them solely by verbal means (components 1 and 3). Indeed, the major differences in performance occur with the two-model and the three-model problems, where accuracy depends on the ability to construct alternative mental models (component 2). This constructive skill should correlate with spatial ability rather than verbal ability. The process of manipulating mental models must also depend on the capacity of working memory (Baddeley and Hitch, 1974), and a recent unpublished study by my colleague Jane Oakhill has established a significant correlation between a simple measure of the efficiency of working memory and accuracy in syllogistic inference.

Conclusions

This chapter has examined two main areas of psychological investigation: the measurement of deductive reasoning ability and the study of its underlying mental mechanisms. Tests of reasoning ability have been in use since the turn of the century, and have had some profound effects on educational practice in both the United States and Europe. Although psychologists can, in principle, measure something even if they do not know what it is, there are clear limits to the usefulness of the practice. It is sensible to measure an individual's likely aptitude as a rear-gunner; there is an obvious way to check the validity of the test. Unfortunately, there is no comparable criterion for deductive ability, since skill in reasoning shows up in a variety of ways, many of which may not be measurable by reasoning tests. In the past, psychologists have had a naive faith in the power of such methods. They have believed that merely by collecting data from a whole battery of tests and validating them against some external criterion, they could uncover the intellectual components of the mind. However, the mind cannot be measured by so crude an instrument. Commenting on the failure of the great French mathematician Galois to pass the entrance examination of the Ecole Polytechnique, his biographer wrote, "A candidate of superior intelligence is lost with an examiner of inferior intelligence." The same comment might aptly be made about tests of reasoning ability. They have added little to our knowledge of human mentality. Only when we turn to the theoretical and experimental study of thinking do we find that progress has been made.

Until recently, psychologists have studied reasoning in a piecemeal fashion. They have hardly considered what it is that the mind does in drawing a deductive inference, and they have assumed tacitly that formal logic provides a useful model of the enterprise. I have tried to challenge this view in this chapter. The effects of the content of a rule on subjects' attempts to test it argue against any simple doctrine of mental logic. This challenge might be countered, however, by arguing that the rules of mental logic are not formal, but take content into account. Such a scheme might be feasible, and certainly computer programs have been devised that work in this way (Winograd, 1972). The main problem with this idea as a psychological hypothesis is to explain how such rules are acquired by the mind without invoking other, purely formal, rules.

A more radical explanation of deductive ability depends on the notion of mental models. This theory assumes that the mind has procedures for interpreting premises as models, which are analogous to scenes of actors, and for searching for alternative models of premises that are counterexamples to conclusions. The search is guided by the fundamental principle of deductive inference, which governs all formal logics, though it is not directly expressed in any of them: a conclusion is valid if there are no counterexamples to it. The process of constructing a model depends on the ability to understand the premises and on general knowledge. The virtue of this account of deductive reasoning is that it is compatible with the human propensities both to think rationally and to err.

References

Arieti, S. 1965. Contributions to cognition from psychoanalytic theory. *In* J. H. Masserman, ed., *Communication and Community* (New York: Grune and Stratton).

Baddeley, A., and G. Hitch. 1974. Working memory. In G. H. Bower, ed., *The Psychology of Learning and Motivation, Vol. 8* (New York: Academic Press).

Beth, E. W., and J. Piaget. 1966. *Mathematical Epistemology and Psychology*. Dordrecht, Holland: Reidel.

Brown, C., J. A. Keats, D. M. Keats, and I. Seggie. 1980. Reasoning about implication: a comparison of Malaysian and Australian subjects. *Journal of Cross-cultural Psychology*, 11, 395–410.

Bryant, P. E., and T. R. Trabasso. 1971. Transitive inferences and memory in young children. *Nature*, 232, 456–458.

Chapman, I. J., and J. P. Chapman. 1959. Atmosphere effect re-examined. *Journal of Experimental Psychology*, 58, 220–226.

Clark, H. H. 1969. Linguistic processes in deductive reasoning. *Psychological Review*, 76, 387–404.

Cox, J. R., and R. A. Griggs. 1982. The effects of experience on performance in Wason's selection task. *Memory and Cognition*, 10, 496–502.

De Soto, C. B., M. London, and S. Handel. 1965. Social reasoning and spatial paralogic. *Journal of Personality and Social Psychology*, 2, 513–521.

Dixon, N. F. 1976. *On the Psychology of Military Incompetence*. London: Jonathan Cape.

Donaldson, M. 1978. *Children's Minds*. London: Fontana.

Egan, D. E., and D. D. Grimes-Farrow. 1982. Differences in mental representations spontaneously adopted for reasoning. *Memory and Cognition*, 10, 297–307.

Erickson, J. R. 1974. A set analysis of behavior in formal syllogistic tasks. In R. L. Solso, ed., *Theories in Cognitive Psychology: The Loyola Symposium* (Potomac, Md.: Erlbaum).

Frandsen, A. N., and J. R. Holder. 1969. Spatial visualization in solving complex verbal problems. *Journal of Psychology*, 73, 229–233.

Fromm-Reichmann, F. 1959. Problems of therapeutic management in a psychoanalytical hospital. In P. M. Bullard and E. V. Weigert, eds., *Psychoanalysis and Psychotherapy: Selected Papers of Freida Fromm-Reichmann* (Chicago: Univ. of Chicago Press).

Gilhooly, K. J., and W. A. Falconer. 1974. Concrete and abstract terms and relations in testing a rule. *Quarterly Journal of Experimental Psychology*, 26, 355–359.

Goldman-Eisler, F. 1968. *Psycholinguistics: Experiments in Spontaneous Speech*. London: Academic Press.

Goldstein, K. 1959. Functional disturbances in brain damage. In S. Arieti, ed., *American Handbook of Psychiatry, Vol. I* (New York: Basic Books).

Guyote, M. J., and R. J. Sternberg. 1981. A transitive-chain theory of syllogistic reasoning. *Cognitive Psychology*, 13, 461–525.

Henle, M. 1978. Foreword to R. Revlin and R. E. Mayer, eds., *Human Reasoning* (Washington, D.C.: Winston).

Hunt, E. B. 1978. The mechanics of verbal ability. *Psychological Review*, 85, 109–130.

Hunter, I. M. L. 1957. The solving of three-term series problems. *British Journal of Psychology*, 48, 286–298.

Huttenlocher, J. 1968. Constructing spatial images: A strategy in reasoning. *Psychological Review*, 75, 550–560.

Inhelder, B., and J. Piaget, 1958. *The Growth of Logical Thinking from Childhood to Adolescence*. New York: Basic Books.

———. 1964. *The Early Growth of Logic in the Child*. London: Routledge.

Jacobson, E. 1954. On psychotic identifications. *International Journal of Psychoanalysis,* 35, 102–107.

Johnson-Laird, P. N. 1972. The three-term series problem. *Cognition,* 1, 57–82.

———. 1982. Ninth Bartlett Memorial Lecture: Thinking as a skill. *Quarterly Journal of Experimental Psychology,* 34A, 1–29.

———. 1983. *Mental Models: Towards a Cognitive Science of Language, Inference, and Consciousness.* Cambridge, Mass.: Harvard Univ. Press.

Johnson-Laird, P. N., and B. Bara. In press. Syllogistic inference. *Cognition.*

Johnson-Laird, P. N., P. Legrenzi, and M. S. Legrenzi. 1972. Reasoning and a sense of reality. *British Journal of Psychology,* 63, 395–400.

Johnson-Laird, P. N., and M. J. Steedman. 1978. The psychology of syllogisms. *Cognitive Psychology,* 10, 64–99.

Johnson-Laird, P. N., and P. C. Wason. 1977. A theoretical analysis of insight into a reasoning task, *and* Postscript. *In* P. N. Johnson-Laird and P. C. Wason, eds., *Thinking: Readings in Cognitive Science* (Cambridge Mass.: Cambridge Univ. Press).

Luria, A. R. 1977. *The Social History of Cognition.* Cambridge, Mass.: Harvard Univ. Press.

MacLeod, C. M., E. B. Hunt, and N. N. Mathews. 1978. Individual differences in the verification of sentence-picture relationships. *Journal of Verbal Learning and Verbal Behavior,* 17, 493–508.

McReynolds, P. 1960. Anxiety, perception, and schizophrenia. *In* D. D. Jackson, ed., *The Etiology of Schizophrenia* (New York: Basic Books).

Mandler, J. M. 1980. Structural invariants in development. *In* L. Liben, ed., *Piaget and the Foundations of Knowledge* (Hillsdale, N.J.: Erlbaum).

Manktelow, K. I., and J. St. B. T. Evans. 1979. Facilitation of reasoning by realism: effect or non-effect? *British Journal of Psychology,* 70, 477–488.

Markman, E. M., and J. Seibert. 1976. Classes and collections: Internal organization and resulting holistic properties. *Cognitive Psychology,* 8, 561–577.

Matte-Blanco, I. 1965. A study of schizophrenic thinking: Its expression in terms of symbolic logic and its representation in terms of multi-dimensional space. *International Journal of Psychiatry,* 1, 91–96.

Mayer, R. E. 1979. Qualitatively different encoding strategies for linear reasoning premises: Evidence for single association and distance theories. *Journal of Experimental Psychology: Human Learning and Memory,* 5, 1–10.

Murray, J. P., and J. Youniss. 1968. Achievement of inferential transitivity and its relation to serial ordering. *Child Development,* 39, 1260–1268.

Mynatt, B. T., and K. H. Smith. 1977. Constructive processes in linear order problems revealed by sentence study times. *Journal of Experimental Psychology: Human Learning and Memory,* 3, 357–374.

Newell, A., and H. A. Simon. 1972. *Human Problem Solving.* Englewood Cliffs, N.J.: Prentice-Hall.

Ormrod, J. E. 1979. Cognitive processes in the solution of three-term series problems. *American Journal of Psychology,* 92, 235–255.

Pollard, P. 1981. The effect of thematic content on the "Wason selection task." *Current Psychological Research,* 1, 21–29.

Pollard, P., and J. St. B. T. Evans. 1981. The effects of prior beliefs in reasoning: An associational interpretation. *British Journal of Psychology,* 72, 73–81.

Polya, G. 1957. *How to Solve It.* New York: Doubleday, 2d ed.

Revlis, R. 1975. Two models of syllogistic reasoning: Feature selection and conversion. *Journal of Verbal Learning and Verbal Behavior,* 14, 180–195.

Scribner, S. 1977. Modes of thinking and ways of speaking: Culture and logic reconsidered. *In* P. N. Johnson-Laird and P. C. Wason, eds., *Thinking: Readings in Cognitive Science.* Cambridge: Cambridge Univ. Press.

Shaver, P., L. Pierson, and S. Lang. 1974. Converging evidence for the functional significance of imagery in problem solving. *Cognition,* 3, 359–375.

Sternberg, R. J., and E. M. Weil. 1980. An aptitude-strategy interaction in linear syllogistic reasoning. *Journal of Educational Psychology,* 72, 226–239.

Störring, G. 1908. Experimentelle Untersuchungen über einfache Schlussprozesse. *Archiv Gesellschaft Psychologie,* 11, 1–127.

von Domarus, E. 1944. The specific laws of logic in schizophrenia. *In* J. S. Kasinin, ed., *Language and Thought in Schizophrenia* (Berkeley: Univ. of California Press).

Wason, P. C., and P. N. Johnson-Laird. 1972. *Psychology of Reasoning: Structure and Content.* London: Batsford. Cambridge, Mass.: Harvard Univ. Press.

Weinstein, E. A., and R. L. Kahn. 1959. Symbolic reorganization in brain injuries. *In* S. Arieti, ed., *American Handbook of Psychiatry, Vol. I* (New York: Basic Books).

Winograd, T. 1972. *Understanding Natural Language.* New York: Academic Press.

Wood, D. J. 1969. The Nature and Development of Problem-Solving Strategies. Ph.D. thesis, Univ. of Nottingham, England.

Woodworth, R. S., and S. B. Sells. 1935. An atmosphere effect in formal syllogistic reasoning. *Journal of Experimental Psychology,* 18, 451–460.

Young, R. M. 1978. Strategies and the structure of a cognitive skill. *In* G. Underwood, ed., *Strategies of Information Processing* (London: Academic Press).

9

INDUCTIVE
REASONING ABILITY

James W. Pellegrino
University of California at Santa Barbara

One of the most pervasive aspects of human thought and intellect is the capacity to generalize from specific experiences and to form new, more abstract concepts. Although individual experiences differ, we all develop a shared set of concepts ranging from concrete ideas, such as what a chair is, to more abstract ideas, such as truth or justice. The existence of such generalizations is critical for understanding each other and the world around us. What is it that allows us to do this from birth onward? Essentially, we engage in a general cognitive activity known as *induction*. Induction is defined as the development of general rules, ideas, or concepts from sets of specific instances or examples. By analyzing the similarities and differences between specific experiences, we extract the general characteristics of classes of objects, events, and situations. We apply these generalizations to new experiences, refine and modify them, and make them part of our permanent knowledge base.

195

Given the importance of induction in human learning, it is not too surprising that inductive reasoning ability has been central in theories of human intelligence (Thurstone, 1938, considered induction to be one of the primary mental abilities). It is also not surprising that inductive reasoning has played a central role in the formal assessment of intelligence. A variety of tasks have been used to assess this ability. These tasks have come to be viewed as measures of a more general ability known as g_f or *fluid analytic ability* (Brody and Brody, 1976).

All inductive-reasoning tasks have the same basic property. We present a set of stimuli to an individual, and his or her task is to infer the pattern or rule structure for the item, so that he or she can generate or select an appropriate continuation of the pattern. This general testing procedure is exhibited in different task forms, ranging from simple classification problems to highly complex matrix problems. Figure 9.1 shows examples of the different types of problems used to measure inductive reasoning ability. It also shows the variety of content (ranging from letters to numbers, words, and complex figural designs) that can be involved in such problems. For verbal and figural classification problems, the task is to discover the relationship (semantic, logical, or geometric) between the inital three terms (the *stem*), and then to select the alternative that is consistent with the inferred rule. With number and letter series problems, the task is to discover the relational and periodic structure of the string of letters or numbers, and then to continue it by filling in the blank spaces. Verbal and figural analogy problems require the individual to choose the alternative that is related to the third term in the stem in the same way that the second term is related to the first. Numerical analogies use two initial item pairs to reduce uncertainty about the appropriate relationship governing the problem. Finally, figural matrix problems require the individual to select the alternative that completes the matrix. The choice must be consistent with rules governing both the row and the column structure.

One or more of these tasks can be found on virtually any current aptitude or intelligence test at any age level, including tests such as the Stanford-Binet for individual administration, as well as group-administered tests, such as the Cognitive Abilities Test (CAT). The latter provides a good example of the pervasiveness and importance of inductive reasoning in measuring intellectual ability. The CAT includes separate verbal analogy, verbal classification, figural analogy, figural classification, and number series subtests in its multilevel battery intended for grades three to twelve. These five subtests represent 50 percent of the entire test!

Information Processing and Inductive Reasoning

Instruments such as the CAT show that individuals differ widely in their ability to solve analogy, classification, and series problems. This is demonstrated by a score on a test or subtest reflecting the total number of problems answered correctly. We also learn from such tests that there are two types of individual differences that need to be understood. The first involves differences

Figure 9.1
Examples of typical inductive reasoning problems. (From Pellegrino and Glaser 1982, reprinted by permission.)

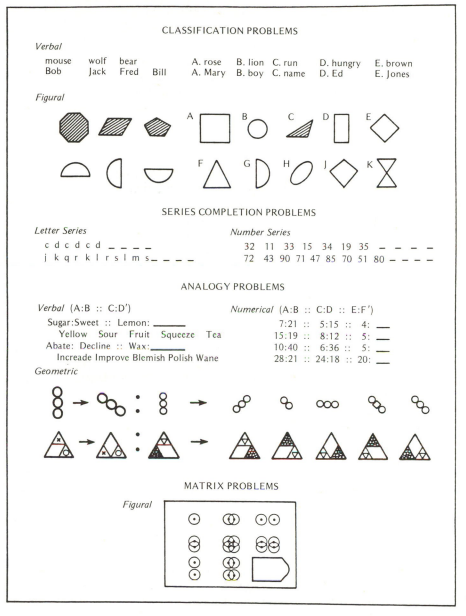

CLASSIFICATION PROBLEMS

Verbal

| mouse | wolf | bear | | A. rose | B. lion | C. run | D. hungry | E. brown |
| Bob | Jack | Fred | Bill | A. Mary | B. boy | C. name | D. Ed | E. Jones |

Figural

SERIES COMPLETION PROBLEMS

Letter Series

c d c d c d _ _ _ _

j k q r k l r s l m s _ _ _ _

Number Series

32 11 33 15 34 19 35 _ _ _ _

72 43 90 71 47 85 70 51 80 _ _ _ _

ANALOGY PROBLEMS

Verbal (A:B :: C:D')

Sugar:Sweet :: Lemon: _____
    Yellow Sour Fruit Squeeze Tea
Abate: Decline :: Wax:_____
    Increade Improve Blemish Polish Wane

Numerical (A:B :: C:D :: E:F')

7:21 :: 5:15 :: 4: __

15:19 :: 8:12 :: 5: __

10:40 :: 6:36 :: 5: __

28:21 :: 24:18 :: 20: __

Geometric

MATRIX PROBLEMS

Figural

197

between age groups. Invariably, adults can solve correctly more items (as well as problems of greater complexity) than eighth-grade children, who in turn perform better than third-grade children. The second type of individual differences involves individuals within the same age range.

The information-processing approach to inductive reasoning attempts to provide answers to questions that we can not answer by simply looking at overall test-score differences. The first major question is "Just what *are* the basic psychological processes involved in solving inductive reasoning problems?" To answer this, we may propose a theory about which mental processes are necessary to deal with the content and structure of a problem such as analogy or series completion. Part of the theory will include assumptions about the sequence in which these processes are performed or executed. Once we have a theory of performance, we can ask the second major question, "What are the predictions of this theory, and how can we test its validity?" Usually, the theory provides explicit predictions about differences between items, such as the length of time it will take to solve each item and/or which items will be more difficult to answer correctly. We can then do experiments to test the theory. When we have a theory that adequately predicts and explains performance, we can deal with the third major question, "How do individuals differ?" The theory provides a basis for detailed analyses of individuals' differences in the speed and accuracy of executing separate mental processes. We can also explore the issue of differences in their overall strategies for performing the task. Strategy differences would include different sequences for executing mental processes, using alternative sets of mental processes, or perhaps failure to execute the appropriate processes.

The three broad issues we have outlined provide the basis for our discussion of inductive reasoning. We will first consider how each of these issues has been addressed in terms of analogy problems, because more work has been done on this type of induction problem than on any other. Our second major illustration of the information-processing approach will be series-completion problems. At the end of this chapter we will return to consider the general area of inductive-reasoning ability.

Analogy

"Analogy" is a Greek term first defined by Aristotle (in *Metaphysics*) as "an equality of proportions . . . (involving) at least four terms . . . when the second is related to the first as the fourth is to the third." The focus on *proportional* relations, combined with the structured form, allowed analogies to be used in precise and technical analyses of the world. They were used extensively by Plato, Aristotle, and Aquinas, among others, to help develop and explicate meanings of mathematical, philosophical, and metaphysical concepts (Lyttkens, 1952). Scientists continue to use analogies to help understand new phenomena, and teachers frequently explain ideas to students "by analogy."

The first appearance of analogy items in intelligence testing occurred simultaneously in Woodworth and Wells' (1911) Mixed Relations test in the

United States and Burt's (1911) Completing Analogies test in England. Wood-worth and Wells considered their test to be a measure of "flexibility of mental performance." Burt described his test as a measure of "higher mental processes" intended to draw on "rational inference" skills in terms of "association by similars." Whipple (1915) listed analogies in his *Manual of Mental and Physical Tests* as a measure of complex processes. These items were included in tests because of the assumed importance of analogical reasoning as an aspect of intelligence. Raven defined intelligence itself as the "ability to reason by analogy from awareness of relations between experienced characters" (Esher et al., 1942, cited in Burke, 1958). He designed the Progressive Matrices (1938) to "test . . . a person's present capacity to form comparisons, reason by analogy, and develop a logical method of thinking" (Raven, 1938). Spearman (1923) considered analogy tasks as measures of general intelligence, or *g*, basing his theory of cognition on three components: the "apprehension of experience," the "eduction of relations," and the "eduction of correlates."

The first topic in our discussion of analogy solution is the mental processes required for dealing with these problems. However, before we can consider any theory of processing, some terminology needs to be defined. We typically see analogies in a forced-choice format with a three-term stem, denoted as $A:B::C:("A$ is to B as C is to _"), and a set of options denoted as $D(1)$, $D(2)$, $D(3)$, etc. Sometimes, however, we may see analogies in a true-false format, that is, a completed analogy *(A:B::C:D)*, and the testee must decide if it is valid or acceptable.

Processes

What are the mental processes for solving analogies? We can derive a general description of the processes required for analogy solution from the work of several individuals (Pellegrino and Glaser, 1982; Spearman, 1923; Sternberg, 1977; Whitely, 1977). The processes fall into three general classes. The first class consists of attribute discovery or encoding processes; the important attri-butes of each individual term in the analogy problem must be represented in memory. For verbal items, this involves activating a set of semantic features associated with a concept. Given the term "dog," encoding would involve activation of semantic features representing superordinate, subordinate, proper-ty, and other relationships. For figural items, encoding constitutes a description of individual shapes or elements, their specific properties, and relationships; an example might be a rectangle containing two adjacent circles, one shaded and the other unshaded. Attribute discovery or encoding is essential for execution of other component processes.

The second class of processes consists of attribute-comparison processes used for specific pairs of terms. The first such process is called *inference,* and deals with the relationship between the first two terms of the analogy (*A* and *B*). For verbal stimuli, the inference process discovers semantic features that directly or indirectly link the two concepts. For an *A-B* pair like "dog-wolf," this might include common features such as *animal* and *canine,* as well as differentiating features such as *size, ferocity,* and *domesticity*. When figural stimuli are involved, the inference process involves defining a set of feature changes or transformations that are applied to the *A* term to produce the *B* term. If the *A* term is a rectangle containing two adjacent circles, and the *B* term consists of only two adjacent circles, then the inference process yields a transformation consisting of the deletion of the external shape. *Mapping* is a similar type of attribute-comparison process. It refers to finding correspondences between the first and third terms (*A* and *C*) of an analogy. Yet another attribute-comparison process is referred to as *application*. This is applying the specific rule inferred for the *A-B* pair to the attributes of the *C* term to produce a candidate or "ideal" *D* term for item solution. Inference, mapping, and application are component processes associated with the stem terms of an analogy, i.e., the *A, B,* and *C* terms.

The third major class of processes necessary for analogy solution consists of evaluation processes. These determine the appropriateness of any completion or *D* term. In simple analogies, where the ideal *D* term can be generated easily, evaluation is a confirmation process in which features of the completion term are matched against the ideal answer. This process leads to rejection of inappropriate completions and to selection of the correct response. However, many analogies involve ambiguous rules, or may have several possible answers. Evaluation of the alternatives may yield two or more completion terms that partially match the features of an acceptable answer; then rule comparison and discrimination processes are required. This general aspect of performance has been labeled *justification*. The final process in solving analogies is, of course, executing an overt response.

Process Sequencing

How and in what sequence are all these processes executed? Two general sequences for process execution are shown in Figure 9.2. The sequence shown on the left assumes that the *A* and *B* terms are encoded, and that execution of the *A-B* inference process follows. Next, the *C* term is encoded, and the *A-C* mapping process is executed. Then a *D* term is encoded, and a combined application-confirmation process is executed, leading to acceptance or rejection of the given *D* term. If the item is in a verification format, then a true or false response is emitted. If the item is in a forced-choice format, then another completion term is encoded with execution of a combined application-confirmation process. This cycle continues until all the options have been evaluated and the correct response identified. For both verification and forced-choice items, a unique response may not be identifiable, so a justification process will be needed prior to final response. A slightly different sequence is shown on the right in Figure 9.2. The process sequence remains essentially the same, except that application occurs prior to encoding the *D* term, which is followed by a confirmation process.

A concrete example of the sequence of process execution is provided by Figure 9.3. The figural analogy shown at the top represents the true-false verification format of the analogy task. To solve the item shown, you must

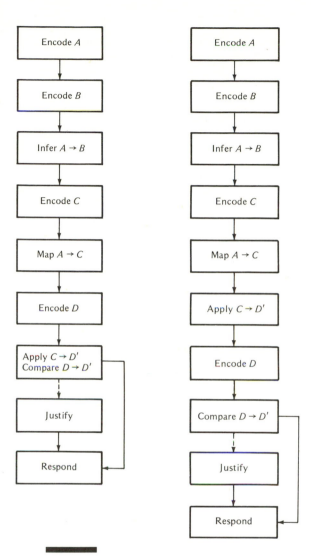

Figure 9.2
Simplified process models for analogy solution. (From Goldman and Pellegrino 1984, reprinted by permission.)

encode the first term (*A*); i.e., the individual shapes or elements of the entire figure must be represented in your memory. We assume that this representation is an exhaustive element-value list that fully describes the presented figure. Next you must thoroughly encode the second term (*B*), and represent it in your memory. The time to execute each separate encoding process will vary with the number of elements to be represented. After the initial two terms have been encoded, you will go through an inference process that exhaustively proceeds through the element list for *A* and *B*, comparing the values and finding differences or transformations that are present. This inference process will take you a

Operation	Result	
1. Encode *A*	Large circle	Two small crosses
2. Encode *B*	Small circle	One small cross
3a. Infer transformation on element 1(t_1)	Size change large to small	
b. Infer transformation on element 2 (t_2)		Number change two to one
4. Encode C	Large square	Two small triangles
5. Map *A-C* change on element 1	Large circle to large square	
6. Apply t_1 to C yielding *D'* value	Small square	
7. Encode *D*	Small square	One small triangle
8. Compare *D* to *D'*	Match	
9. Map *A-C* change on element 2		Two small crosses to two small triangles
10. Apply t_2 to C, yielding *D'* value		One small triangle
11. Compare *D* to *D'*		Match
12. Respond TRUE		

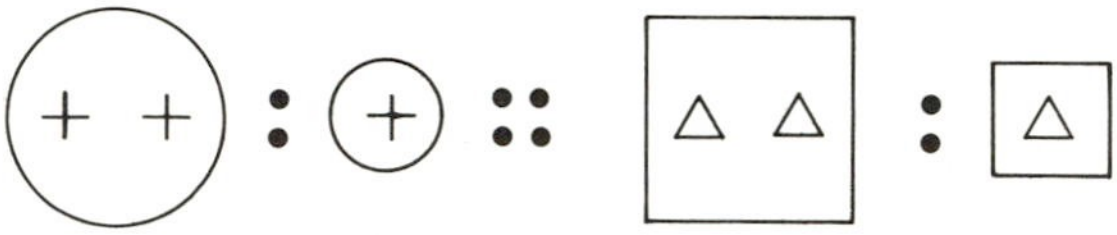

Figure 9.3
Representation of the solution steps for a simple figural analogy.

certain amount of time for each element on which the values for A and B do not match, that is, for elements on which a transformation has occurred. The next phase of processing requires you to exhaustively encode the elements of the C term. You follow this by a mapping process that selects the first element of A and generates its corresponding value in C. No other elements are mapped yet. Instead, the next step is an application process, in which the appropriate transformation in the A-B pair is applied to the corresponding element value of C, to yield an element value for an ideal answer D'. You then exhaustively encode the D term. This is followed by a comparison of D and D' on the values of the designated element. If these do not match, you *do* give a "false" response, and the problem is solved. If a match is obtained, then you return to the mapping process, to find the value change (if any) for the next A to C element comparison. The sequence continues with an application of the appropriate A-B transformation to yield the value of D' to be compared to D. If the analogy is true, then your mapping and application processes will work through all the elements, with the time for each process being a function of the number of transformations that must be processed. The final process is your response selection and execution, which will take you the same amount of time for each item.

Theory and Model Testing

Our next concern is how to test the adequacy of our theory. We begin with the basic assumption that the total time needed for you to verify the truth of an analogy, such as the one shown in Figure 9.3, is the sum of the times associated with each of the processes you sequentially executed. Our theory also tells us that the time you take to execute each process will depend on how complex the item is. Consider the different types of items shown in Figure 9.4. They differ in two ways. First, the individual terms have different numbers of shapes or elements. According to the theory, you should take longer to encode each of the terms in the more complex items. Second, the items vary in the number of elements that are changed or transformed in each pair of terms (A-B and C-D). The more feature changes that exist, the longer you should take for attribute-comparison processes such as inference, mapping, and application. These two factors, the number of elements and the number of transformations, should combine in a systematic way to produce the increased times it takes you to solve various items. This is exactly what happened, as shown in Figure 9.5. When tests were done (Mulholland et al., 1980), each stimulus element depicted in Figure 9.4 added approximately 300 milliseconds to the average subject's solution time, and each feature change (transformation) added approximately 400 milliseconds.

Our theory also generates the prediction that it will take less time to fals an item than to accept a true item of comparable complexity (see Figure 9.2 Although not shown in Figure 9.5, data also support this prediction (Mulholland et al., 1980). By varying the complexity of items and the way in which they are presented, we can test predictions of a theory while simultaneously obtaining estimates of the time needed to encode stimuli, infer, map, and apply relations, and respond (Sternberg, 1977).

Figure 9.4
Examples of true and false figural analogies varying in item complexity. (From Mulholland et al., 1980, reprinted by permission.)

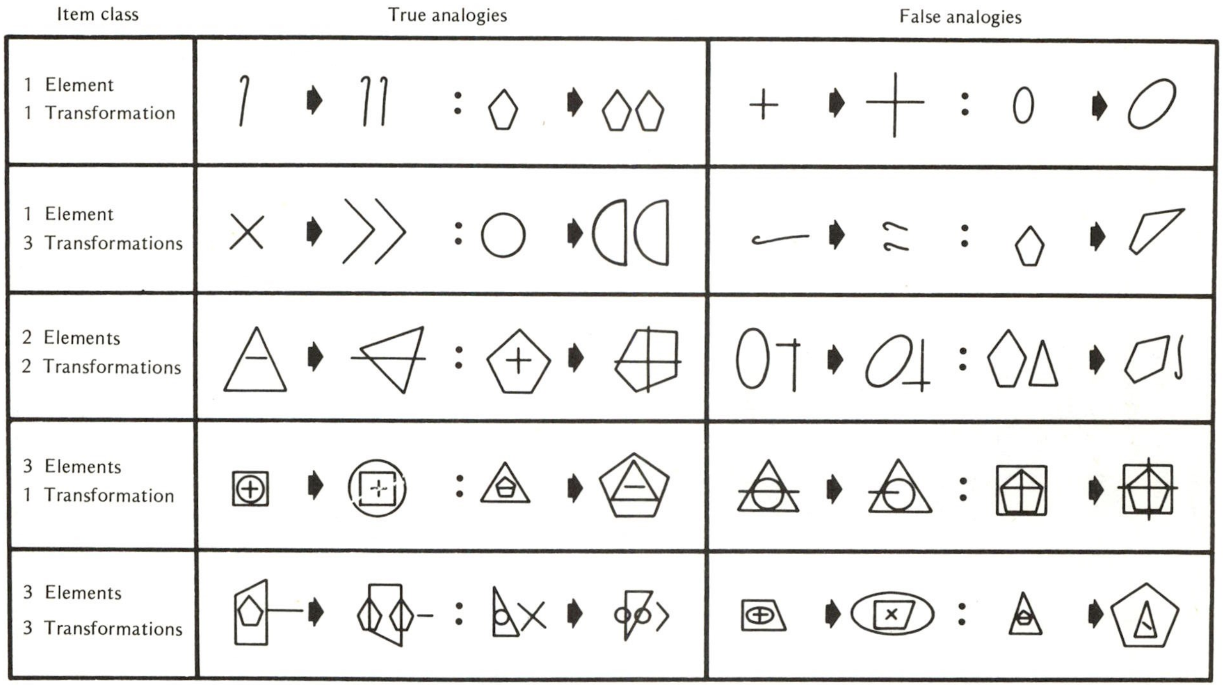

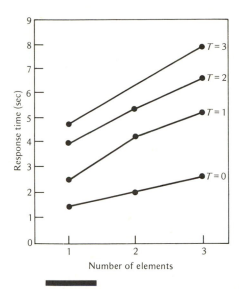

Figure 9.5
Reaction times for figural analogy solution showing the separate effects of number of elements and number of transformations (I). (Adapted from Mulholland et al., 1980.)

Several studies have been conducted with adult, college-age individuals to examine actual performance on verbal, figural, schematic-figure, and "people-piece" (human-like figure) items (Sternberg, 1977; Mulholland et al., 1980; Pellegrino and Glaser, 1982; Sternberg and Gardner, 1983). A major goal of these studies was to evaluate different possible sequences for process execution and to obtain estimates of the time needed to execute individual component processes. All the studies of adult performance have found support for self-terminating process execution for item falsification. When a completion term violates a critical feature of the *A-B* relation, processing of that term ceases, and it is rejected. In a verification task, item processing terminates, and a "false" response is emitted. In a forced-choice task, processing shifts to consideration of the remaining alternatives.

Another general result of these studies was to clarify overall differences between item types in the time for solution. Schematic-figure analogies are solved more rapidly than verbal analogies, with an average total time of 1.5 seconds; and verbal analogy items tend to be solved more rapidly than figural items. In Sternberg's (1977) study of verbal analogy solution, the average total time was approximately 2.5 seconds, which is consistent with data obtained in studies conducted by Pellegrino and Ingram (1977). Figural analogies require considerably longer average total times, on the order of 4 seconds for verification tasks (Mulholland et al., 1980) and 7 seconds for forced-choice tasks (Sternberg, 1977).

A second difference between item types is the distribution of time for different types of processes. Since schematic-figure and people-piece items are relatively simple, with a well-defined set of properties, most of the processing time is distributed over the encoding and response components (70 percent), and their attribute-comparison processes require only 30 percent of the total solution time. In contrast, geometric analogies require 44 to 57 percent of the total solution time for their attribute-comparison processes. Some studies of verbal analogies have shown that more than 60 percent of the total solution time can be required for their attribute-comparison processes.

Modeling Performance Accuracy

An information-processing approach can also be applied to the analysis of solution accuracy. Such a focus is important for several reasons related to both developmental and individual differences analysis. This can be illustrated by considering a prototypical standardized test of analogical reasoning. The CAT developed by Thorndike and Hagen (1972) contains a set of 60 verbal and 60 geometric analogies. The structure of this group test consists of overlapping item sets for successive age groups starting at grade three and continuing through grade twelve. Each age group solves a set of 25 items. The third graders solve problems 1 to 25, fourth graders solve problems 6 to 30, and so on; so children of several different ages solve similar subsets of items. Normative data on item solutions reveal two important things. First, children typically complete all 25 items within the time allotted. Second, the probability of correct solution of a given item increases with age. Developmental changes in analogical reasoning performance are therefore more a function of accuracy than speed. To maintain the same average accuracy over age groups, each age group is required to solve successively harder sets of items. Given that children within an age group attempt to solve all 25 items, the major factor associated with individual differences is accuracy. If we are to understand developmental and individual differences in analogical reasoning, we must consider the accuracy of executing component processes as well as speed.

There are three possible relationships between accuracy and latency for individuals. The first of these would be a speed-accuracy tradeoff, such that individuals who show lower average solution times would have higher average error rates, producing a negative (inverse) correlation between latency and errors. The second would be a complete independence of latency and accuracy, yielding a zero correlation of the two measures over individuals. The third possibility would be a positive (direct) relationship, such that individuals who make more errors would also be slower in average solution latency. Research results tend to support the last relationship. As an example, Holzman (1979) examined the performance of adults on three types of inductive reasoning items: geometric analogies, numerical analogies, and number-series problems. For all three tasks, an individual's average solution time for a set of items was positively correlated with average errors. The implication of these results is that skill is often associated with faster *and* more-accurate process execution. The data obtained in a number of studies of analogy solution support a similar relationship between latency and accuracy at the level of individual items. An item that is predicted to have a longer solution latency, because of increased time for execution of encoding, attribute comparison, or response-evaluation processes, also has a higher average error rate (Sternberg, 1977).

Whitely (1980) has developed a very powerful method of analyzing solution accuracy that is based on the general theory of analogy solution. She refers to the method as *multicomponent latent-trait modeling*. The essence of this approach is to treat performance on a task such as analogy or classification as the result of two factors. The first consists of the probabilities of success in executing each of the separate component processes necessary for item solution. These probabilities are used to create a prediction equation in which the likelihood of overall success in item solution is a function of the individual's ability on each of the separate component processes. The second factor deals with the difficulty of executing each separate process in solving a given item. Items are assumed to differ in the ease or likelihood of inferring the appropriate rule and/or in selecting the best alternative completion term. A model of item difficulty can be derived that is then combined with a model of individual ability to provide a composite model. The performance of an individual on a specific item is described in terms of both subject and item variables. Process-outcome models can be tested, and the result is a characterization of those components of performance that contribute to both item difficulty and individual differences.

Developmental Differences

We can now consider the issue of how individuals differ in solving analogy problems. First we will deal with differences associated with age and intellectual maturity. A variety of studies have indicated that both qualitative and quantitative changes occur with age. *Qualitative changes* are changes in the strategies used for solution, as well as changes in understanding and following task rules. Such changes are demonstrated by data indicating that some processes present in adult performance may not be present in children's performance. *Quantitative changes* are changes in the efficiency with which a process is executed. Efficiency may be indexed by speed or accuracy of process execution. From studies of analogy tasks using figural and verbal materials, it can be concluded that the development of analogical reasoning involves all the previously mentioned areas of change.

One of the first efforts to apply process theories to children's performance was conducted by Sternberg and Rifkin (1979). They presented two types of analogies to eight-, ten-, twelve-, and nineteen-year-olds. The task was to choose the better of two completion terms. Both types of analogies are shown in Figure 9.6, and they differed in four attribute dimensions. For the schematic-picture analogies shown at the top, these attributes are separable, that is, the presence or absence of one attribute does not directly affect the presence or absence of any other. In contrast, the second type of analogy shown involves integral-stimulus dimensions. These were human-like figures (people-piece analogies), and in order to depict any one attribute, the other three must be assigned some value.

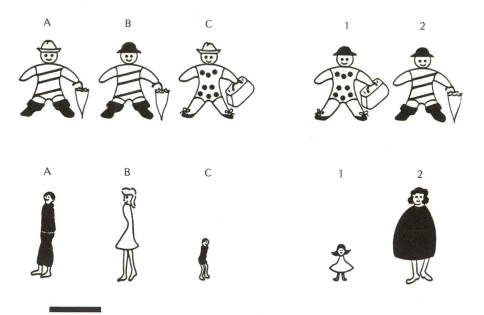

Figure 9.6
Examples of schematic-picture (top) and people-piece (bottom) analogies. (From Sternberg and Rifkin, 1979, reprinted by permission.)

Figure 9.7 shows the results obtained by Sternberg and Rifkin (1979) for both types of items. There was a developmental change for both types in the overall time to solve the problems. Also shown in Figure 9.7 are developmental changes in the time for executing each separate process. Encoding, inference, and application were used at each age level for both types of analogies. Mapping was used only for people-piece analogies, and, although it is required when attributes are integrated, the eight-year-olds did not use this process. Sternberg and Rifkin (1979) concluded that mapping .is unavailable or inaccessible to eight-year-olds, who appear to solve analogies in ways that bypass mapping.

The Sternberg and Rifkin study, together with other studies by Bisanz (1979) and Stone and Day (1981) with figural analogy and matrix problems, indicate that the basic component processes of encoding, inference, and application are executed by children as young as eight. The speed of executing these processes appears to increase with age. Furthermore, as age increases, there is an increased tendency to adjust information-processing activities to stimuli that differ in complexity, in terms of either separability of attributes, number of attributes, or transformations.

Research with verbal analogies has indicated developmental changes in analogical reasoning representing both qualitative and quantitative differences in how items are solved. Sternberg and Nigro (1980) had twenty children at each of four age levels (nine, twelve, fifteen and eighteen years) solve forced-choice verbal analogies. They used different item forms that varied the number of missing terms. The simplest type was the standard forced-choice item with A:B::C: and a set of four choices. This has only one missing term. The most

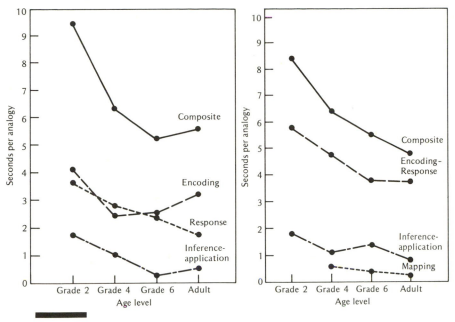

Figure 9.7
Latency data for analogy solution components as a function of analogy type and grade level. (From Sternberg and Rifkin, 1979, reprinted by permission.)

complex type was a forced-choice item with A: and a set of four choices each representing a B::C:D combination. These problems have three missing terms. Of particular importance for development is that Sternberg and Nigro (1980) found differences between the age groups in how they performed on the problem types. This is shown in Figure 9.8. The 15- and 18-year-olds showed increasing times for items with more missing terms. The 9- and 12-year-olds showed both an initial increase and then a decrease in time and errors for items with more missing terms. Three processes accounted for solution times at each age level: encoding, application, and mapping. However, the degree of association between the stem and alternatives was also predictive of the nine- and twelve-year-olds' performance. Sternberg and Nigro (1980) interpret their data as indicating two levels of performance. At the first level, processing partially reflects analogical reasoning. However, when memory demands are great because of several missing terms, then processing is affected by associative relatedness. This level characterizes the nine- and twelve-year-olds. At the second level of performance, there is complete encoding of relations, such that the two halves of the analogy are fully related to one another. In essence, verbal reasoning overrides verbal association, and this level characterizes fifteen- and eighteen-year-olds.

Goldman et al. (1982) also found evidence for both quantitative and qualitative changes in children's solution of verbal analogies. They conducted two experiments with eight- and ten-year-olds, and obtained significant age differences on several measures of processing. Older children were more accu-

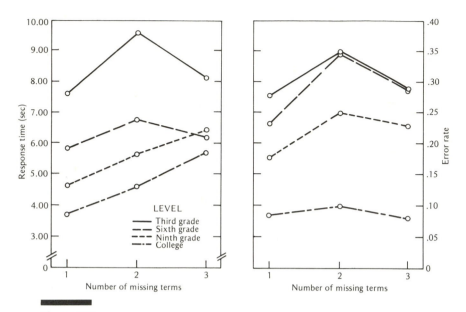

Figure 9.8
Latency and accuracy for verbal analogy solution as a function of number of missing elements in the analogy and grade level. (From Sternberg and Nigro, 1980, reprinted by permission.)

rate in inference and application processes, and also more likely to recognize the correct response from among a set of alternatives when inference and application had been incorrect. In addition, the ten-year-olds were less likely to be distracted by associative choices in the alternative set.

In both experiments, the children were also asked to state why they picked the answer they did. Three major categories were used to classify the responses: parallel relations, nonparallel relations, and no relation. Those statements which indicated an understanding that the *A:B* and *C:D* relations must match were classified in the first category. The nonparallel category comprised statements that violate the property of matching relations. In the no-relation category were statements about the chosen response that did not relate it to anything else. When justifications for all responses were considered, ten-year-olds had significantly more statements in the parallel relations category (.50) than eight-year-olds (.34). Goldman et al. (1982) interpreted these results as indicating that younger children are aware of the constraints or the "rules of the game" that are supposed to hold in analogical reasoning, but that their understanding and compliance is often weak. When they do choose the correct alternative, they are as likely as older children to verbalize appropriate reasons. However, they choose an inappropriate answer more frequently than older children, and their rationalizations often reflect little awareness of the relational properties of the four terms.

The data of Sternberg and Nigro (1980) and Goldman et al. (1982) support the idea that mature analogical reasoning involves an understanding of the "rules of analogy" as well as the efficient and appropriate management of inference, application, and evaluation processes. Less-mature reasoning performance typically involves some type of associative-processing component. An associative-processing strategy seems to be present when item complexity exceeds the child's capacity to coordinate and compare multiple relations. Such coordination and comparison demand the ability to deal with a higher-order relation-of-relations. It was this ability that Piaget (1977) cited as a critical feature in the acquisition of analogical reasoning, and one typically acquired by adolescence.

Individual Differences

Analyses of individual differences between adults have focused on the speed and accuracy of executing all the different processes necessary for solving analogies. Process speed or accuracy for an individual are estimated by fitting a model to a large set of data representing performance on many different items. The estimates for the time to execute separate processes are then used in either correlational analyses, where performance on a reference test of reasoning ability is the criterion variable, or in a contrastive analysis, comparing high- vs. low-reasoning groups. The purpose is to discover the measures of processing that are most related to differences in reasoning skill.

One of the most consistently observed sources of individual differences is part of the response component. Skilled reasoners have shorter latencies for this component of processing when solving people-piece and verbal analogies (Sternberg, 1977, 1981) and figural analogies (Mulholland et al., 1980). Although the response component may not appear to be a terribly significant aspect of inductive reasoning, it has been argued (Sternberg, 1977; Mulholland et al., 1980) that this measure also reflects certain executive or higher-level functions associated with executing and monitoring the entire analogy solution strategy.

Ability differences in encoding speed have also been observed. The direction of the difference shows that skilled reasoners are actually slower at encoding than less-skilled reasoners! Sternberg (1977) suggested that such counterintuitive results might reflect a strategy difference between ability groups. High-ability individuals spend more time on encoding, since more precise encodings facilitate or speed up subsequent processing operations. Accurate encodings seem to increase subsequent processing speed greatly as indexed by attribute comparison and response components.

Attribute-comparison components such as inference, mapping, application, and justification have all shown significant latency differences that favor skilled over less-skilled reasoners. In verbal analogy solution, Sternberg (1977) obtained data indicating that skilled reasoners were 243 milliseconds (msec) faster than less-skilled reasoners for a combined estimate of inference, mapping, and application. Pellegrino and Ingram (1977) obtained a 181-msec difference for inference, mapping, and application, as well as a 120-msec difference for justification. Geometric analogies have also yielded similar reasoning-skill differences for application and justification components (Sternberg, 1977).

The individual difference data we have summarized are based on different groups of individuals performing a single analogy task. Recently, Sternberg and Gardner (1983) reported the results of an extensive individual differences study examining the performance of eighteen adults over a series of nine inductive-reasoning tasks. The eighteen individuals solved 2,880 individual induction problems representing the crossing of three task forms (analogy, classification, and series completion), with three types of content (verbal, figural, and schematic). When performance on all nine tasks was considered together, reasoning scores from a set of reference tests were correlated with three aspects of processing. A component score representing inference, mapping, and application yielded a correlation of −.79, and one representing confirmation yielded a correlation of −.75. The component score for justification yielded a correlation of −.48. All of these represent attribute comparison and evaluation processes, and the results are generally consistent with those obtained in earlier studies. Apparently, adult individual differences in inductive reasoning ability are partly attributable to more efficient execution of component processes involving the attribute relationships between individual pairs of analogy terms.

Studies focusing on adult individual differences in the accuracy of executing individual processes match the results obtained from latency studies. Two studies have examined the performance of several adult subjects on verbal analogy problems (Alderton et al., 1982; Whitely, 1980). Table 9.1 contains a summary of the major results from the Alderton et al. (1982) study. Results are shown for the twenty highest-ability individuals and the twenty individuals who scored the lowest on a forced-choice analogy test. The measure of inference and application accuracy showed a 33 percent difference between the high- and low-ability individuals. Of particular interest are the data for the two measures

Table 9.1
Adult ability differences on analogy performance measures

Item	High-ability adults	Low-ability adults
Overall accuracy	.90	.55
Stem processing:		
Probability of correct execution of inference and application processes	.67	.34
Option processing:		
Probability of distraction when stem processing was correct	.01	.09
Probability of recognizing the correct choice when stem processing was incorrect	.52	.14

reflecting how individuals dealt with the alternatives in a forced-choice situation. The overall probability of recognizing a correct solution when inference and application were incorrect was .33, and there was a three-fold difference in performance between the high- and low-ability individuals. In contrast, the probability of distraction was extremely low for all adults. This is very different from children's performance, which tends to show a high susceptibility to distraction. The Alderton et al. (1982) results show that high-ability individuals are more accurate in initial encoding and attribute comparison processes, and are also more accurate in subsequent response-evaluation components. These conclusions are supported by Whitely's (1980) study, which examined the performance of 104 adults on similar types of problems.

Individual differences between adults largely reside in the efficient and accurate execution of the same set of processes. Studies of high-school students (Heller, 1979), as well as within-age group comparisons of elementary-school children (Goldman et al., 1982), indicate that there are also qualitative individual differences in task performance. When we examine a range of skill levels wider than that typically found among college students, individual differences are observed in what people are doing, as well as in how well they are doing it.

Heller (1979) examined the verbal analogical-reasoning performance of vocational high school and college students. Protocols of solution episodes were analyzed to find out whether behaviors were appropriate to solving the problems. Two major types of solutions were identified. Analogical solutions showed no behaviors that violated any of the "rules of analogy": consistent attention was given to the relations contained in the A-B and C-D word pairs, and to the match between these pairs of relations. Nonanalogical solutions violated one or more task rules. For example, relations between "illegal" pairs of terms (A-D, B-C) were the only ones considered, or the match between relations was disregarded consistently. These two solution types were observed differentially across ability groups. High-ability solvers (twenty college students) used analogical solutions 99 percent of the time. Intermediate-ability solvers (six tenth-grade students in the upper 25 percent of verbal ability) used analogical solutions 71 percent of the time. Low-ability solvers (nine tenth-grade students in the lower 25 percent of verbal ability) were analogical only 34 percent of the time.

Ability differences between children of the same age have also been found to parallel overall developmental differences between age groups. In their work with eight- and ten-year-olds, Goldman et al. (1982) found significant individual differences in the accuracy of executing several component processes. Three different process-accuracy measures—inference-plus-application, recognition, and distractor interference—were significant predictors of overall forced-choice performance differences between children within each age group. The recognition and distractor-interference processes were relatively more important than the combined inference and application processes. The former are associated with the coordination and comparison of multiple relations, whereas the latter is basically a stem process involving fewer relationships. To illustrate the magnitude of the individual differences on these measures, the data for the top and bottom scores within each grade are shown in Table 9.2. There is greater similarity between ability groups across grades than between ability groups within grades. In addition to differences in process accuracy, analyses of verbal justification data indicated individual differences in the ability to justify correct responses in terms of parallel relations. The low-ability individuals in each grade justified only half of their correct responses in terms of parallel relations.

Heller's (1979) individual difference work with adolescents and Goldman et al.'s (1982) with eight- and ten-year-olds indicate that solution strategies often do not conform to the rules governing analogical reasoning. In addition to a weaker understanding of the task, individuals differ in the accuracy of process execution. The factors that seem to characterize general developmental differences in analogy solution also characterize individual differences between children and adolescents. In contrast, individual differences in college-age adults are associated largely with differences in the efficiency of process execution. The fact that adults are not easily distracted and that they consistently use an appropriate solution strategy indicates that understanding and following the rules of analogical reasoning is not a particular problem for college populations. A less-mature or weaker understanding of analogy manifests itself in inconsistent use of analogical solutions. The coordination and comparison of multiple relations often appears difficult for adolescents and children. Mature analogical reasoning involves the ability to manipulate second-order and sometimes third-order relationships. Less-mature forms of analogical reasoning are characterized by failure to deal successfully or efficiently with this manipulation. A typical manifestation is reasoning associatively rather than analogically.

Series Completion

Series-completion problems can be found on many aptitude and intelligence tests, although they are less frequent than analogy problems. The induc-

Table 9.2

Children's ability differences on analogy performance measures

Item	Eight-year-olds		Ten-year-olds	
	High-ability	Low-ability	High-ability	Low-ability
Probability of correct execution of inference and application processes	.37	.22	.52	.29
Probability of distraction when stem processing was correct	.26	.52	.18	.41
Probability of recognizing the correct choice when stem processing was incorrect	.21	.01	.34	.03

tion of serial patterns has also been identified as an important component of major scientific discoveries (Banet, 1966; Kedrov, 1966), artistic endeavors (Simon and Sumner, 1968), and language organization (Lashley, 1951). During the past fifteen years, psychologists have analyzed many different instances of series-completion performance, including the types of items found on mental tests. This includes letter and number series, musical-note sequences, and sequences of light patterns (Simon and Kotovsky, 1963; Restle, 1970; Kotovsky and Simon, 1973).

Processes and Sequencing

A theory of performance that specifies both the processes required for series completion and their sequence of execution has been developed by Simon and Kotovsky (1963). This theory was explicitly intended for performance on the letter-series problems found on the Primary Mental Abilities Test. However, it also applies to other problems, such as number series.

The basic components of series completion are schematically represented in Figure 9.9. The first component, *relations detection,* requires the individual to

Figure 9.9

Representation of processing stages for solution of series completion problems. (From Holzman et al., 1983, reprinted by permission.)

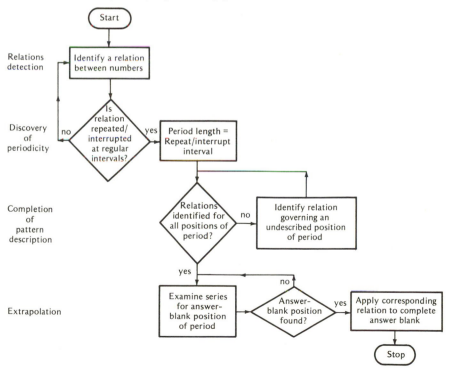

scan the series and hypothesize how one element of the series is related to another. For letter-series problems, only three relations need be considered: identity (repetition of a letter), next (movement to the next letter of the alphabet, as in BC), and backward next (reverse alphabetical order, as in CB). Number-series problems normally exhibit a greater variety of relations. They can involve any category of arithmetic operation (e.g., addition, subtraction, multiplication, division, exponentiation), and can also vary the magnitude of the arithmetic operation that interrelates the elements of the series (e.g., +2 versus +9). Number-series relations can be further complicated by use a hierarchic sequence of arithmetic operations. For example, the problem 36, 34, 30, 22, . . . involves subtraction, but the magnitude of the subtrahend is repeatedly multiplied by 2.

The second solution component is *discovery of periodicity*. The period length of the series is the number of elements that constitutes one complete cycle of the pattern. For example, the series 3, 7, 11, 15, 19, 23, . . . has a period length of one, because the same relation applies to each consecutive element. On the other hand, the series 12, 12, 13, 13, 14, 14, . . . has a period length of two, because two numbers occur before the cycle of relations begins again.

Two principal methods can be used to discover the periodicity of the series. The *adjacent* approach defines the period length by discovering regularly occurring breaks in relations between adjacent elements. For instance, the periodicity of the series 12, 12, 13, 13, 14, 14, . . . could be discovered by noting that the identity relation is regularly interrupted at two-number intervals. The *nonadjacent* approach defines the period length by discovering some regular interval at which a relation repeats itself. For example, the periodicity of the series 45, 36, 44, 36, 43, 36, . . . could be determined by noticing either a −1 relation or an identity relation repeating at two-number intervals. As shown in Figure 9.9, if the initially detected relation is neither repeated nor interrupted at regular intervals, the individual must search for a new relation that is characterized by such regularity.

The third principal component depicted in Figure 9.9 is *completion* of the pattern description. After the period length of the series has been found, the individual must identify the relations governing all remaining positions within the period in order fully to define the rule for the sequence. This rule is then used to *extrapolate* (continue) the sequence. Extrapolation is done by identifying the position of the period occupied by the answer blank(s), isolating the part of the rule governing that position, and subsequently applying that part of the rule in order to generate the number(s) for the answer blank(s).

Theory Testing

How do we evaluate a theory like that illustrated in Figure 9.9? The solution of series problems can not be easily broken down into discrete times for each of the different components, as we could do with analogy problems. There is repeated cycling through processes such as relations detection and pattern description. Therefore, no attempt is made to obtain estimates of the time for each stage of solution. However, the theory does allow for general predictions about differences between items in the overall time and difficulty of solution. The predictions arise from a structured system for representing the pattern description that must be developed and held in memory by the subjects. Simon and Kotovsky developed this system for representing pattern descriptions for letter-series problems. The main features of these pattern descriptions can be illustrated with a few examples.

First, consider the relatively simple series c, d, c, d, c, d, ... This pattern may be described as consisting of two-letter periods, with a constant letter occurring in each position of each period, in this case, a c in position 1 and a d in position 2. This series is simply denoted as:

$[C, D]$

A somewhat more complicated series is u, r, t, u, s, t, u, t, t, u, ... Here the period length is three. The first position of one period is related to the first position of the preceding period by identity. Likewise, the same letter always occupies the third position of each period. The second position, however, is governed by a next relation. Thus, the series is represented as follows:

$[U, M_1, N(M_1), T]$

In this pattern description, "M_1, $N(M_1)$" indicates that the letter in the second position of one period is related to the letter in the second position of the following period by the *next* relation, symbolized as N. The subscripted Ms stand for slots or placekeepers in memory. For each new cycle or period of the series, the individual recalls a letter from Memory 1 (notated as M_1) and uses that letter as the second letter of the period. Then the individual finds the next letter of the alphabet, and places that letter in Memory 1 for recall in the next cycle of the series. This operation of finding the next letter of the alphabet and placing it in Memory 1 is notated as $N(M_1)$.

The pattern descriptions for different series are a way to represent the information that an individual must assemble and hold in memory to solve a problem. Problems will differ in the complexity of the pattern description and how much information must be held in memory to solve a problem. The result is a prediction that problems with complex pattern descriptions containing many memory components will be more difficult to solve. This has been supported in studies of adult and children's performance on letter-series problems (Kotovsky and Simon, 1973; Holzman et al., 1976).

Pattern-description rules for number-series problems can be represented by extending the notational scheme proposed originally by Simon and Kotovsky (1963) for letter series. Examples of different types of number series and the representations of their patterns are shown in Table 9.3. The first pattern involves no transformation of the series elements; so the pattern description is notated simply by the repeated element. The second pattern entails consecutive additions by 4. The description and extrapolation of this series involves reading an element of the series into a location in memory, incrementing the content of that

Table 9.3
Examples of number series and pattern description notation

Problem	Pattern description	Pattern-description length[a]	Period length	Working-memory placekeepers
1. No numerical operation (identity) 64, 64, 64, 64, 64, 64, —	[64]	4	1	0
2. One addition (+4) 3, 7, 11, 15, 19, 23, —	$[M_1, +4(M_1)]$	11	1	1
3. Two hierarchically related operations (subtraction, ×2) 36, 34, 30, 22, —	$[M_1, -N_1(M_1), ×2(N_1)]$	19	1	2
4. One identity, one subtraction (−1) 22, 22, 21, 21, 20, 20, —	$[M_1, M_1, -1(M_1)]$	14	2	1
5. One subtraction (−1), one identity 45, 36, 44, 36, 43, 36, —	$[M_1, -1(M_1), 36]$	14	2	1
6. Two subtractions (−1, −3) 32, 21, 31, 18, 30, 15, —	$[M_1, -1(M_1), M_2, -3(M_2)]$	21	2	2
7. Two divisions (÷2, ÷3), one identity 64, 36, 24, 32, 12, 24, 16, 4, 24, —	$[M_1, ÷2(M_1), M_2, ÷3(M_2), 24]$	24	3	2
8. Two subtractions, one addition (−1, +4, −5) 72, 43, 90, 71, 47, 85, 70, 51, 80, —	$[M_1, -1(M_1), M_2, +4(M_2), M_3, -5(M_3)]$	31	3	3

[a]Pattern-description length is determined by counting the total number of individual characters in the pattern description including brackets parentheses, commas, subscripts, and arithmetic operations.

location by 4 [notated by +4(M_1)], and then outputting the new content of that location (M_1).

The third series of Table 9.3 is more complex, because it involves a hierarchic relation in which the size of the subtrahend is repeatedly multiplied by 2. The solution of this series again requires that a number be read into a location in memory. The individual must then reduce that number by a sub-trahend of changing value, which must also be kept track of in memory [repre-sented by $-N_1(M_1)$]. Finally, the value of the subtrahend itself must be in-cremented [represented by $\times 2(N_1)$], and the current value in location M_1 should be output.

The examples in Table 9.3 also show that solution difficulty for series items may be related to a number of factors. Among them are the complexity of the relations constituting the solution rule, the period length of the pattern, and the number of pieces of information that must be coordinated and manipulated in memory.

Developmental and Individual Differences

How do individuals of different ages and mental-ability levels differ in solving series-completion problems? A study conducted by Holzman et al. (1983) provides some answers to these questions. It also allows us to look at differences in overall accuracy of solution for problems such as those shown in Table 9.3. Holzman et al. presented a large set of number-series problems to adults and children in the fourth and fifth grades. Eighteen of the children were of average IQ; another eighteen had very high IQ scores (130 to 158).

One of the most important factors affecting solution accuracy for number-series problems was the number of memory slots required to represent the pattern for an item. The effect of memory slots or placekeepers is shown in Figure 9.10. For adults and children, performance was poorer on problems requiring

Figure 9.10
Solution accuracy for number series problems as a function of memory-place-keepers and subject group. (From Holzman et al., 1983, reprinted by permission.)

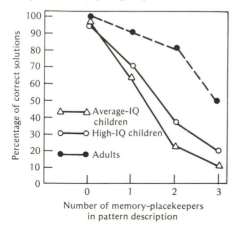

several memory placekeepers. However, the effect was much greater on the performance of both the average and the high-IQ children; so one major developmental difference is the ability to handle series problems that place large demands on working memory. One way to view this result is in terms of greater memory capacity for adults (Pascual-Leone, 1970; Case, 1974).

The ability to handle larger amounts of information and more complex rules may also be attributable to knowledge differences. Adults may be able to handle more complex numerical rules because of their efficiency in accessing numerical information. In fact, Holzman et al. (1983) found evidence for age and ability differences associated with knowledge of numerical relations. Figure 9.11 shows the results for problems that involved different types of relations. The category of relation made virtually no difference in adults' performance. However, the children performed better on series problems based on addition and subtraction relations than they did on those based on multiplication and division relations. Figure 9.11 also shows that the high-IQ children did better than the average-IQ children on the series problems with multiplication and division relations.

There was one other area that showed both age and ability differences. Series problems with hierarchic relations were especially difficult for the average-IQ children, and only 16 percent of these problems were answered correctly. The high-IQ children were able to solve 38 percent of these problems, and

Figure 9.11
Solution accuracy for number series problems as a function of arithmetic relation and subject group. (From Holzman et al., 1983, reprinted by permission.)

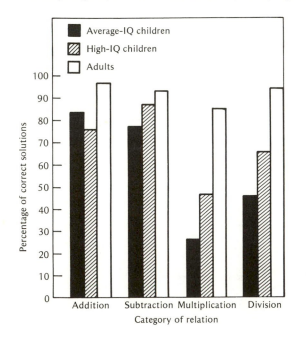

the adults correctly answered 85 percent. It seems that children, particularly those of average ability, experience special difficulties in recognizing and formulating new or unusual kinds of concepts even when their components are familiar. Hierarchic-relations problems require that individuals operate with numerical relations in a nonstandard form; that is, they must seek out and use second-order relations, such as an operation on an operation. Adults and high-IQ children are more able to induce and apply such novel relationships, although adults are clearly superior.

The Holzman et al. (1983) study shows that several factors, directly related to the theory of performance, affect the solution accuracy of adults and children. Series-completion problems appear to be sensitive indices of problem-solving and inductive-reasoning ability. As novelty and task complexity increase, major differences appear between older and younger reasoners, and between skilled and less-skilled reasoners.

Summary

We raised three broad questions about inductive reasoning:

1. What psychological processes are involved in solving analogy or series-completion problems?
2. How do we test information-processing theories of performance?
3. How do individuals of different ages and abilities differ?

Although the focus has been on analogy and series completion, these issues can be summarized for all the induction tasks illustrated in Figure 9.1.

Inductive-reasoning tasks of the type found on intelligence tests all require encoding processes which create mental representations of alphanumeric, verbal, or figural stimuli. The individual terms of analogy, classification, series, or matrix problems must be encoded so that various inference or attribute comparison processes can operate. The latter involve systematic analyses of the way(s) in which individual terms are related to each other. In analogy, this includes how the first term is related to the second, how the first term is related to the third, and how the third term is related to a final term. In classification problems, the inference process searches for a common relationship among three or four terms, such as dog, cow, horse, cat. The relationship is typically some higher-level category encompassing all the terms or some common property. In figural analogy and matrix problems, the inference process is an analysis of the transformations or changes that logically relate sets of figures. Finally, in series problems, the inference process involves discovering the sequential or mathematical relationship between a letter or number and other letters or numbers in the series.

Inference processes are not sufficient to solve induction problems. They only specify how pairs or sets of terms are related. Solution also depends on processes that evaluate the consistency and comparability of relations with each other. In an analogy, this means that the relationship inferred between the third and fourth terms is *identical* to the relationship inferred between the first and second terms. In a figural matrix problem, it means that the relations inferred for one row must be identical to the relations inferred for all other rows, and that the relations inferred for each column must be identical to the relations inferred for all other columns. Series-completion problems require that relations inferred for all elements of a "period" be consistently repeated. One of the most important aspects of inductive reasoning is the creation in memory of complex relationship structures and a comparison of their consistency. Often, the relationship structures or "rules" are too complex for the individual to keep track of and errors occur.

The other processes required for solving induction problems are decision and response processes. All these processes are executed in a sequential fashion. Often there are multiple cycles through the various processes before a decision can be reached and a response made.

A theory of how analogy, classification, matrix, or series problems are solved can be tested by finding out how well it predicts differences between items in the time or accuracy of solution. Such a theory must have many aspects, since it must explain the processes that must be executed, their sequence, and the amount of information that must be held in memory for an individual problem to be solved. Experiments are then done to see how well the theory actually predicts the performance of adults or children. In a task like analogy, where the processes can be neatly separated, measures can be taken of the time or accuracy of executing each process. Another way in which theories are sometimes tested is by developing a computer program to simulate the performance of individuals in solving problems. Built into the simulation program are all the assumptions of the theory. If the simulation program can mimic how humans perform, then it is considered to be a reasonable representation of what humans actually do. The theory for solving series problems was initially tested in this way. Other tests of the theory include predictions and explanations of the difficulties that adults and children have on letter- and number-series problems.

One of the most important features of information-processing theories of performance on inductive reasoning problems is their applicability to the individual-differences issue. The theories and methods of analyzing performance provide detailed answers to questions about ability that can not be addressed just by looking at overall scores on intelligence tests. Studies of individual differences focusing on age and ability contrasts lead to several conclusions regarding inductive reasoning. First, ability is often associated with faster and more accurate execution of processes such as inference and application of rules. Second, ability involves being able to infer novel and complex rules that place large demands on memory. Third, ability includes the capacity to coordinate and compare multiple relationships. Younger and less-skilled reasoners often seem to falter in coordinating and comparing multiple relationships. At times, they demonstrate appropriate behaviors, but often their performance demonstrates a less sophisticated strategy that violates the rules of analogical or inductive reasoning, sometimes because they do not understand the "rules of the game," sometimes because the problem complexity exceeds their mental resources.

The study of inductive reasoning is not limited to the types of problems found on intelligence tests. As we noted at the outset, induction seems to be a general characteristic of human cognition and a powerful learning mechanism. Recently, cognitive psychologists have begun to explore the role of analogical thinking in solving problems, question answering, and scientific reasoning (Rumelhart and Norman, 1981; Gentner, 1982; Gick and Holyoak, 1983; Holyoak, 1984). One goal of this research is to understand how individuals generate and use analogies in dealing with new material that must be comprehended. Another goal is to examine how new information is learned by making use of analogy to existing knowledge. For both, the interest is in the generative use of analogy where the two "halves" of the analogy are not specified ahead of time. The basic idea, however, is one of mapping the structure of information in one knowledge domain into another domain. In science, this often leads to a "model" of how things are related or operate in the new domain, with testable predictions. If we have chosen a good analogy or model, then our predictions will be confirmed. If not, we will need to modify our model or seek a new one. How individuals use such models as part of their normal thinking processes is not well understood. Nevertheless, it seems clear that analogy and the use of mental models is an important characteristic of human attempts to understand new concepts and systems. An example is the use of a flowing-waters or teeming-crowds analogy to think about electricity and current flow (Gentner and Gentner, 1982). Analogy is also an important tool for teaching new concepts or ideas. Often when we try to explain something unfamiliar to someone else, we spontaneously make use of analogy and simile. It is not uncommon to hear expressions such as "Let me give you an analogy," "An example is when . . .," or "It's just like . . . ."

There are many aspects of inductive reasoning that remain unexplored. One interesting question is whether the spontaneous use of analogy in comprehension, problem solving, and learning is related to more formal assessments of inductive-reasoning ability. Perhaps a more easily answered question is whether the ability to understand and learn from analogy is related to performance on tests of inductive-reasoning ability. We might suspect that it is, since scores on inductive-reasoning tests are significantly correlated with levels of academic achievement. One possible reason for such a relationship is that learning from instruction may be largely an inductive process (Norman et al., 1976). Structures of interrelated concepts are communicated to students by a teacher or through some other instructional medium such as a textbook. In order to comprehend and remember the material, the student must induce the structure of the new information by detecting the relational pattern of the presented concepts, and then discover connections between the newly communicated material and knowledge structures already in his or her permanent memory. Instruction often relies heavily on the use of analogy and simile to help the learner establish connections to knowledge structures already available. However, to profit from analogy, the learner must be able to distinguish between relevant and irrelevant relations. Teachers assume that relational features common to both domains can be identified, and that dissimilar relations will be ignored. This comparison and coordination of relations is exactly the problem area for less-skilled reasoners on inductive-reasoning tests. Perhaps these individuals experience similar problems in learning situations that also depend upon these capabilities. This potential link between formal inductive-reasoning and learning from instruction and example is an hypothesis worth study, since it has practical implications for improving cognitive skills and educational practice.

References

Alderton, D. C., S. R. Goldman, and J. W. Pellegrino. 1982. Multitask assessment of inductive reasoning skill. Paper presented at the annual meeting of American Educational Research Association, New York, March, 1982.

Banet, L. 1969. Evolution of the Balmer series. *American Journal of Physics,* 34, 496–503.

Bisanz, J. 1979. Processes and Strategies in Children's Solutions of Geometric Analogies. Unpublished doctoral dissertation, Univ. of Pittsburgh.

Brody, E. B., and N. Brody. 1976. *Intelligence: Nature, Determinants, and Consequences.* New York: Academic Press.

Burke, H. R. 1958. Raven's progressive matrices: A review and critical evaluation. *Journal of Genetic Psychology,* 93, 199–228.

Burt, C. 1911. Experimental tests of higher mental processes and their relation to general intelligence. *Journal of Experimental Pedagogy,* 1, 93–112.

Case, R. 1974. Structures and strictures: Some functional limitations on the course of cognitive growth. *Cognitive Psychology,* 6, 544–573.

Gentner, D. 1982. Are scientific analogies metaphors? *In* D. S. Miall, ed., *Metaphor: Problems and Perspectives* (Brighton, England: Harvester Press).

Gentner, D., and D. R. Gentner. 1983. Flowing waters or teeming crowds: Mental models of electricity. *In* D. Gentner and A. L. Stevens, eds., *Mental Models* (Hillsdale, N.J.: Erlbaum).

Gick, M. L., and K. J. Holyoak. 1983. Schema induction and analogical transfer. *Cognitive Psychology,* 15, 1–38.

Goldman, S. R., and J. W. Pellegrino. 1984. Deductions about induction: Analyses of developmental and individual differences. *In* R. Sternberg, ed., *Advances in the Psychology of Human Intelligence, Vol. 2* (Hillsdale, N.J.: Erlbaum).

Goldman, S. R., J. W. Pellegrino, P. E. Parseghian, and R. Sallis. 1982. Developmental and individual differences in verbal analogical reasoning. *Child Development,* 53, 550–559.

Greeno, J. G. 1978. Natures of problem-solving abilities. *In* W. K. Estes, ed., *Handbook of Learning and Cognitive Processes, Vol. 5* (Hillsdale, N.J.: Erlbaum).

Heller, J. I. 1979. Cognitive Processing in Verbal Analogy Solution. Unpublished doctoral dissertation. Univ. of Pittsburgh.

Holyoak, K. J. 1984. Analogical thinking and human intelligence. *In* R. J. Sternberg, ed., *Advances in the psychology of human intelligence, Vol. 2* (Hillsdale, N.J.: Erlbaum).

Holzman, T. G., R. Glaser, and J. W. Pellegrino. 1976. Process training derived from a computer simulation theory. *Memory & Cognition,* 4, 249–256.

Holzman, T. G., J. W. Pellegrino, and R. Glaser. 1983. Cognitive variables in series completion. *Journal of Educational Psychology,* 75, 602–617.

Kedrov, B. M. 1966. On the question of the psychology of scientific creativity. H. A. Simon, trans. *Soviet Psychology,* 5, 18–37. (Reprinted from *Veprosy psikhologii,* 1957, 3, 91–113.)

Kotovsky, K., and H. A. Simon. 1973. Empirical tests of a theory of human acquisition of concepts for sequential patterns. *Cognitive Psychology,* 4, 399–424.

Lashley, K. S. 1951. The problem of serial order in behavior. *In* L. A. Jeffress, ed., *Cerebral Mechanisms in Behavior* (New York: Wiley).

Lyttkens, H. 1952. *The Analogy between God and the World.* Uppsala, Sweden: Almquist and Wiksells.

Mulholland, T. M., J. W. Pellegrino, and R. Glaser. 1980. Components of geometric analogy solution. *Cognitive Psychology,* 12, 252–284.

Pascual-Leone, J. 1970. A mathematical model for the transition rule in Piaget's developmental stages. *Acta Psychologica,* 32, 301–345.

Pellegrino, J. W., and R. Glaser. 1982. Analyzing aptitudes for learning: Inductive reasoning. *In* R. Glaser, ed., *Advances in Instructional Psychology Vol. 2* (Hillsdale, N.J.: Erlbaum).

Pellegrino, J. W., and A. L. Ingram. 1977. Components of verbal analogy solution. Paper presented at the annual meeting of the Midwestern Psychological Association, Chicago, May, 1977.

Raven, J. C. 1938. *Progressive Matrices: A Perceptual Test of Intelligence.* London: Lewis.

Restle, F. 1970. Theory of serial pattern learning: Structural trees. *Psychological Review,* 77, 481–495.

Rumelhart, D. E., and D. A. Norman. 1981. Analogical processes in learning. *In* J. R. Anderson, ed., *Cognitive Skills and Their Acquisition* (Hillsdale, N.J.: Erlbaum).

Simon, H. A., and K. Kotovsky. 1963. Human acquisition of concepts for sequential patterns. *Psychological Review,* 70, 534–546.

Simon, H. A., and R. K. Sumner. 1968. Pattern in music. *In* B. Kleinmuntz, ed., *Formal Representation of Human Judgment* (New York: Wiley).

Spearman, C. 1923. *The Nature of Intelligence and the Principles of Cognition.* London: Macmillan.

Sternberg, R. J. 1977. *Intelligence, Information Processing, and Analogical Reasoning: The Componential Analysis of Human Abilities.* Hillsdale, N.J.: Erlbaum.

Sternberg, R. J. 1981. Intelligence and nonentrenchment. *Journal of Educational Psychology,* 73, 1–16.

Sternberg, R. J., and M. K. Gardner. 1983. Unities in inductive reasoning. *Journal of Experimental Psychology: General,* 112, 80–116.

Sternberg, R. J., and G. Nigro. 1980. Developmental patterns in the solution of verbal analogies. *Child Development,* 51, 27–38.

Sternberg, R. J., and B. Rifkin. 1979. The development of analogical reasoning processes. *Journal of Experimental Child Psychology,* 27, 195–232.

Stone, B., and M. C. Day. 1981. A developmental study of the processes underlying solution of figural matrices. *Child Development,* 52, 359–362.

Thurstone, L. L. 1938. *Primary Mental Abilities.* Chicago: Univ. of Chicago Press.

Whipple, G. M. 1915. *Manual of Mental and Physical Tests, Part II: Complex Processes.* Baltimore: Warwick and York.

Whitely, S. E. 1977. Information processing on intelligence test items: Some response components. *Applied Psychological Measurement,* 1, 465–476.

———. 1980. Modeling aptitude test validity from cognitive components. *Journal of Educational Psychology,* 72, 750–769.

Woodsworth, R. S., and F. L. Wells. 1911. Association tests. *Psychological Monographs,* 13, No. 5.

10

PROBLEM-SOLVING ABILITY

Micheline T. H. Chi
Robert Glaser
University of Pittsburgh

Solving problems is a complex cognitive skill that characterizes one of the most intelligent human activities. From childhood onward, we actively solve problems presented to us by the world. We acquire information about the world, and organize this information into structures of knowledge about objects, events, people, and ourselves that are stored in our memories. These structures of knowledge comprise bodies of understanding, mental models, convictions, and beliefs that influence how we relate our experiences together, and how we solve the problems that confront us in everyday life, in school, in our jobs, and at play.

This research program, conducted at the Learning Research and Development Center, University of Pittsburgh, is supported in part by Contract no. N00014–79–C–0215, NR 157–430/12–19–80, of the Office of Naval Research, Personnel and Training Research Programs, Psychological Sciences Division, and in part by the National Institute of Education. The authors are grateful to Ted Rees for comments and editing.

How do humans develop their abilities to solve problems in these situations? People differ, children from adults, and experts from novices, and these differences are based on cognitive processes and mental organizations that humans have in common, and that characterize their problem-solving abilities. In this chapter we emphasize the general characteristics of human problem-solving ability. Systematic theory on the mechanisms of human problem solving is a relatively recent advance in psychological science, and knowledge of fundamental processes provides a basis for understanding the development and acquisition of our abilities to think and solve problems.

Scientists interested in problem solving have studied various classes of problems, each having its own task characteristics, which determine to a large extent the behavior of the problem solver and the strategies appropriate to finding solutions. In addition, as we have seen in the preceding chapters, the experience and knowledge brought to the situation by the problem solver determine whether and how a solution will be reached. Puzzle problems, like tic-tac-toe or combining the links of several small chains into a larger chain with the minimal number of moves, require little knowledge of a subject-matter domain. Solving problems in elementary physics, however, requires more subject-matter knowledge, such as knowledge of force diagrams and of certain laws of physics. Puzzle problems have been studied largely because they are not complicated by needing much background knowledge, and because they reveal the strategies that people employ in searching for a solution. Detailed observations of performance in puzzle situations have been accompanied by computer simulations of these performances that precisely describe certain general strategies or *heuristics* that people use when they are confronted with novel situations. As a result of extensive work with these computer models of problem solving, the main mechanisms for solving these well-structured puzzle problems are fairly well understood. The strategies used depend on attention to perceptual cues, the goals and subgoals held in memory, and the discovery of sequential patterns of correct moves.

Research has also been carried out on the nature of expert problem solving in knowledge-rich domains like chess playing and school problems in physics and mathematics. Investigation of the performance of experts and novices in domains requiring extensive knowledge has deepened our understanding of the kinds of knowledge required for efficient problem-solving ability. In particular, the investigation of problem solving in domains requiring extensive knowledge has shown how the knowledge organizations acquired by the problem solver, which are stored in long-term memory, influence the perceptual processes and strategies of problem solving.

Two important factors, then, that influence problem solving are the nature of the task (the *task environment*) and the kind of knowledge brought to the problem by the solver. These two factors dictate the organization of this chapter. In the first main section, we will consider puzzle problems and general processes of solution. In the second, we will discuss solving of problems that require domain knowledge. We will also consider various task environments that involve insight, creativity, and ill-structured problems. Our goal, in the problem-solving task of writing this chapter, is to give you an understanding of some of the mechanisms that underlie problem-solving abilities. We can now begin by defining the various types of problems that have been studied.

What Is a Problem?

A problem is a situation in which you are trying to reach some goal, and must find a means for getting there. Figuring out puzzles, solving algebra problems, deciding how to budget a limited amount of money, trying to control inflation and reduce unemployment, are all examples of problems that we as individuals and as a society frequently encounter. Clearly, these problems cover an enormous range of difficulty and complexity, but they do have some things in common. They all have some *initial state,* whether it is a set of equations or the state of the economy, and they all have some *goal.* To solve the problem, you must perform some *operations* on the initial state to achieve that goal. Often there are some rules that specify allowable operations, and these are generally called *constraints.*

Puzzles are one form of problem with which we are all familiar. The Tower of Hanoi puzzle (shown in Figure 10.1) is a typical example, and has received a great deal of attention from psychologists. It consists of three pegs and a set of disks of different sizes. In the initial state, the disks are stacked up on the first peg (the top display in Figure 10.1) in order of decreasing size (like a pyramid), and the goal is to move all the disks onto the third peg, maintaining the pyramid (the bottom display in Figure 10.1). The constraints in this problem are that the solver can never place a larger disk on top of a smaller one, and that only one disk may be moved at a time.

Although puzzles are interesting, the kinds of problems that we most frequently encounter fall into two types: classroom problems and real-world problems. An algebra problem where we have to find the unknown quantity typifies our standard notion of a problem. Students spend a good deal of time learning to solve various kinds of classroom problems in such areas as mathematics, physics, and chemistry. A distinct difference between puzzles and classroom problems is that a fair amount of knowledge of a specific subject area is necessary for the solution of the classroom problems. Although even a young child can move a disk from one peg to another, solving an algebra problem requires knowing when and how to apply a whole set of rules for manipulating equations. An example of a fairly complex algebra problem can be found in Box 10.1.

Often the most important and difficult problems we have to solve are those that we encounter in everyday life outside the classroom. Such problems range from finding our way about in a city, to elevating ourselves out of a period of depression. In both cases, we have a clear initial state (being lost at location *A* or feeling depressed), and a clear goal (wanting to be at location *B* or feeling elated). The solution for the first problem might be either calling a taxi, asking directions, or reading a map.

Figure 10.1
The Tower of Hanoi.

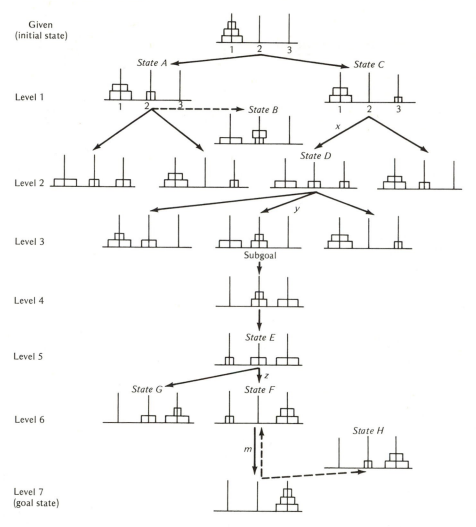

The puzzles, classroom, and real-world problems described so far are all *well defined.* That is, you can readily recognize when the problem is solved. We know that the Tower of Hanoi problem is solved when the disks have all been transferred to the third peg. An algebra problem is solved when a quantity for the unknown is found (although it could be the wrong answer). Likewise, we know when we feel less depressed, and we know that we have accomplished our goal of finding our way when we are at location *B.*

There is another class of problems, called *ill defined.* These are generally problems in which one or several aspects of the situation is not well specified. Examples are composing a poem, or designing a house. The general nature of

---

Box 10.1
The Smalltown problem

Because of their quiet ways, the inhabitants of Smalltown were especially upset by the terrible New Year's Eve auto accident which claimed the life of one Smalltown resident. The facts were these. Both Smith and Jones were New Year's Eve babies, and each had planned a surprise visit to the other one on their mutual birthday. Jones had started out for Smith's house traveling due east on Route 210 just two minutes after Smith had left for Jones' house. Smith was traveling directly south on Route 140. Jones was traveling 30 miles per hour faster than Smith even though their houses were only five miles apart as the crow flies. Their cars crashed at the right-angle intersection of the two highways. Officer Franklin, who observed the crash, determined that Jones was traveling half again as fast as Smith at the time of the crash. The crash occurred nearer to the house of the dead man than to the house of the survivor. What was the name of the dead man?

---

these problems is that their descriptions are not clear, and the information needed to solve them is not entirely contained in the problem statement; consequently, it is even less obvious (than in well-defined problems) what actions to take in order to solve them.

Puzzle Problems and Processes of Solution

Well-structured puzzle problems have been traditionally studied by psychologists and have received particular attention in the last two decades. Their popularity arose from two related considerations.

First, with the advent of computer science and its accompanying notions and techniques of computer simulation of human behavior (Newell et al., 1958), psychologists were particularly interested in rigorous investigation of the basic processes of solving problems. The technique used was to have a subject "think out loud" while solving a given problem. This problem-solving protocol is tape-recorded, transcribed, and then intensely analyzed to find out just how the subject tried to solve the problem. The problem-solving strategies used by the subject are then simulated in a computer program, to see if the program can produce similar solution patterns.

Second, puzzle problems require very little background knowledge and yet can be very difficult to solve. In such tasks, differences in individuals' abilities to solve problems can be attributed to differences in some basic underlying problem-solving processes rather than to greater or lesser subject-matter knowledge. Puzzle problems therefore lend themselves particularly well to uncovering the underlying solution processes, by tracing the sequence of operations applied to transform the initial state to the goal state.

The focus of modern cognitive psychologists on processes is in contrast with the earlier problem-solving research by Gestalt psychologists of the 1930s. The early work dealt mostly with *insight* problems, and emphasized how appropriate changes in the representation of a problem could lead to solution. A typical insight problem is the two-string problem (Maier, 1931). Two strings are hung from the ceiling. The object is to tie them together, but they are too far apart for a person to reach both of them at the same time. A book of matches, a few pieces of cotton, and a screwdriver are on the table nearby. The necessary insight for solving this problem comes from a person recognizing that the screwdriver can be used in other than its usual function. Here it may be tied to one string, to create a pendulum that can be swung to the other string. This early research focused on the conditions that impeded or facilitated problem solving, and on how intuitively improbable responses could become more probable. For example, would putting the screwdriver among a different set of items on the table make it easier for the solver to recognize that a screwdriver can be used in an unfamiliar way, as a weight?

The information-processing approach, represented by the work of Newell and Simon (1972), significantly changed problem-solving research, by turning attention away from the conditions under which solutions can be reached, and toward the component cognitive processes involved that transform the initial state of the problem to the final goal state. In order to make this problem a manageable one to study, many researchers in the late 1960s and early 1970s concentrated on a class of puzzle-like problems called *move* or *transformation* problems. These problems all have clear initial and goal states, and a small set of well-defined operations (moves) that can successively transform the initial state to the goal state.

The Tower of Hanoi is one such problem, and it has been extensively studied. A spatial metaphor is useful in analyzing this kind of problem. The states of the problem are represented as points in a space. The possible operations on each state are represented by lines leading to the states that these operations produce. Because there is only one initial state, and typically more than one operation can be applied to each state to generate several plausible transformed states, this *solution space* resembles an upside-down tree. Part of the solution space for the Tower of Hanoi is shown in Figure 10.1.

One way to look at the process of solving a problem is to think of it as a search through the solution space. The space contains many possible paths, but only one (or a few) leads to the goal state. The distance traveled down a particular branch of the tree, the levels in Figure 10.1, is often referred to as the depth (D) of search, and the number of alternatives at each point is the breadth (B). The total number of possible paths is equal to B^D (if B is the same number at every state). That is, the number of alternative paths to be considered explodes exponentially.

Representation

The *representation* of a problem consists essentially of the solver's interpretation or understanding of the problem. Researchers have found that the representation is very important in determining how easy a problem is to solve. In the two-string problem, for example, insight is really representation. The initial representation of the screwdriver must be broadened to include the fact that it is a heavy object, which can therefore be used as a pendulum weight.

The representation of move problems, like the Tower of Hanoi, is fairly straightforward, because the initial and final states (and the permissible moves) are clearly spelled out. However, we can conceive of situations where the representation fails to embody one or more aspects of the problem. For example, if the constraints on the operations are not properly encoded, then the solution space could be enlarged unnecessarily. For example, when children try to solve the Tower of Hanoi problem, they may have trouble remembering the constraint that a larger disk may not be placed on a smaller disk, or they may forget what the goal state should look like (Klahr and Robinson, 1981). If the children forget a constraint, they essentially add branches to the solution space, making the correct path harder to find. The resulting search space is referred to as the solver's *problem space.* The dotted path from State A to State B in Figure 10.1 shows an illegal addition to the solution space.

In certain problems, a solver might also add unnecessary constraints, thereby taking away branches, so that the proper solution path is not even present in the problem space. The problem thus becomes impossible to solve. Adding or deleting branches because of improper representation is common. One example of adding a constraint to the representation is to be seen in the problem of drawing four straight lines through nine dots arranged as three rows of three without retracing or lifting the pencil (see Figure 10.2a). Almost invariably, solvers unconsciously add the constraint that the line cannot go outside of the square indicated by the dots, as shown in Figure 10.2b.

The representation of a problem can also be faulty if solvers encode the goal state improperly. This makes the problem impossible to solve, because solvers then do not know what to search for. An illustration of a problem in which the goal state is improperly encoded is the well-known sixteen-matches problem (see Figure 10.3a). The goal is to form four squares, given the constraint that only three matches may be moved. One of the common causes of error is that the goal is often represented as in Figure 10.3b, instead of in arrangements

---

Figure 10.2
The nine dots problem: (a) initial figure; (b) typical attempts at solution; (c) correct solution.

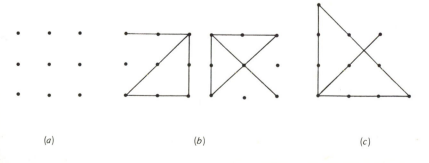

(a)   (b)   (c)

like those in Figure 10.3c, where each square uses up four sticks. That is, the initial representation of the goal does not emphasize that sixteen sticks can make up four squares perfectly, so that no stick should be shared by two squares. (Another way to look at this is that the representation did not contain the constraint that no stick should be shared by two squares.)

The difficulty in solving move problems is not generally related to solvers' misrepresenting the initial state, but rather to their omitting constraints or not having a clear representation of the goal state, as just described. However, other puzzle problems, such as the two-string problem, are difficult precisely because of initial-state representation. For problems of greater complexity, the initial representation is even more important, as we will discuss later in this chapter.

Searching for a Solution

The process of finding a solution to a problem can be visualized as a search through the paths in the problem space until one that leads to the goal is found. Since move problems are generally not difficult to represent, research on solving move problems has tended to concentrate on uncovering the strategies that effective problem solvers use to find a solution in the problem space. There are a variety of strategies for carrying out this search.

One strategy is to try paths randomly, hoping to stumble on the goal. A *random search* is adequate if your search space is small. However, since the search space expands exponentially for most problems, the chance of a random search being successful is quite small.

Another obvious strategy is that of systematically searching the entire tree. In a *depth-first search,* for instance, you search a particular path all the way to the bottom. If this state is not the goal, you back up one level and then start searching down again via an untried path. When all paths from a particular state have been tried, you back up one more level and start down again, and so on. This method (and any such exhaustive method) requires much recordkeeping to keep track of which paths you have tried, and which state you should back up to when all current links have been tried. Except for very simple problems, the memory required for this recordkeeping is too great for human beings. Exhaustive methods are often not feasible even for computers to use.

The key to the effective strategies actually used by humans is to reduce the search space by considering only one branch or a very few branches at each point. For instance, de Groot (1966) found that chess players use a strategy that can be called depth-first, because they initially follow one path straight down for

Figure 10.3
The move three matches problem (see text for discussion).

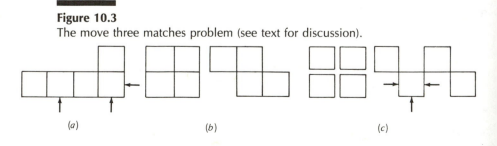

(a)   (b)   (c)

a few moves. They make no attempt to be exhaustive or to backtrack systematically, however. Instead, they tend to jump back to the beginning position or to some important intermediate point and gradually explore just a few alternative branches. Obviously, if only a few alternatives at each point are going to be explored, they had better be good ones; so good strategies are those that guide the selection of promising moves or the elimination of unpromising ones.

Means/ends analysis.   A powerful strategy for finding good alternatives, which takes the goal state into account, is *means/ends analysis.* This strategy was used as an important search strategy in one of the earliest attempts to create a computer program to solve problems, the General Problem Solver (Ernst and Newell, 1969). The general idea is to discover what differences there are between the current state and the goal state, and then to find operations that will reduce them. If there is more than one such operation, the one that reduces the largest difference is applied first. In other words, find the best means to achieve the desired end.

In the Tower of Hanoi, the differences are simply that disks are not on the proper peg in the proper order. At the initial state, the move that does the most to reduce the difference is placing the small disk on the third peg (see state *C* in Figure 10.1). Note, however, that this move actually introduces a new difference, because the disk is in the wrong (bottom) position on the correct (third) peg. Being in the wrong position must therefore be defined to be a smaller difference than not being on the correct peg. That is, state *C* is the correct move, because there is less of a difference between state *C* and the goal state than between state *A* and the goal.

Means/ends analysis, however, is not guaranteed to find the solution. At state *D* in Figure 10.1, for example, the correct move is to take path *y*, even though it does not reduce the overall difference. General methods like this one, which reduce the number of moves that must be considered but are not guaranteed to succeed in all situations, are called *heuristics.*

Means/ends analysis can be used to work not only from the initial state to the goal, but also backward from the goal. In this situation, the strategy is to find an operation (such as path *m* in Figure 10.1) that can produce the goal state when it is applied to a state which is closer to the initial state (e.g., state *F*). In the Tower of Hanoi example, to find state *F,* we can transform state *E* via path *z,* working forward. To work backward from the goal, we want to find the transformation (here, path *m*) that, when applied in a forward manner, will take us from state *F* to the goal. Working backward, however, two states (states *F* and *H*) can be transformed from the goal, only one of which (state *F*) overlaps with one of the two states (states *F* and *G*) generated in a forward way, from state *E*. So by combining forward and backward searches, we can select the right move almost by default.

An additional benefit of working backward (which is unfortunately not true in the Tower of Hanoi problem), is that often the number of "backward branches" to be considered is smaller than the number when working forward. Another difference between the forward and backward strategy is that we can try out moves as soon as they are decided on in the forward strategy, whereas backward strategy requires a chain of moves to be selected first. We then apply them in the same order as they would have been applied if we had been using the forward strategy. So working backward requires planning, and is therefore more sophisticated than forward strategy.

Although the Tower of Hanoi is quite a simple puzzle, means/ends analysis is useful in more-complicated situations. Newell and Simon (1972) observed subjects using it in solving *cryptarithmetic* problems (in which an arithmetic problem is presented with letters standing for numbers, and the solver must discover which letter stands for which number). Reed and Simon (1976) show how it is used on the missionaries and cannibals problem (in which one boat of limited capacity must be used to transport missionaries and cannibals across a river without anyone being eaten), and Atwood and Polson (1976) demonstrated its use in the water-jug problems. Simon and Simon (1978) noted a subject who worked backward while solving distance-rate-time problems; and Larkin et al. (1980) observed similar solution strategies being used to solve physics problems.

Means/ends analysis does have limitations, of course. In particular, it will fail if there is no operation that will reduce the remaining differences. Such an occasion will arise when a problem requires a *detour* to get to the goal. The term *detour* generally refers to a path that *increases* the differences between the current and goal states, at least temporarily. This is the situation that was mentioned in state *D* in Figure 10.1. Here the differences from the goal state are that the large and medium disks are on the wrong pegs, and the small one is in the wrong position even though it is on the correct peg. None of the available moves actually reduces the overall difference. The correct move, which is moving the smallest disk (taking path *y*), actually produces a larger difference than the previous state.

Subgoaling. A very useful strategy, which can be used in conjunction with means/end analysis, is *subgoaling.* Subgoaling is simply picking out an intermediate state on the solution path to reach as the temporary goal. In effect, subgoaling divides a problem into two or more subproblems, thus transforming the entire search space into two or more spaces of smaller depth.

Choosing a subgoal well can allow you to use means/ends analysis in situations where, by itself, it might not reduce a difference (as when a detour is needed). In the Tower of Hanoi, one useful subgoal is for you to get the largest disk onto its proper peg, because you must put it there before you can place the others on top of it. Look at state *D* in Figure 10.1 again, with that subgoal in mind. Now the differences for you to consider are that (a) the large one is on the wrong peg and (b) the small one is blocking it. By using means/ends analysis now, you will see that the correct move (taking path *y*) does reduce the difference, whereas the less-efficient ones do not. Subgoaling can therefore remove the apparent need to move away from a goal in order to get to it. In effect, when you use subgoaling with means/ends analysis, you remove the limitation of means/ends analysis.

Subgoaling also reduces the search space significantly. Remember that the size of the space increases exponentially with its depth. If the subgoal we have selected is on the solution path, then, once we have reached it, we have reduced significantly the number of alternative paths to be considered to reach the goal, as Figure 10.4 shows. The obvious advantage to subgoaling is that we have divided a larger problem into smaller ones.

A pragmatic difficulty, though, is how to choose useful subgoals. There are several heuristics for finding them. One way is for you to work backward first, and then use the new state that you have reached as the subgoal to work forward to. Another method is to *decompose* the main goal. In the Tower of Hanoi problem, the goal is for you to have the set of disks on the third peg in a certain order, and an obvious subgoal is for you to first put the larger disk on the third peg. In order for you to achieve this subgoal, the third peg must be empty and the large disk must be uncovered. In other words, the other disks must be on the middle peg. Because large disks can never be on top of small ones, a two-disk subgoal is generated, with the middle peg as the goal peg. This form of the subgoal is very useful when there are more than three disks in the problem, because it decomposes the puzzle into a hierarchic series of smaller problems.

Another heuristic for setting subgoals is for the solver to consider only one constraint at a time, which serves systematically to narrow down the problem space. Actually, this may be the way most people solve some everyday problems, since they may not initially think of all the constraints involved. Suppose, for example, that you are buying your first house. Your initial constraint is that the price be under $50,000. After looking around at a few houses, you realize that in order to cut down on the heating bills, you need a well-insulated contemporary house rather than one of those old mansions. Thus, your next

Figure 10.4
Reducing the search space with a subgoal.

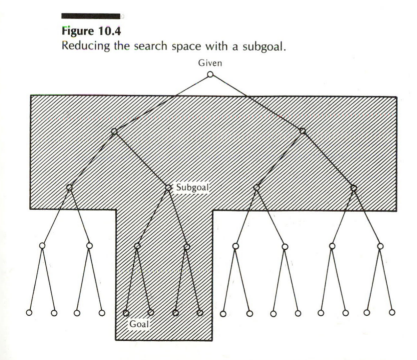

search will be limited only to smaller contemporary houses, but still under the initial price constraint of $50,000.

Although subgoaling seems theoretically to be an ideal strategy, research on the effect of providing a subgoal shows that it does not always help. Providing a subgoal for problem solvers can instead increase their confusion, because they do not seem to know how to continue after the subgoal has been reached. Hayes (1966), for example, found that people took longer to solve problems when a subgoal was provided in the statement of the problem, even though the subgoal helped them reach the situation quite easily, than when they were allowed to solve the problem by their own methods.

Generate-and-test. A heuristic that is often useful in many cases is for you to generate a set of possible solutions to a given problem directly, and then to test each one to see if it is the correct solution. Consider the task of opening a small combination lock. Possible solutions are all short series of numbers (usually three) that fall between the smallest and largest numbers on the dial. These are easy to generate. Testing is also easy: just turn the dial and see if the lock opens. Fortunately (or unfortunately, depending on your situation), the total number of possible solutions is quite large; success is certain, but testing all 999 combinations (at one per second) would take 17 minutes.

Generate-and-test is a useful technique only when it is reasonably easy for you to generate the set of potential solutions and test them. This may occur, for example, when the set is fairly small and the path from the current state to the solution is unimportant to you, or when you have difficulty generating the search space.

Particularly relevant examples of the generate-and-test strategy are scientific research and medical diagnosis. In research, an investigator will generate a hypothesis to explain some observed phenomena (the behavior of humans solving problems, for instance) and then devise experiments to test it. In medicine, physicians typically make a tentative diagnosis (or hypothesis) based on a partial description of the initial state (the patient's symptoms), and then order various examinations and laboratory tests to confirm or disconfirm the diagnosis. Even if the initial hypothesis is disconfirmed, the testing process generally adds new information about the initial state and can lead to new hypotheses. These examples lend themselves particularly well to a generate-and-test heuristic, mainly because it is obviously difficult for us to find a set of operations that can transform the initial state into the goal state. In the medical diagnosis example, the initial state consists mainly of symptoms, and the goal state is to explain what causes them. Typically, this initial state is incompletely known; some of the symptoms may be irrelevant; and there may be multiple causes at work (a patient may be suffering from heart, lung, and kidney problems, for instance). In such a situation, it is much easier to hypothesize a particular cause, find out what its effects would be, and compare them with the known symptoms.

In sum, the outcome of the research on puzzle-type problems has been very useful in uncovering several standard and powerful general-purpose problem-solving techniques: means/ends analysis, subgoaling, and generate-and-test. These heuristics have been observed to be used across a wide range of problems, including puzzles, physics problems, and medical diagnosis.

Domain Problems and Knowledge

Although research on puzzle problems, particularly move problems, flourished well into the 1970s and provided valuable insights into the kinds of general problem-solving strategies people use, researchers found, when studying more-complicated kinds of problems, that strategies did not, by themselves, sufficiently describe problem-solving performance. Knowledge of the problem domain is also important, and can influence the use of general problem-solving heuristics. Striking demonstrations of the influence of knowledge on problem-solving processes were provided by researchers in both cognitive psychology and artificial intelligence. In cognitive psychology, de Groot (1966) and then Chase and Simon (1973a,b) explored what makes master chess players different from less-expert ones. De Groot obtained protocols from former world champions and from some fairly skillful club players as they tried to find the best move in a given situation. Surprisingly, he found no strategy differences. All players tended to consider the same number of moves. They also looked ahead about the same number of moves as they tried to evaluate each move, and they used the same strategy to guide this search. In contrast to other players, experts simply recognized the best move and gave it first consideration, evaluating the other moves only as a way of double-checking themselves. This ability to perceive the problem in a way that restricts the problem space has since been shown to occur in other areas as well. For instance, in medical diagnosis research, both experts and novices are found to use the same kind of generate-and-test heuristic. The experts, however, start with a more accurate hypothesis (Elstein et al., 1978). So what differentiates an expert problem solver from a nonexpert is not the use of different or more powerful heuristics, but an ability to choose the best path to solution without considering all the others.

Research in artificial intelligence aimed at creating chess-playing programs (e.g., Wilkins, 1980) has further demonstrated that human skill is not based on strategies to guide search through the solution space. The number of possible moves at a given position can be fairly large, perhaps 30 or 35, and because the size of a search space increases exponentially with each subsequent move on a given possible path of play, the size of the chess space is extremely large (somewhere around 10^{120} paths). Even the most powerful computers cannot search this large space entirely, and it must be drastically reduced by using sophisticated computational strategies to evaluate and eliminate moves. Although these programs can play at tournament level, they succeed because they can do far more searching than humans, using complex statistical strategies to compute and evaluate the best move in a way that humans do not. Even with these advantages, they still cannot match the best players. Clearly, good chess players do something very different from searching through the space for a good move.

The evidence indicates that what humans actually do is to build up an extremely large store of knowledge about typical chess positions through years of experience. De Groot (1966) provided a clue when he found that chess masters, when shown a chess position for only five seconds, were able to remember it with very high accuracy, whereas the less-expert players could not. This difference could not be attributed to the experts' superior visual memory, because when random board positions were used that were not like chess patterns, masters did as poorly as novices (Chase and Simon, 1973a). Using very simple techniques, Chase and Simon showed that the masters were actually perceiving groups of pieces, or *chunks*. They asked subjects to reproduce from memory board positions that had just been shown to them, or to copy a position from one board to another. During the reproduction task, groupings could be detected if significantly longer pauses occurred after the placement of several individual pieces in quick succession. Because the contents of a chunk are closely associated in memory, once a chunk is accessed, recall of its component pieces will be rapid. However, more time is needed to access another chunk. When masters were copying a position, clear evidence of grouping could be detected by their periodic glances at the board. The subject would turn to look at the board, place a series of pieces, then look back again, place the next series of pieces, and so on.

Significant pauses and head turns, as evidence of chunking, were observed with both expert and novice subjects. However, expert groupings contained three to six pieces, whereas novice groupings contained only one or two. It is the larger sizes of the experts' chunks that enabled them to remember so many more pieces from a chessboard than did novices. Moreover, the pieces in the expert patterns were related in identifiable ways to chess knowledge. They constituted very common patterns, such as a castled-king or a pawn chain, or local clusters of pieces. Additional support for the existence of chunks comes from eye-movement studies. When experts were asked to analyze a board position, their eye fixations showed that they were concentrating on groups of pieces, such as those in important attack and defense relationships (Simon and Barenfeld, 1969).

Differences in chunking between experts and nonexperts have been observed in other domains, as well. In electronics, Egan and Schwartz (1979) found that skilled technicians reconstructed symbolic drawings of circuit diagrams according to the functional nature of the elements in the circuit, such as amplifiers, rectifiers, and filters. Novice technicians, however, produced chunks based more on the spatial proximity of the elements. When Akin (1980) asked architects to reconstruct building plans from memory, several levels of patterns were produced. First, the architects recalled local patterns consisting of wall segments and doors, then rooms and other areas, then clusters of rooms or areas. In other words, the reconstruction processes exhibited a hierarchic pattern of chunks within chunks.

The important implication of this research is that when experts look at an apparently complicated situation, they are able to represent it in terms of a small number of patterns or chunks. If the situation is very intricate, as with the architectural drawings, their knowledge is further organized into embedded sets or hierarchic structures.

How Structured Knowledge Facilitates Problem Solving

Although understanding the cognitive processes involved in finding a good chess move is clearly a difficult and challenging problem for analysis, we are especially interested in what these findings tell us about solving the kinds of problems we encounter in the classroom and in life in general. Remember that the initial representation of a problem is very important in determining how easy the problem is to solve. Just as a chess player's knowledge allows a representation of a given situation to be formed, a problem solver's knowledge somehow determines the problem representation. Then the proper problem-solving procedures, if they are known, must be retrieved from memory and applied. It is the problem solver's representation that guides retrieval of appropriate solution procedures.

In order to consider this process of representation in more detail, we will find it very helpful to use the concept of a *schema*. Recall that a schema is a theoretical construct which describes the format of an organized body of knowledge in memory. Researchers conceive of a schema as a modifiable information structure that represents generic concepts stored in memory. Schemata represent knowledge that we experience, such as the interrelations between objects, situations, events, and sequences of events that normally occur. In this sense, schemata contain prototypical information about frequently experienced situations, and they are used to interpret new situations and observations (Rumelhart, 1981). Often a great deal of relevant information is not apparent, so that you may have trouble understanding a situation without filling in the missing data by means of prior knowledge. Estes (National Academy of Sciences, 1981) explains this point by describing the following vignette:

> *At the security gate, the airline passenger presented his briefcase.*
> *It contained metallic objects.*
> *His departure was delayed.*

In order to understand this commonplace incident, an individual must already know a good deal about air terminals. Such *prior knowledge* is represented in memory by a schema that specifies the relations between the roles played by various people in the terminal, the objects typically encountered, and the actions that typically ensue. Schema theory assumes that there are memory structures *(schemata)* in memory for recurrent situations that are experienced, and that a major function of schemata is to construct interpretations of new situations.

The objects of a schema may be thought of as variables or slots into which incoming information can fit. If enough slots of a particular schema are filled, it becomes *active*. An active schema can then guide you to seek information to fill its remaining slots. If such additional information is not available in the environment, then you will fill its slots with information typical of a particular situation, activate its procedures, and access as needed any other knowledge it contains. In effect, the schema is a prototypical structure that can incorporate observed phenomena. People often react very rapidly and effectively to incoming stimuli. Recognizing a familiar face (for example) seems to happen almost instantaneously, and the speed is independent of the number of faces one knows. The features of a face fit into slots in "face schemata," and one of these schemata becomes active and provides the person's name.

Schemata are closely related to chunks. When a chess player looks at the board, the individual pieces can fit into the slots of "chess-pattern schemata." These schemata then provide the names or symbols that represent the patterns in memory, and later enable the player to retrieve the individual pieces when they are needed. Further, a set of active schemata can activate some higher-level "position schema," which provides the optional move. With the concept of schemata in mind, we can look in more detail at how knowledge and its organization affect problem solving.

It is now easier to think about how problem representations are formed. Essentially, they are formed in terms of the existing schemata and the slots they contain. If a problem is of a very familiar type, it can trigger an appropriate problem schema; if not, some more-general schema will be triggered. In any event, the slots in the schema control what features of the problem are incorporated into the representation; features that do not fit into a slot will be ignored.

Once a schema is triggered, a solver can decide on the solution if the schema contains the necessary information. If it is a specific and appropriate schema, it might contain precisely the right procedures, enabling the solver to proceed easily and rapidly. If it is a general schema, it might only contain a general prescription for how to proceed. In this situation the solver will have to search for procedures which fit the given problem and the general prescription. The solution will then be much more difficult to achieve, and may be impossible to achieve if the proper procedures can not be found. If an inappropriate schema is somehow triggered, the solver will not make any progress at all. Thus the importance of the knowledge structure, how it is organized into schemata, becomes clear. It is the organization and structure provided by schemata that allow relevant knowledge to be found in memory. Thus either lack of knowledge or lack of access to knowledge because of inadequate structure may be the reason for failure to solve a problem.

There is some experimental support for this interpretation. For instance, Hinsley et al. (1978) asked high school and college students to classify 76 algebra problems in any way they wished. There was considerable agreement among the students on the types of categories. Problems were grouped that would be solved in the same way, such as triangle problems, ratio problems, and river-current problems. Furthermore, students could classify these problems after hearing only the first sentence. For example, a problem starting with "John walked three miles east and then four miles north" could readily be classified as a triangle problem, that is, one using the Pythagorean theorem for solution. The rapidity with which problems are classified appears to rule out the possibility that problem categories are identified after the students have formulated a solution. Instead, it is suggested that the problems were indeed triggering some appropriate schemata in memory.

The existence of specific schemata can also be uncovered by showing how they can be mistakenly accessed. For example, poorer students, in particular, will classify problems erroneously if they contain "cover stories" that trigger a specific schema (Silver, 1981). A problem used by Hinsley et al. (1978) might be mistakenly identified as a triangle problem, even though it is actually a distance-rate-time problem, because irrelevant information about the triangular relation between the three problem elements has been introduced. Good students were not fooled, however.

A similar contrast was found by Chi et al. (1981). Students who had completed introductory physics with an A grade and physics instructors both grouped typical physics problems. The students tended to group problems that contained similar physical entities (as shown in Figure 10.5), whereas the instructors grouped problems according to the underlying principle (as shown in Figure 10.6). These studies show that good problem solvers are not fooled by the superficial features of a problem statement.

The results of these categorization studies, which show that good problem solvers are not deceived by cover stories, indicate that the skill of expert problem solvers arises from the complexity and completeness of their schemata. Their schemata must contain rules that are more complex than simple linking of superficial (or *primary*) cues in the problem statement with solution procedures. The schemata of the novice learners may be developed initially with these simple rules, but in order for novices to learn not to be misled by cover stories, they must also develop *secondary* knowledge (Chi et al., 1981), that is, knowledge that incorporates the interaction between the primary cues in the problem statement. Hence, a complete schema must contain not only the procedures (such as the equation to compute the hypotenuse of a triangle), but also the primary and secondary cues needed to identify the problem type appropriately.

Another way to illustrate these separate components of schemata is to use *problem isomorphs.* These are sets of problems whose underlying structures and solutions are all the same, but whose context can be quite different. An example of a problem isomorph is the tea ceremony (Hayes and Simon, 1974). In it, three people are conducting an oriental tea ceremony, and they must distribute responsibility for various parts of the ceremony among themselves according to certain rules. In actuality, this puzzle is the familiar Tower of Hanoi, with the pegs replaced by people, and the disks by parts of the ceremony. Anyone who is familiar with the Tower problem and who notices the correspondence can solve the Tea Ceremony quite easily. However, studies show that virtually no one notices the similarity. One way to interpret this finding is that the slots of the Tower of Hanoi schema were designed specifically for pegs and disks. When people and ceremonies were presented instead, the Tower of Hanoi solution schema was therefore not accessed, even though it contained very efficient procedures for solving the tea-ceremony puzzle.

In sum, studies on the solution of problems where a great deal of domain knowledge is involved indicate clearly that a very relevant part of success in

Diagrams depicted from problems categorized by novices within the same groups	Novices' explanations for their similarity groupings

Problem 10 (11)

Novice 2: "*Angular* velocity, *momentum, circular* things"

Novice 3: "*Rotational* kinematics, *angular* speeds, *angular* velocities"

Novice 6: "Problems that have something *rotating; angular* speed"

Problem 11 (39)

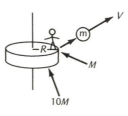

Problem 7 (23)

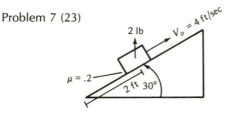

Novice 1: "These deal with blocks on an *inclined plane*"

Novice 5: "*Inclined-plane* problems, coefficient of *friction*"

Novice 6: "Blocks on *inclined planes* with angles"

Problem 7 (35)

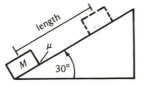

Figure 10.5

Examples from novices' problem categories. Problem numbers represent problem and chapter number from Halliday and Resnick (1974) (Taken from Chi, Feltovich, and Glaser, 1981.)

Diagrams depicted from problems categorized by experts within the same groups	Experts' explanations for their similarity groupings

Problem 6 (21)

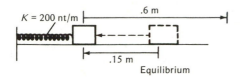

Expert 2: *"Conservation of Energy"*
Expert 3: *"Work-Energy Theorem.* They are all straight forward problems."
Expert 4: "These can be done from energy considerations. Either you should know the *Principle of Conservation of Energy,* or work is lost somewhere."

Problem 7 (35)

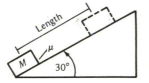

Problem 5 (39)

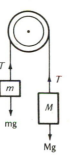

Expert 2: "These can be solved by *Newton's Second Law"*
Expert 3: "*F = ma; Newton's Second Law"*
Expert 4: "Largely use *F = ma; Newton's Second Law"*

Problem 12 (23)

$F_p = Kv$

mg

Figure 10.6

Example from experts' problem categories. Problem numbers represent problem and chapter number from Halliday and Resnick (1974). (Taken from Chi, Feltovich, and Glaser, 1981.)

problem solving is the ability to access a large body of well-structured domain knowledge. Therefore, one important direction of current research is to explore how a large body of knowledge is organized and represented, so that it can be easily accessed for successful solving of problems.

Ill-Defined Problems

Perhaps the best way to define an ill-defined problem is by default. That is, problems which do not fall into the class of well-defined problems, such as those that have been studied and described in the preceding discussion, may be considered ill-defined problems. One framework that can be used to conceptualize ill-defined problems draws on the information-processing approach we mentioned earlier in discussing puzzle problems. In that framework, a problem has a clear initial state, a set of permissible operators, and a goal state. A problem qualifies as *ill*-defined if any one or all of the three components are *not* well specified.

For example, the initial state may be vague, as in economics problems. Our economy is so complex that we really do not understand it very well. For any given economics problem, we have only a partial picture of the initial state, based on all the various statistics the government and other agencies collect. Not only do we have incomplete data to describe the initial state, but even professional economists cannot agree on the interpretation of the statistics that we do have.

A problem can also be considered ill defined if the operators are not well specified. In our economics problem, the various actions that might be taken to modify the initial state are not clear, and many possible actions have not yet even been formulated.

Finally, the problem is ill defined if the goal state is not clear. What conditions of controlled inflation and unemployment are to be attained? How much is too much? As you know, experts disagree vehemently on the answer to these questions. In fact, one prominent characteristic of the ill-defined problem is that there is generally a lack of consensus even among experts about what the appropriate solution is.

There has been very little research done on ill-structured problems. One interesting piece of work, recently conducted by Voss and his associates (Voss et al., 1983a; Voss et al., 1983b), used problems from the social sciences, much like the economics problem we have just described. Imagine you are the Minister of Agriculture for the Soviet Union. Crop productivity has been too low for the past several years. What would you do to increase crop production? This ill-structured problem has all the components unspecified. The initial state is far more complicated than just bad crops. Among other things, the Soviet political system, current agricultural methods, the amount of arable land, and the weather are all part of it. The task is to find some actions or operations that might improve the situation, but there is no mention at all of what they might be. And, finally, the goal is vaguely stated. How much of an increase is an appropriate goal? 5 percent? 20 percent? 200 percent?

In order to try to disentangle the various effects of knowledge, Voss and colleagues used subjects who were political scientists specializing in the Soviet Union, students who were taking a political-science course on Soviet domestic policy, and chemistry professors. Not surprisingly, they found strong knowledge effects. The most comprehensive and detailed solutions were produced by the Soviet experts, and the worst were produced by the students and the chemists. About 24 percent of the solution protocols of the Soviet experts focused on elaborating the initial state of the problem, as opposed to 1 percent for the students and the chemists.

Prominent in the experts' protocols at the initial phase of problem solving were the identification of possible constraints, such as the Soviet ideology and the amount of arable land. Defining constraints will provide a means of testing possible solutions, such as fostering private competition (a capitalist solution) or increasing planting, which can be rejected immediately under these constraints.

The obvious way to solve a problem of this sort is to eliminate its causes; so it is important to enumerate causes in the problem representation. If you realize that there are a series of separate causes, you will naturally decompose the problem into subproblems, that is, use subgoaling. All the subjects, from expert to novice, used this strategy. The differences, however, were that the experts tended to create a few very general subproblems that might encompass several related causes, whereas the novices related solutions very directly to individual causes. For instance, one expert identified the Soviet bureaucracy, the attitudes of the peasants toward agricultural practices, and the lack of infrastructure (railroads, fertilizer plants, fuel-distribution networks, etc.) as the main subproblems. In the most extreme examples of this tendency, the problem was recast into a single "subproblem," such as inadequate technological development.

There are at least two conclusions we can draw from this research. First, even in dealing with ill-defined problems, solvers use heuristics not unlike those, such as subgoaling, that they use in well-defined problems. Second, the very nature of ill-defined problems means that solvers define the problems better for themselves. This suggests that knowledge of the problem domain really makes it easier for a solver to define the problem, such as in identifying the constraints. For example, Reitman (1965) found from his protocols of a composer writing a fugue that, at any moment in time, the composer was really dealing with a very well-defined subproblem, even though the subproblem required some initial work to define it.

Because ill-defined problems require this special component, that is, a process for adding information to the problem situation, sometimes people refer to the solution of these problems as a creative act (Newell et al., 1964). Another name for a creative act is *insight*. This term often seems to imply that the solution was achieved in one single step, rather than in a series of discrete transformations, as happens with well-defined problems. The two-string problem we mentioned earlier seems to match this description. However, contemporary research is just beginning to explore the process of insight, and it appears that insight itself can be decomposed into several component processes, such as encoding the information in a selective way, combining information in a novel way, or comparing certain aspects of two objects (Sternberg and Davidson, 1983). For example, Fleming's discovery of penicillin required him to notice that the bacteria in the vicinity of a moldy dish containing a culture that had been destroyed. We could therefore say that Fleming was simply more insightful or creative than the other researchers. However, encoding information selectively requires that a person *know* which piece of information is relevant. That is, Fleming must have had some stored knowledge that only certain potent substances could destroy bacteria. Two tentative conclusions can thus be gleaned from the current preliminary research. First, creative and insightful acts may not necessarily be discrete and unitary; they may actually be composed of a sequence of subprocesses. Second, the execution of these subprocesses in an apparently creative way may require some existing stored knowledge.

Summary

Over the years, psychologists have learned a lot about the nature of the problem-solving process. The importance of the initial representation of a problem was discovered quite a few years ago by the Gestalt school in its examination of insight problems. The actual nature of initial representations and their influence on problem solving was made clear only in the last few decades, however, when the notion of a solution space was developed. Not too long ago researchers, especially those in artificial intelligence, thought that effective problem solving might result mainly from applying general strategies for guiding a searching process through problem spaces. Early attempts to create computer programs to solve problems, such as the General Problem Solver, took this approach.

As we have seen, though, this picture of problem solving has recently been shown to be far too simple. Specific knowledge of a domain is of overriding importance in the effective solution of problems. In addition, this knowledge must be well-structured, so that relevant knowledge can be accessed at the proper time. Research is beginning to uncover just what "well structured" means, but considerable work is left to be done on how we can retrieve information in a rapid and effective manner from the wealth of knowledge we all possess.

Even more work needs to be done on the kinds of problems that are probably the most important to us: ill-structured, real-world problems. The process of solving such problems is difficult, complex, and thus difficult to study, especially because it is often not clear whether an ill-structured problem has been solved. In addition, the most important real-world problems are often solved (or made worse) by means of complex (and little understood) social interactions.

References

Akin, O. 1980. *Models of Architectural Knowledge.* London: Pion.

Atwood, M. E., and P. G. Polson. 1976. A process model for water jug problems. Cognitive Psychology, 8, 191–216.

Chase, W. G., and H. A. Simon. 1973a. Perception in chess. *Cognitive Psychology,* 1973, 4, 55–81.

————. 1973b. The mind's eye in chess. *In* W. G. Chase, ed., *Visual Information Processing* (New York: Academic Press).

Chi, M. T. H., P. J. Feltovich, and R. Glaser. 1981. Categorization and representation of physics problems by experts and novices. *Cognitive Science, 5,* 121–152.

de Groot, A. 1966. Perception and memory versus thought: Some old ideas and recent findings. *In* B. Kleinmuntz, ed., *Problem Solving: Research, Method, and Theory* (New York: Wiley).

Egan, D. E., and B. J. Schwartz. 1979. Chunking in recall of symbolic drawings. *Memory and Cognition, 7,* 149–158.

Elstein, A. S., L. S. Shulman, and S. A. Sprafka. 1978. *Medical Problem Solving.* Cambridge, Mass.: Harvard Univ. Press.

Ernst, G. W., and A. Newell. 1969. *GPS: A Case Study in Generality and Problem Solving.* New York: Academic Press.

Halliday, D., and R. Resnick. 1974. *Fundamentals of Physics.* New York: Wiley.

Hayes, J. R. 1966. Memory, goals, and problem solving. *In* B. Kleinmuntz, ed., *Problem Solving: Research, Method, and Theory* (New York: Wiley).

Hayes, J. R. and H. A. Simon. 1974. Understanding written problem instructions. *In* L. W. Gregg, ed., *Knowledge and Cognition* (Hillsdale, N.J.: Erlbaum).

Hinsley, D. A., J. R. Hayes, and H. A. Simon. 1978. From words to equations: Meaning and representation in algebra word problems. *In* P. A. Carpenter and M. A. Just, eds., *Cognitive Processes in Comprehension* (Hillsdale, N.J.: Erlbaum).

Klahr, D. and M. Robinson. 1981. Formal assessment of problem-solving and planning processing in preschool children. *Cognitive Psychology, 13,* 113–148.

Larkin, J. H., J. McDermott, D. P. Simon, and H. A. Simon. 1980. Models of competence in solving physics problems. *Cognitive Science, 4,* 317–345.

Maier, N. R. F. 1931. Reasoning in humans, II: The solution of a problem at its appearance in consciousness. *Journal of Comparative Psychology, 12,* 181–194.

National Academy of Sciences. 1981. *Outlook for Science and Technology: The Next Five Years.* Washington, DC: N.A.S.

Newell, A., J. C. Shaw, and H. A. Simon. 1964. The processes of creative thinking. *In* H. E. Gruber, G. Terrell, and M. Wertheimer, eds., *Contemporary Approaches to Creative Thinking, Vol. 3* (New York: Atherton Press).

————. 1958. Chess-playing programs and the problem of complexity. *IBM Journal of Research and Development, 2,* 320–335.

Newell, A., and H. A. Simon. 1972. *Human Problem Solving.* Englewood Cliffs, N.J.: Prentice-Hall.

Reed, S. K., and H. A. Simon. 1976. Modeling strategy shifts in a problem solving task. *Cognitive Psychology, 8,* 86–97.

Reitman, W. 1965. *Cognition and Thought.* New York: Wiley.

Rumelhart, D. E. 1981. *Understanding Understanding.* La Jolla: Univ. of California, Center for Human Information Processing.

Silver, E. A. 1981. Recall of mathematical problem information: Solving related problems. *Journal for Research in Mathematics Education, 12,* 54–64.

Simon, D. P. and H. A. Simon. 1978. Individual differences in solving physics problems. *In* R. Siegler, ed., *Children's Thinking: What develops?* (Hillsdale, N.J.: Erlbaum).

Simon, H. A., and M. Barenfeld. 1969. Information processing analysis of perceptual processes in problem solving. *Psychological Review, 76,* 473–483.

Sternberg, R. J., and J. E. Davidson. 1983. Insight in the gifted. *Educational Psychologist,* 18(1), 51–57.

Voss, J. F., T. R. Greene, T. A. Post, and B. C. Penner. 1983a. Problem solving skill in social sciences. *In* G. Power, ed., *The Psychology of Learning and Motivation: Advances in Research and Theory,* Vol. 17. New York: Academic Press.

Voss, J. F., S. W. Tyler, and L. A. Yengo. 1983b. Individual differences in the solving of social science problems. *In* R. F. Dillon and R. R. Schmeck, eds., *Individual Differences in Cognition* (New York: Academic Press).

Wilkins, D. 1980. Using patterns and plans in chess. *Artificial Intelligence,* 14, 165–203.

AUTHOR INDEX*

*Italic numbers indicate pages in which complete reference is given.

SUBJECT INDEX

257